MW00860598

DIOGENES UNVEILED

DIOGENES UNVEILED

A Paul Mankowski Collection

Edited by Philip F. Lawler

IGNATIUS PRESS   SAN FRANCISCO

Cover art:
Detail of a caricature of Diogenes by Honoré Daumier, 1842
Image in the public domain

Cover design by John Herreid

© 2022 by Ignatius Press, San Francisco
All rights reserved
ISBN 978-1-62164-508-5 (PB)
ISBN 978-1-64229-238-1 (eBook)
Library of Congress Control Number 2022934986
Printed in the United States of America ∞

CONTENTS

INTRODUCTION

In the 1990s, *Catholic World Report*, the monthly magazine that I then edited, ran a regular back-of-the-book feature that we entitled Last Word. The articles that appeared on that final page were a mixed bag, including some personal reflections, some lighthearted commentary, even some statistical analysis. Sometimes these pieces were signed by their authors; sometimes we used a pseudonym. One of those pseudonyms, which was used by several different writers, was Diogenes.

A full generation later, I can no longer confidently match all those Last Word pieces with their true authors. At least a few, I know, were written by the Diogenes to whose pseudonymous work this book is dedicated. I strongly suspect that he penned "Exorcism a la Mode" for the March 1999 issue, and probably "Rectory Parlor Games" in May 2000. (Readers of this book might enjoy browsing through old copies of *Catholic World Report*, to see if they can detect his distinctive style.) But the only piece that I *know* to be his work, and therefore appears in this volume, was written under the unlikely nickname of Trixie Bonvivante.

Early in 2003, *Catholic World News* (CWN), the daily online service that I had begun, inaugurated an experimental new section that offered pithy commentary on current news stories. Entitled Off the Record (OTR), this section proved popular with our readers, and when CWN became a part of the Catholic Culture website (catholic culture.org), OTR continued as a regular feature there.

At first OTR included comments by several different contributors, who sometimes wrote under their own names and sometimes used pseudonyms. But one personality soon emerged as our readers' favorite. Writing as Diogenes, our star analyst delighted readers for several years before he mysteriously disappeared from our site.

While he was contributing nuggets of insight to Off the Record, Diogenes was popular for his wit. Reading his comments now, more than a decade later, knowledgeable Catholics will recognize that he was remarkably prescient as well. He identified public figures who would later be caught up in scandals, and he anticipated the nature of those scandals too. Was he remarkably well informed? Yes, but the secret to his success lay in his ability to do what American bishops have often adjured the faithful to do: read the signs of the times.

Actually several different people contributed to OTR under the Diogenes byline, and to this day I am the only person who can say with certainty which author wrote which comments. But perceptive readers came to recognize the style of one writer. This particular Diogenes—Uncle Di, to his friends—displayed a broad knowledge of current affairs, particularly in the Catholic Church; a graceful writing style; and above all a biting wit that often tiptoed along the outer boundaries of good taste.

Who was this Diogenes? For years we kept his identity secret. But knowledgeable Catholic readers heard rumors that it was Father Paul Mankowski, S.J. After his untimely and sudden death on September 3, 2020, I felt free to confirm that those rumors were—like his commentary—on target. I could also explain (see my tribute below, "Farewell, Uncle Di") why he had written under a pseudonym, why his OTR comments had ceased without any real explanation, and why this brilliant writer was not better known.

Despite the constraints that were placed upon him by his superiors, Father Mankowski did write a number of serious essays and reviews under his own name. These works are collected in a separate volume by Ignatius Press, *Jesuit at Large*, edited by George Weigel. This present collection is devoted exclusively to Father Mankowski the satirist, and to his pseudonymous writing.

In compiling this collection of commentary by Diogenes, I have faced several challenges:

First, the sheer volume of material was daunting. Father Mankowski wrote over 2,600 posts for OTR. Even after eliminating the comments that were not suitable for this book (for reasons listed below), I had enough posts to fill several volumes. I strived to choose the best of them, sometimes wincing as I made the cuts. I have no doubt that some readers, the most ardent of Diogenes fans, will recall favorites that they think should have been included.

Second, the nature of Uncle Di's comments did not always lend themselves to reproduction in printed form. He often used visual props—links to images on other websites—that would not display in written form, even if we could secure the appropriate permissions.

Third, Diogenes typically wrote about current headline stories, about events that have now, a decade or more later, faded in memory. Many of his comments might be lost on today's readers—and especially on younger readers, who until now may not have been introduced to Uncle Di.

Fourth, OTR was written for an online audience, and most posts contained links to stories from other media outlets. In some cases the comments would be incomprehensible without those links. But of course a printed book cannot contain a clickable link, and by now many of those links are no longer working.

Finally, I might as well confess, there were questions of taste. Diogenes was not afraid to use provocative imagery and salty language. He sometimes went too far, and since I appreciate earthy humor, I would rarely censor his online commentary. But maybe I'm getting old; a few of his more hilarious ribald comments now struck me as inappropriate for a book published by a house as distinguished as Ignatius Press.

In what follows I have reproduced the OTR contributions of Diogenes / Father Mankowski as they appeared, with minimal editing, including fair-use quotations from other sources. I trust that readers will be able to piece together the context. I have divided these posts into sections, according to the subject matter, with a very brief editorial introduction to each section. Hoping to reproduce for readers the experience that OTR provided for our online audience, I have let Diogenes speak for himself. His stylistic peculiarities—including occasional oddities in voice, usage, capitalization, and even spelling—are part of the package, and I have left them mostly untouched.

Philip F. Lawler

TRIBUTES

In the week following Father Mankowski's death, my tribute appeared on the Catholic Culture site; Tony Abbott's appeared in First Things. *Both appear here with permission.*

Farewell, Uncle Di: Father Paul Mankowski, RIP

Philip F. Lawler

September 4, 2020

My editorial career has brought me into close contact with quite a few impressive thinkers. I have worked with famous authors, with noted theologians and philosophers, with canny political strategists, with at least a half dozen Nobel Prize winners. Among them all, for sheer full-spectrum intellectual wattage, none was more brilliant than my friend Father Paul Mankowski, S.J., who died suddenly this week.

You may well ask: If he was such a world-class genius, why wasn't his death front-page news? Why wasn't he a celebrity? Why is the only book available under his name an obscure work on *Akkadian Loanwords in Biblical Hebrew*? Those are good questions. The answers make his life story all the more interesting.

That he was a prodigious intellect is beyond dispute. He earned advanced degrees at Harvard and Oxford. He was fluent in multiple languages. He advised Vatican prelates, and more than once I detected a familiar style of prose in an official document from the Holy See. He taught biblical languages at the Pontifical Biblical Institute. He maintained a lively correspondence with philosophers and political leaders. And if you have read "The Tragedy of MacDeth", which he wrote just for fun under a pseudonym, you know that you are not dealing with an ordinary mind.

Born into a middle-class family, Paul worked in steel mills to help pay his college tuition, and never abandoned his blue-collar approach to work. He was unimpressed with academic colleagues who, he chuckled in wonderment, "wouldn't even know how to change a shock absorber." Then again he was also unimpressed with his own academic achievements, and congenitally incapable of self-promotion.

As a young man Paul Mankowski developed a deep admiration for the Society of Jesus. He noticed, in his readings of history, that the Jesuits always turned up in crucial battles, defending the Catholic faith "where the fighting was fiercest." Determined to do the same, he joined the Jesuits after graduating from the University of Chicago. He did not foresee that in our days the fiercest fighting would take place *inside* the Church and inside the Society of Jesus, and that—at least during his lifetime—he would be on the losing side.

For years Paul worked under constraints imposed by his Jesuit superiors. Having ruffled feathers with his unapologetic defense of traditional Catholic teaching, he was directed to avoid public controversies. Faithful to his vow of obedience, he hewed to the order he was given. When told that he could not write under his own name without censorship, he used pseudonyms. When told that he could not write under a pseudonym, he stopped. And so the Catholic world was denied what might have been a treasure trove of lively and insightful prose. Do not be surprised if some memorable work now leaks out posthumously.

At this point there is no reason to maintain what is already an ill-kept secret: that Father Mankowski, writing as Diogenes, was the guiding light of the Off the Record feature that long delighted readers on this Catholic Culture site. He was not the only contributor—others wrote under the Diogenes byline—but he was the most prolific and easily the best. When he withdrew, the quality and quantity of Diogenes' work took a nosedive, and we chose to discontinue the feature.

Diogenes was not universally popular. Father Mankowski had a special gift for satire, and—appropriately for a man who had been a boxer in student days—never pulled his punches. Perhaps at times he went too far, and as his editor I should have toned down his posts. But as it happens I too am a former boxer. Certainly Diogenes was often acerbic. At times his work was also hilariously funny, and

Catholic Culture readers learned not to take a sip of hot coffee before reading Off the Record. Maybe it wasn't always as charitable as it should have been. But it sure was fun.

We were friends for so long, I honestly don't recall how we became acquainted. We had many mutual friends while he was studying at Harvard and I was working in Boston, but I think our first face-to-face meeting was in jail in Brookline, Massachusetts, after we had both been arrested during an Operation Rescue blockade of an abortion clinic. We quickly became friends, stayed in touch when he moved to Rome to teach at the Biblicum, and developed a regular pattern of exchanging ideas and suggestions and observations by e-mail.

In the past twenty years or so, my wife, Leila, and I have counted on these e-mail exchanges with Paul and a few other friends for analysis, advice, and perspective—as well as for comedy and commiseration. They have helped furnish the material for dozens of columns and a couple of books. We recognized Father Mankowski as a demanding yet constructive critic. If I sent him a draft of something I was writing, I would almost invariably make the changes he suggested; if he wrote with an "attaboy" about something I had posted, it made my day.

(How often were we in touch? I asked myself that question yesterday, and counted the number of e-mails that I had sent to Paul in the month before his death. I found fifty-six—but then he had been on retreat for a week during that time.)

But now I wonder whether I am painting an inaccurate picture of my friend, because I am portraying a scholar and a counselor but not necessarily a Catholic priest. Father Mankowski's feisty defense of the faith was motivated by a deep and rock-solid personal conviction. As Leila observed in her own tribute, he was granite. Yet he could and did empathize with confused teenagers and elderly dementia patients and the many ordinary parishioners whose confessions he heard as a "supply priest" on weekends.

Paul had recently volunteered to bring the sacraments to COVID-19 patients, whatever the risks. That was predictable. While he was stationed in Rome, teaching, he would use school breaks to travel to different countries and work with the Missionaries of Charity. As editor of Catholic World Report I published his memorable, moving accounts of service to "the poorest of the poor"—written again pseudonymously, to deflect attention from himself—in Romania and Armenia. He lived very simply himself. Leila noticed his threadbare clerical shirts. Once when I visited Rome, and asked him to recommend a good restaurant, he couldn't. Is there another priest who, after a few years in Rome, cannot tell a friend where to get a spectacular dinner?

In their obituary notice, for their colleague, the Jesuits of the Midwest Province unintentionally revealed something about themselves in their praise for Father Mankowski. "Paul was deeply devoted to the Mass and the sacraments," the obituary noted. And again: "When men in formation would live at Woodlawn, Paul would offer to celebrate Mass for them." Why would it be remarkable—indeed, why would it be worthy of particular mention—that a Catholic priest was devoted to the Mass, and willing to say Mass for men in formation? Unfortunately Paul's sort of active faith was remarkable in the Jesuit community to which he devoted his life. Nevertheless he persevered. He, at least, could certainly be found "where the fighting was fiercest."

Was he wrong to fight so fiercely? Let me give my old friend (almost) the last word, by quoting in its entirely a piece that he posted as Diogenes back in 2003:

Maybe in the long run Church historians will conclude that among orthodox Catholics concerned about reform one can identify two main approaches to the job: nutrition and surgery.

Nutritionists believe that the Church's ills can be cured by fresh air, moderate exercise, and green leafy vegetables. Surgeons believe the patient has an aggressive cancer that demands cutting and cautery— the sooner the better.

Both nutritionists and surgeons understand that Christ's Church cannot die. We've all had a peek at the last chapter of The Book (see Rev 22:1ff.) and know that she ultimately triumphs in the bottom of the eleventh inning. We realize too that there's much suffering ahead of her in the interim.

The history of the Church shows that every crisis is confronted by nutritionists and surgeons. Sometimes the nutritionists are right, and the surgeons cause unnecessary damage by overreacting and amputating still-healthy members. Sometimes the surgeons are right, and the nutritionists cause unnecessary damage by underestimating the virulence of the disease and delaying the needful intervention, so that once-savable limbs rot off.

With hindsight it's easy to say when the nutritionists were wrong and when the surgeons were. But at the time of the crisis the evidence is almost always equivocal: some aspects of the Church appear healthy or on the mend; other aspects appear corrupt and progressively toxic to the entire organism. Today nutritionists point to signs of vitality found in thriving new congregations, excellent papal catechesis, the comparative orthodoxy of younger priests, and a documentary commitment to reform. Surgeons are more impressed by the nature and scale of clerical depravity, the incapacity of bishops to remove heretics and criminals from their own number (plus their apparent unwillingness to deal with any corruption except under pressures of public scandal), and the widening gap between the Holy See's instruction on doctrine, morals, and liturgy and the actual efforts of bishops and priests, who defy this instruction with impunity.

Note too how even undisputed truths are ambiguous in interpretation; the fact that most bishops side with nutritionists and very few with the surgeons is taken by each side as corroborative of its own diagnosis.

Nutritionists and surgeons have the same goal: the full health of the patient. But each believes the other is almost willfully obtuse in ignoring the important symptoms and in talking up the marginal ones. Each believes the other impedes the cure by giving the patient bad advice. "Why do you discourage the faithful by publicizing scandal?" ask the nutritionists. "Why do you divert the Church's eyes from her danger by minimizing it?" the surgeons reply. Each can point to innocent persons who have left the Church in disgust because of blundering by the other side. A certain mutual exasperation is inevitable.

Most Off the Record contributors are surgeons. In blogdom, at least, we (entirely predictably) provoke dismay and unfriendly comment among nutritionists. Speaking for myself, I don't think that's a bad thing. While I believe the surgeons are right and the nutritionists mistaken, I admit to fallibility in matters big and small, nor do I doubt that nutritionists want the Faith to prosper. They may not return the compliment, but that doesn't especially bother me. Those who lance festering boils (or indulge in sarcasm when untreated boils burst of their own accord) must expect to be viewed with suspicion and alarm; it comes with the job.

A final point. The OTR surgeons of my acquaintance share this characteristic: we wish we were wrong. We would be ecstatic if it

turned out that the apparent villainy we decry had an innocent explanation, that ecclesial corruption was a phantasm, that we had misread
the signs and had a long list of apologies to make. Where the important matters are concerned, we would love to eat crow.

Was Catholicism not seriously corrupted in our time, such that
the intransigence of Father Mankowski was not warranted? I doubt
it. When he is seated at the celestial banquet—soon, I pray—I don't
think he'll be eating crow.

Remembering Father Paul Mankowski

Tony Abbott

September 4, 2020

Paul Mankowski, a Jesuit of the Chicago Province, who has just died—too soon at only sixty-six—was probably the most striking man I have ever met. My friendship with Paul crept up on me, toward the end of Michaelmas term at Oxford in 1981. He was a Jesuit scholastic, two years into Latin and Greek philosophy at Campion Hall; I was a politics and philosophy freshman at the Queen's College. We met through the Australian priest and doctoral student John Honner, who'd taken me under his wing as a newly arrived Jesuit alumnus.

Paul was not exactly your average student for the priesthood: handsome, athletic, not very abstemious, and capable of devastating locker room humor. He'd had at least one serious girlfriend before joining the Jesuits. As someone then wrestling with the prospect of a vocation, once I'd gotten used to his occasional intensity, I craved his company not just as a friend but as a role model too. At twenty-four, I'd decided that the priesthood was the greatest calling to which a Catholic man could aspire, in part because of the priests I'd come to admire; but Paul was the first contemporary I'd found who was both an utterly committed Jesuit and a "normal" human being.

To call him a "muscular Christian" wouldn't do justice to his intellect and his emotional depth, or to his capacity for friendship with women while remaining chaste. But his ability to keep the faith through thick and thin and to live a life of relentless self-discipline must have required singular inner strength. Earlier, at Sydney University, I'd been ready enough to assert the Church's teaching (on the sanctity of life, for instance) while usually conceding that "hard cases make bad law." Unlike me, Paul never felt the need to curry favor by making intellectual concessions—and to this day, almost forty years on, I've never quite lost that sense of being the lesser man.

In January 1982, the pair of us were marking the start of a new term at the old Eastgate Hotel. At some stage, Paul mentioned that the university boxing club, which he'd joined earlier, was short a heavyweight. I'd done a season's sparring at Sydney, mostly to be able to give as good as I got on the rugby field, so a bit reluctantly said yes a couple of beers on. After one session, I'd decided to make my excuses—but Paul then turned up to present a brand-new skipping rope. His vow of poverty mattered so much that his clothes were mostly hand-me-downs from dead Jesuits; so this was a big deal, and I didn't have the heart to quit. The two Oxford "blues" I would never have had without him are among the highlights of my life. In the ring, Paul's practice was less to throw punches than to keep standing: a stoicism that he was to need soon after.

Regular letters from Paul subsequently helped to keep me going during three years of being a square peg in a round hole as a student for the diocesan priesthood back in Sydney. It was readily apparent, though, that he was already "on the outer" with his Jesuit superiors. His was a robust, straight, manly faith that respected Scripture and tradition. Theirs, in Paul's eyes at least, was shape-shifting and far too attuned to the "signs of the times". At times, I wondered whether he didn't "protest too much", but the scales fell from my eyes after a few days spent at the Jesuit house at Harvard, where he was then doing further studies. The contrast between Paul and the other residents circa 1990 could hardly have been sharper; and, to me, all in his favor.

By the time of his ordination, Paul was well on the road to becoming the Jesuits' fiercest internal critic. Sometimes writing under his own name and sometimes using a pseudonym, he excoriated priests and bishops who'd only wear a clerical collar to a protest meeting or who thought that celibacy could be selective. His satire was devastating, his judgments uncompromising, his logic impeccable. For all their commitment to Christian charity, religious superiors have never coped well with criticism, especially when it's justified, so Paul endured years of ostracism within the order. Literally for decades, he was on the verge of expulsion and denied the opportunity to take final vows.

Meanwhile, he was a professor of ancient Semitic languages to students in the Vatican, no doubt inspiring many of them to become better priests. For about a decade until 2012, he was an annual visitor to Australia, teaching a much-in-demand two-week course in practical apologetics at the John Paul II Institute in Melbourne. I recall an intellectually rigorous and personally challenging sermon to the sleepy church of Saint Martin de Porres in Sydney. It was hard to grasp all he said and impossible to live up to what he asked, but the parishioners mobbed him afterward all the same.

Why did he have to be so unappreciated by his own colleagues? Why not join the less militantly progressive Australian Province, or be incardinated into the Sydney Archdiocese where George Pell was a friend and fan? I sometimes asked. But this, of course, would have been taking too worldly or too self-centered an approach. Paul's self-appointed mission was to prod the Jesuits into once more being the special forces of faith, and if that meant that he was often a lonely outcast, so be it.

The hardest battles are with the people who are supposed to be on the same side. There are no medals for internal fights, however necessary. The strength of character and the moral courage required is all the more heroic because it's invariably recognized only posthumously. I hope the Jesuits grasp what they've lost and start to give him the respect he always deserved. Especially because prayer is not my forte, this tribute is my way to honor a man I loved.

Tony Abbott was the prime minister of Australia from 2013 to 2015.

AMONG THE POOREST OF THE POOR

While teaching in Rome, rather than come home for Christmas, Father Man-
kowski chose to spend his vacations working among the poor with the Mission-
aries of Charity. His visits to Romania and Armenia produced these diaries,
which originally appeared under the pseudonym Father X in Catholic World
Report. I offer them first in this collection not only because of their vivid report-
ing but also as a reminder that while Diogenes was often a cynical commentator,
the man behind this persona was a dedicated and self-sacrificing Catholic priest.

Romania Diary

Father X

Monday, December 23, 2002

Landed at Otopeni Airport in Bucharest at dusk, eastward, in the
middle of a snowstorm. The tarmac appeared to be unplowed, with
about 3 inches of new snow collecting. As we taxied to the gate I
saw four or five old Tupolev-154s parked in the grass with Tarom
(Romanian Air) markings just visible in the gloom: 727 lookalikes.
The fuselage-mounted engines were stripped, leaving only the cowl-
ings, which were clearly hollow when we passed behind and gave the
aircraft, and the airport in general, an eerie and decrepit look. For-
malities were swift, as ours was the only flight in the immigration and
customs area, and the border official stamped my passport without a
question or a look in my direction.

I was met by Sister Subasia (Slovak) and Sister Albertine (Polish),
who briskly loaded me onto a bus for the city center, where I was to
catch a minibus north to Moldavia. Traffic was not heavy but barely
crawling, and when we got off the bus Sister Subasia was convinced
we had missed the 6:15 departure. However, we decided to make a

dash for it and ran and jogged through the unplowed streets for about
a mile. We arrived panting at the bus stop exactly in time, and were
met by an English volunteer named Abby Flavell, and a Romanian
boy named Marius, whom the sisters had cared for in past years.
There was no bus. Once the heat of our run wore off it got cold fast.
I was still dressed for Rome, and pulled on a sweater I had in my bag.
The bus stop had a rudimentary shelter that served as a windbreak,
but even so we were stamping our feet in the cold, and the snow
swirled over the top of the shelter and collected on the leeward side
of our coats, pants, luggage, so that we all appeared to be frosted on
one side.

An hour and ten minutes later the minibus arrived, a stretched Ford
van with 17 seats, and Abby and I squashed into places in the back,
luggage on our laps. After fueling at an Agip gas station we reversed
course and drove steadily north for five hours, through intermittent
snow flurries, often slowed behind trucks and tractors. The terrain
was flat and, to my eye, featureless—though to be fair it was dark and
I had to scuff the frost from the inside of the window to see anything
at all. The other passengers spoke in low voices, eating candy and
drinking Czech beer and letting the empty bottles bounce around
our feet. We passed through two medium-sized towns en route. The
heating worked sporadically and the radio, regrettably, nonstop. I was
amused when at one point the disc jockey's Romanian patter gave
way to a track from *The Blues Brothers*: "We would especially like to
welcome all the representatives of Illinois' law enforcement community that have chosen to join us here tonight ..."

We reached Bacau at 12:30 and got a taxi to take us the two miles
to Casa Sfantul Iosif, the MC's [Missionaries of Charity] house. The
superior Sister Maria (Indian) and Sister Joseret (Rwandan) showed
me to the chapel, where a bed had been prepared for me in a 10' × 5'
room off the sacristy. I said Compline and was asleep by 1:00.

Tuesday, December 24

Up at 5:00, said OR [Office of Readings] and Lauds, and hosed myself
down rapidly with tepid water from the spray nozzle in the adjoin-
ing bathroom. Breakfast of bread and Nescafé. At about 6:40 people
began to assemble in the chapel for the 7:00 Mass: poorly clothed and

clearly not well fed. Father Sergio, a Salesian from Venice, showed up to celebrate. He heard the people's confessions first, and I concelebrated with him in Romanian. The Moldavian Catholics are pious (in demeanor, at least) and unselfconsciously give priests the greeting "*Lauda sa fie Iesus Christus*" (Jesus Christ be praised), to which the priest responds "*Invece vacilor amin*" (For ever and ever, amen).

Sunny, clear, and quite cold. There's about four inches of snow on the ground. A turquoise sweater draped over the clothesline outside has 6-inch icicles hanging off the sleeves.

10:00 Lecture to the sisters.

After the Rosary, the sisters took me into the main house, where they take care of 28 mentally and physically damaged "children"—they range in age from 11 to 26—almost all of whom are were taken in from the state institutions shortly after the fall of the Ceausescu regime. The building is of cement block and patterned stucco (through which rusty wire mesh was visible), two stories, clean and spare both inside and out. There was a Christmas tree in the entranceway and crepe paper festoons, balloons, and foil angels hanging in most of the rooms.

On the ground floor is a laundry and a room for children who cannot stand or walk. It was explained to me that most of these had come from the state orphanage called Ungerrini. Children judged at a birth to be "irrecuperables"—e.g., brain damaged or blind— were taken from their parents and kept in a special asylum. There they were clothed only in a shirt, and their wrists and ankles were kept crossed and bound together underneath the chin, so that they couldn't move from their cots and would be easy to wipe. Feeding and cleaning were the only human contact provided until they were old enough to be moved to the adult hospital. The effects of this treatment were obvious in the grossly underdeveloped legs of every child in the house. Perhaps half a dozen of those I saw in their late teens and early twenties had never learned to walk at all. One little boy was asleep on his back with his arms and tiny legs folded across his chest in a disturbingly insectile manner. Sister Marie told me that he was 15, although he looked 6 or 7 to me, and that he tended to sleep with his limbs roughly in the position in which they had been bound while he was at Ungerrini. Most of the ground-floor children displayed some pronounced autism, constantly flexing the trunk forward from the waist, chewing or sucking their fingers.

There was sporadic whimpering and screaming from some and a kind of repeated half hum, half moan from others. None of these children could speak, but one girl, when prompted, would smile and repeat her name in a kind of sob.

This room contained two standing-boxes, which looked like hollow pillars or adjustable-height lecterns. Children are placed inside so that most of their weight is borne by their arms, and bit by bit they are supposed to develop leg muscles strong enough to stand. I was told that one boy, who in several years had given no earlier indications of progress in this regard, took it into his head one day that he wanted to blow out the candles after Mass, and astonished everyone by leaving the toy tractor on which he was seated and walking over to the altar to do so.

Alida is blind, deaf, very prettily complected, with no legs to speak of, lying on her back. When Sister Marie took her hand she gave a far-off smile. She is thought to be about 18, though I would have put her at half that. The sisters make sure she gets taken to Mass with the rest of the children.

A lunch of bits of bread soaked in soup and apple slices was being prepared. Sister Marie explained that they try to teach these children to feed themselves to the extent possible. They're not up to spoons, so it's always finger food of some sort. She also mentioned the difficulty with the fact that the Missionaries of Charity rarely work in the same place for more than four years: children naturally form attachments to particular sisters, then they too are taken from them. It hurts to think about.

Next I was taken to the upper floor (all female), where there are children who can walk to some extent, as well as young adults. Four of the latter were seated hip to hip on the side of a bed, staring at me quietly. There was something oddly familiar about their appearance that I couldn't quite place. Later, walking back to the chapel, it came to me: Tenniel's illustrations in Lewis Carroll's Alice books, with his overlarge heads and adult faces on top of puny children's bodies.

Sister Szymon Jozef (Polish) said that the problem here was protecting the nonviolent girls from the violent ones, and protecting the self-damaging ones from themselves. Without interrupting her explanations she had to pounce three or four times around the room like a boxing ref, breaking the clinches that formed here and there, keeping the girls from biting and so forth, always addressing them in an even and soothing voice. Here too there was weeping and shrieking from some, quiet smiles or burbling from most. A woman with Down syndrome named Maria (of unknown origins, estimated by a doctor to be 24) gently took my hand and quietly and earnestly spoke to my chest for several minutes, saying I don't know what. Cristina joined us, wearing a badly mended sweater, and I was told that she rips her clothes off herself from time to time and so is made to stitch them back together (with supervision), so as to develop her motor skills on the one hand and to discourage her shredding act on the other. Dana, in her late teens, came up from nowhere with tears in her eyes and gave Maria a shove. She is aphasic and self-mutilating, and has clawed the skin clean away from her left cheekbone, baring the flesh underneath. Her fingers are badly bitten and swollen like franks on a grill.

At times the smell of rotting teeth was overpowering. Sister Marie said that this is an insuperable problem. The children cannot cooperate with a dentist in the usual way, and have to be anesthetized to have any work done whatsoever—for which there is neither the money nor the inclination on the part of the public health dentists. Abscessed and impacted teeth just rot away, and the pain, and the inability to understand the pain, must add considerably to their misery.

When a lay worker came to take charge of these girls, Sister Szymon Jozef took me to see their two babies: one, a newborn girl, tightly swaddled in pink flannel, being taken care of for a drug-addict mother; Iosif, a 7-month-old, was (I think she said) a foundling. He had a green cotton crab that, when squeezed, played "Old MacDonald". I gave him my clerical collar to chew, which he took in both tiny hands and gnawed with the total concentration and equanimity befitting the season.

4:00 Lecture.

Adoration and Vespers in the sisters' chapel. Heard sisters' confessions. An early supper in the sacristy.

8:00 Lecture.

At 10:30 I said the Christmas vigil Mass, in Italian, with a young woman from Bacau translating my homily into Romanian. The walking children were present, as well as some of the staff and a dozen or so townsfolk. Here, as elsewhere in Romania, I noticed that the people sing extremely well. After Mass there were carols and hot chocolate in the main house, with the most capable of the children joining in the singing and the others licking the frosting off gingerbread reindeer while they watched. To bed about 12:30.

Wednesday, December 25

Sunny, very cold (−10°F). Mass at 8:00, concelebrated in Romanian with the local pastor. A crowded chapel, with many townsfolk and the full complement of children, including many carried or wheeled in. They were remarkably attentive and well disposed, with the occasional whimper or shout quickly hushed by an attendant sister. Afterwards there was carol singing in the chapel, with the children gathered around the crèche. It's disturbing how, in these circumstances, the lyrics of the schmaltziest old-fashioned Christmas hymns lose all their schmaltz and cut right to the heart. I was moved by the sight of Margita, grabbing Abby's sleeve with one hand and cupping her own groin with the other, her blind eyes rolled up under her lids, rocking back and forth from heel to heel and laughing in sheer happiness.

Immediately after Mass we made preparations to set off to the Gisteni Adult Institute—the state hospital for mental defectives about 18 miles southwest of Bacau. The name was pronounced by the sisters with a certain residual horror audible in their voices (as with Treblinka or Birkenau after World War II), and I was told that it was here that the Missionaries of Charity, in the course of a Christmas visit shortly after the 1989 revolution, gave the slip to the guards and came upon the now-notorious Gatosh ("End of the Line") Unit. This consisted of two large unheated basement rooms in which the worst mental defectives were put, men and women together, unclothed, bathed in a common tank once a week, fed by putting buckets of food in the room and letting the strongest fight for it. Four MC sisters started a house nearby simply to care for these patients. In all such matters it's hard to know which recounted horrors were real and which are later exaggerations, but I noticed that the sisters who had actually seen the Gatosh Unit in operation were much less willing to talk about it than those who hadn't.

The sisters took great pains to bundle themselves up warmly for the visit and to dress me adequately as well. I was given extra pairs of thick socks, a stocking cap, a sweater and sweatshirt, a disintegrating

Romanian down-filled parka, and boots on which I sliced open my palm when lacing them up. I thought this might have been overkill for a half-an-hour ride, but they patiently explained to me that Gisteni is only heated for seven hours a day, and that I would be glad of any insulation from the chill. They were right. Six of us piled into a rickety VW van half-filled with cardboard boxes, containing Christmas parcels for the patients, and we headed through Bacau and south towards Bacaciuni.

My first good look at Moldavian building; it is not reassuring. The shoddiness, in almost every important aspect, is staggering. Concrete is far and away the most common building material, but it seems to be salted out and crumbling at every edge. It looks as if every building were erected in sub-zero weather, where the mixing water had frozen and expanded and bred faults in the casting, but of course it couldn't actually be the case. There are the stereotypical rows upon rows of grey six-story apartment buildings, weather-stained and unpainted, drearier even than Chicago's Robert Taylor Homes. One would think they were long-abandoned slums, but for the fact that every single window is intact. Unwashed, but intact. The same was true of a curvilinear futuristic building—a skating rink? an arts center?—put up in the early 1970s perhaps, which because of its pathetic attempt at modernity was even more depressing than the concrete boxes. Its windows were unbroken also, but it looked as dead as a rusting freighter. For reasons I don't grasp, any attempt at beauty has results grimmer than strict functionalism. The roads are fair. Most of the traffic is motorized (old Russian and East German vehicles along with Fiats and Fords), but there was a sizable number of horse-drawn rubber-tired wagons as well. I was surprised to see many (full) old-style corncribs even in the city, presumably storing feed for the draft animals. There were many hitchhikers on the roads, young and old, men and women, and this in every area I visited.

We drove south past snowy fields and shacky farmhouses for twelve miles, turned west at Bacaciuni, began a gentle climb into a village, and entered the gate of Gisteni. Some of the male patients, excited at seeing the sisters, came out to greet us and eagerly helped carry the boxes into the hospital. It is a 1920s building onto which several large wings were added postwar; there are nearly 400 patients, male and female. The corridors were narrow, very dark, low-ceilinged, and icy;

concrete walls and floors. Everything in poor repair but not conspicuously filthy. We made our way to a kind of common room in which there was a Christmas tree with blinking lights. Later I noticed that their blinking was irregular and caused by a short in the wiring, not by a programmed interrupter. We put out the word that Mass was starting, and in about 15 minutes the room was packed solid. Even behind the table that served as a makeshift altar there was barely room for me and Father Manuel, a Portuguese missionary priest who arrived separately and was the principal celebrant. The congregation was predominantly male and middle-aged. There was no uniform garb for the patients, and they were all dressed in several layers of shabby clothes. Both women and men had close-cropped hair, and in fact the women were identifiable solely by their beardlessness. (It then occurred to me that even the severely handicapped women at the Casa had long, well-tended hair with bows, barrettes, and ribbons kept in order by the staff and the sisters.) When they sang it was striking how few teeth, and those brown, they had among them, and again the smell of rot became noticeable with every chorus. About halfway through Mass I became distracted by another smell—the hot wire of the Christmas tree lights—and I began a pessimistic calculation of the chances of orderly egress in the event of fire: a jammed room; a single, small, inward-opening door; bars on the only two windows.

Communion was given to the four Catholic patients; most would have been Orthodox. After Mass I saw one patient with grossly deformed legs pick up another (legless) man—maybe 18 years old—and carry him back to his cell. His ankles bowed out from his calves at about a 160° angle, and he tipped crazily to right and left with each stride; I couldn't see how he could walk himself, much less carry anyone that size. As I took off my vestments a short, broad-shouldered man with close-set eyes and almost no brow came up to me, took me by both elbows, and began speaking softly as he stared into my face; after a few moments his own face clouded and he put his forehead on my chest and blubbered for a minute and then shuffled away, leaving an egg-whitey smear of snot on my clerical shirt. I put my sweater and gloves back on and noticed that my borrowed goose-down parka was leaking brown chicken feathers.

After allowing a few minutes for the patients to return to their cells, the sisters went from room to room to give each one a present of a tangerine, a chocolate bar, a pack of sugar wafers, and a slice of panettone. Some patients appeared catatonic; some carried on arguments with a wall or a bedpost; most ate their tangerines hungrily. Each cell was packed with twelve beds, sometimes stacked as bunks, and there were twelve steel lockers in one corner. I saw no radiators in any of the rooms, and those in the corridors were ludicrously small and few in number; the ones I touched were warm but not hot.

The head nurse, or at any rate the person who seemed to be in charge, sat for most of our visit smoking in the tiny dispensary. Underneath she was dressed conventionally enough, in black slacks, shoes, and turtleneck. But on top of this she wore a white terry cloth bathrobe and an Orlando Magic stocking hat, which added to the weird unworldliness of the atmosphere.

Home for Vespers at 4:00. Afterward I walked over to the main house to visit the children. One girl threw a dinner-table tantrum and swiped her bowl off the table, then stood and screamed for a few minutes, really angry, with the wet white bread visible in her open mouth. The other children seemed unfazed, and one boy meditatively ate the center out of his slice of bread, holding up the intact ring formed by the crust. Maria moved quietly from place to place, picking up the empty bowls and wiping them.

Adoration and Benediction from 6:30 to 7:30. I was just about to get ready for bed when Abby Flavell came by with the girls Illeana and Elena, the latter dressed as Santa Claus with a beard made of cotton gauze. They made me a Christmas present of a card, a Bic razor, and some toffee. Abby's work has been mainly music therapy with the children, by which she tries to overcome some of the mental damage done by the early years of total neglect.

Thursday, December 26

Up at 5:00. A bitterly cold morning (−18°F). Breakfast of bread and taramasalata. All the Bacau sisters are traveling with me to the MC house at Sfantu Gheorghe in Transylvania, to drop me there and visit with their sisters. At 6:10 we got into the same unheated VW van, two sisters in front with the driver, six sisters with me in the back seated facing each other on two bench seats along the sides, with coats and blankets piled on our laps. I was pleased by the company of

Sister Szymon Jozef, who has a dry but lively wit, a characteristically Polish irony in the good-humored concession that things will always turn out to be worse than expected. The first hour was dark; when it became light enough we said Lauds. About an hour and a half into the trip the engine failed and we pulled off the road in a small village. The sisters debated whether it was better to try to catch a bus back to Bacau, to try to catch a bus to Sfantu Gheorghe, or to risk a serious breakdown in the mountains by going forward. Once he got the engine restarted, the driver insisted that the last course was best, and we went on without incident. My feet were burning with the cold as we started to climb into the Carpathians, and our comfort was not increased by the fact that the sliding van door did not close fully and let in a stream of frigid air. Going uphill it would open about ¾"; downhill it would close to a ¼" gap. It was slow going on the icy switchbacks. After three and a half hours we reached Sfantu Gheorghe and the MC house. A welcome smell of coffee in the entranceway as we kicked the snow off our shoes. It's a spacious three-story stucco building, the first floor given to the sisters' community, the second floor to old and dying women ("grannies" in the sisters' technical parlance), and the third floor to catechism classrooms. In one of these a cot was put for me: a large bare room with an Infant of Prague in one corner.

The sisters put out a lunch in the sacristy/parlor for their driver, Ion Herciu, and me, and, given we had no language in common, we had a pleasant and instructive conversation. Pony carts were frequently passing outside in the snow at a fast trot. A tractor came down the streets towing a wagonload of sand, from which a man tossed a shovelful across the road every ten yards or so. The city is located in a valley surrounded by low mountains, with conifers visible here and there among high-pitched rooftops.

After Vespers, Adoration, and Mass, the Bacau contingent said their goodbyes to their sisters and me and got back in the van. There was a kind of schoolgirlish romp as the three Indian sisters ran laughing behind the van in the street trying to pelt it with handfuls of powdery snow.

The superior Sister Szymona (Polish) took me up to visit the grannies. She explained that Transylvania is predominantly Hungarian-speaking and Catholic, whereas Moldavia and the rest of the country is mainly Romanian-speaking and Orthodox. The sisters have to learn both languages, and their work is divided between tending to the grannies in their own house, and care for the large gypsy camp (around 4,000) which begins a hundred yards from their door. One of the grannies, Veronika, had died on Christmas Day, and was to be buried on the 27th—if Szymona could succeed in wrangling the necessary permits from the municipal bureaucracy.

On going to bed, I heard people in the street singing to the music of a squeezebox.

Friday, December 27

Up at 4:50. Very cold. I borrowed a pocket mirror yesterday from Sister Szymona to shave with and, this being my first night passed in Transylvania, checked my neck for telltale punctures. Nothing doing. I shaved badly and took a few twists under the primitive shower head, from which there came a thin but steady trickle of hot water—luxury enough in the circumstances. OR and Lauds in my room, then down to the parlor for breakfast. There was a rich smell of soiled bedding in the stairwell. A pretty sun-up behind the mountains: white slopes, black firs, neon-orange dawn, cobalt sky. I was given an object lesson in Soviet-bloc technology. Partway through a bowl of plain yogurt, I was puzzled to see a pink strawberries-and-cream swirl in the dish. Then it became clear that I was bleeding into it. I had sliced open my lip on the stamping-burr left on the bowl of the teaspoon I was using. It occurred to me that I had congratulated myself too quickly on my unpunctured neck, as I had inflicted on myself a kind of auto-vampirism with my razor, my bootlace guides, and now a teaspoon.

As I have a gruesome collection of bloody handkerchiefs, I washed them and my other laundry in a bucket and hung them to dry in the upstairs bathroom. The local priest was due to say Mass in the grannies' chapel, but was a no-show, so I took it. The sisters have gently intimated that the good father tends to overdose on antifreeze, and they expressed concern that he would also miss this afternoon's burial.

10:30 Lecture to the sisters.

Lunch of polenta and a fried carp. At 3:30 the sisters, three grannies, and I walked to the Catholic cemetery, about seven blocks away. Sister Paula (Indian) carried with her a hammer and nails in her bag, explaining to me her embarrassment on the occasion of her first Transylvanian funeral, when the sextons asked her for nails to close the coffin and she, presuming they would be provided, was caught short. I confessed that this was my first BYO [bring your own] burial as well. The cemetery was snowy and pathless; two or three times one of the grannies slipped and took a fall on her bottom. We entered into an unheated stone chapel in which Veronika's open coffin was lying. The cold was intense. We said a Rosary, the sisters and grannies alternating decades in Romanian and Hungarian and I mumbling to myself in English. After half an hour the pastor showed up, wearing a cassock, biretta, cotta, and pluvial, conducted a (well-sung) 20-minute service in Hungarian, and then walked with us to the grave. After the sextons lowered the coffin by ropes they tried to fill the grave, but the piles of earth were frozen hard, and two had to loosen the soil with mattocks while another pair shoveled it in. After the grave was filled, the pastor and I introduced ourselves and spoke briefly but amicably in clumsy Latin.

At 5:00 a dozen or so gypsy children turned up for catechism: 8- to 12-year-olds. They are astonishingly beautiful; I've never seen such consistently handsome children in a random gathering. Clothes tatty but clean. The sisters had them act out the Annunciation, each reading a part and going through the appropriate motions; then they recited the Annunciation decade of the Rosary in Hungarian. I was impressed with the fact that they all knew all the prayers, including the Fatima prayer, by heart.

8:30 Lecture. Compline, and early to bed.

Armenia Diary

Father X

Sunday, December 21, 2003

After a 10-hour layover in the Vienna airport they finally called my flight, and we boarded a Tyrolean Airways Fokker 70 at about 10:30 p.m. The first-class section was occupied by the kind of flashy hard guys in their late thirties that were later pointed out to me—how accurately, I can't say—as Armenian mafiosi. Certainly they dressed and acted the part, with the swagger and the smirk and the pricey toys—heavy gold watches and leather coats—on conspicuous display. One carried skin mags and a cell phone that sounded the *Addams Family* theme song.

The flight east took 3 hours, and we landed in Yerevan at 4:30 a.m. local time. Oddly, Yerevan is 4 hours ahead of Greenwich, while Baghdad—on the same meridian—is only 3 hours ahead, and Teheran, 7 degrees of longitude to the east, is 3 and a half ahead. We walked down the gangway into darkness and bitter cold and were loaded onto a bus where we waited shivering for a driver to show up. My hand stuck to the metal of the handrail. After ten minutes a man appeared, spat a cigarette onto the tarmac, and moved us no more than 50 yards to the Arrivals doorway. I learned that Armenian includes some very expressive monosyllables. It would have been more amusing if it had been 30 degrees warmer.

Inside, the airport was bare, dirty, and cold. I'd figured that since we were arriving before 5 a.m. there'd be no lengthy queueing for immigration, but in fact two flights had just preceded us, and I stood in line for half an hour. The border police wore Soviet-style wool uniforms; a square female officer in her late thirties had peroxided hair and an ill-fitting grey tunic with three stars on her oversized shoulder boards. She scowled at me and scowled at my passport and stamped it with violent disgust as if squashing a roach.

The Home at Spitak

I was met by the superior Sister Mieke (Belgian), Sister Anne Marie (Indian), and Carlo the driver, and we climbed into a Land Rover and headed north on icy unmarked roads through the mountains for about an hour and a half. It was still dark when we arrived.

Spitak is situated at an elevation of about 5,300 feet in the Bazum Mountains, a spur of the Lesser Caucasus range, about 30 miles east of Turkey and 35 miles south of Georgia. The surrounding mountains are between 8,000 and 9,000 feet at the summit. This was the epicenter of a catastrophic earthquake in December of 1988, which killed 25,000 and destroyed the town's only factories and many of its dwellings. Among the relief efforts was the construction of a cluster of prefabricated houses and other buildings that came to include the Missionaries of Charity's Home of Peace for orphans and handicapped children, four miles to the west of Spitak proper. I was given a room in another prefab building, shared by the MC's chaplain Father Laurier Harvey, a Canadian Jesuit. I felt better after some instant coffee.

It was painfully cold as I walked over to my own quarters—cold enough to hurt my teeth when my mouth was open—and I realized my clothes were inadequate. There is a nearly constant gusting wind blowing a mixture of light snow and grit along the ground. The landscape is monotone and bleak. Everything that is not covered by snow, including the buildings, is the color of dead weeds. My room was clean, bare, and in spite of a weak electric heater, glacial; I put on my gloves and stocking hat and a second sweater and managed to doze in a chair. The building occasionally shook with the wind, which I could feel knifing in through a gap between the wall and floor slab.

Adoration and Benediction in the sisters' chapel, then a tour of the facility. There are roughly thirty children of both sexes, ranging from newborns to 14-year-olds, with a few older special cases. Almost all are mentally impaired: some mildly, some very severely indeed; almost all have some physical defect as well. A few are true orphans; most were abandoned by their parents. As is usual in such places the boys are especially hungry for masculine attention, and I was dragged by the sleeve here and there to admire toy trucks, favorite photos, and Christmas decorations. Those who could speak at all addressed me in broken English learned from the sisters. I was touched by their delight in the Nativity crèche. Every ox and ass and kneeling shepherd was individually plucked from its spot, carefully examined, shown to me for my approval, and then reverently returned to its position. At least once a day I was towed into the playroom to repeat the inspection.

Back at his house Father Harvey showed me a Russian battery charger, with which he was attempting to top up the spare for a veteran VW Golf he'd bought thirdhand. Both cable leads were marked "negative", unhelpfully, and he determined the proper configuration empirically: when the charger started to smoke, he knew the cables had to be reversed.

Living with the MCs are two volunteers: Hilde Vanwesemael, a Belgian in her late twenties, and Jevgenia Veskäilänen, a Finn in her mid-twenties, both pious laywomen, both nearing the end of extensive sojourns here and despondent at the prospect of leaving the sisters and the children.

Vespers in the chapel at 7:00, followed by supper, then Compline. Outside, light snow blown by a stiff breeze. My room still cold, but I piled on the blankets and got four or five hours of sleep.

December 23

Up at 5:50, said the Office of Readings and Lauds, with my breath visible. The water is on the fritz, so I took a bucket from the 55-gallon barrel and bathed very quickly, toweling off as fast as I could and climbing into my clothes. A cold-water shave. Mass at 7:00, with the sisters plus Hilde and Jevgenia, and Communion by intinction, according to the Armenian usage.

After breakfast, Sister Nishakant (Indian) loaded up the Land Rover and took Hilde and me into Spitak. It was sunny and bitter: temperature about 3°F. The devastation left by the earthquake is still obvious everywhere: rusting trestles, buckled train tracks overgrown with weeds, lopsided half buildings used as haylofts. Goats, calves, and dogs were foraging in the alleys and footpaths. Though I'd been told by Sister Mieke that unemployment was roughly 80 percent, I was shocked by the destitution.

The spine of the town is an abandoned factory (for processing sugar beets, I was told) that was erected by the Russians, destroyed by the earthquake, and—since its destruction coincided with the breakup of the Soviet Union—never rebuilt. The poor have scavenged from the ruins whatever they could find for their own use. Several rusting shipping containers were used as houses, as well as wheel-less buses propped up on cinder blocks with the windows sealed with cardboard. In at least two cases an 8-by-20-foot oil storage tank had been laid lengthwise on the ground with broken pieces of concrete to serve as chocks and a door cut in one end of the cylinder. Sanitation took the form of scrap-metal outhouses just big enough for a five-gallon bucket. There were no true roads in the poorer areas, just twin ruts of the kind tractors make, and Carlo moved the Land Rover through the snow in low gear, trying to balance on the crown between the ruts and the bank.

I saw a man carrying what at first looked like a bundle of weeds on his back; they were twigs and bits of sticks he had collected for fuel. Then I was hit by the realization of the treelessness of the hills and the fact that none of the houses was built of wood, but concrete and stone and steel, making for a doubly cold winter. Elsewhere I would see women standing in the snow by the roadside, completely in the open, with a dismal little pile of firewood for sale at their feet.

We made our way into a cluster of shacks and stopped. There was a Dogpatch flavor to the place; the houses were crazily out of plumb and improvised from disparate bits of scrap: corrugated steel, fieldstone, sheet metal scavenged from crane cabs, odd bits of concrete and "pre-owned" cinder blocks. Speckled hens scratched through the snow and scattered when the dogs came out from under the houses to bark at us. Sewerage, running water, and electric power were missing. On the other hand, there was evidence that the poor were still trying—that it was money rather than energy that was lacking. Many houses had laundry hanging from clotheslines; the fences were as heterogeneous as the houses (one included a harrow frame, punch-press scrap, a white enamel range top, and several rocker panels) but were intact. I'm not sure why, but it struck me as heartening that many of the cottages, even the poorest, had curtains hanging in the windows: a flag of defiance.

Carlo lit up a Chesterfield, and Sister Nishakant and Hilde and I took some plastic sacks filled with milk powder, cereal, soap, and some odds and ends of clothing and made our way cautiously down a steep and icy incline between the shacks. We came to a one-room cottage, maybe 18 feet square, with a tiny stove in the middle. Against one wall was a bed with two sick children in it. There were no closets, no chests of drawers, no shelves, no hooks on the walls. All the

clothing of the household, outer- and underwear, was laid flat on top
of the bed, and the children shivered beneath it all.

The cottage was made of concrete—not poured concrete, but
irregular blocks that might have come from a torn-up highway or
factory floor, laid in courses like bricks. I could see daylight through
many of the chinks. The door was a piece of fiberboard hanging by
one hinge in the doorway, providing some privacy, I suppose, but
little else. It was still achingly cold. The mistress of the house was
a very thin woman of about 27, a widow, plainly worried, dressed
in a long skirt and thin wool top. She stood trembling in the cold,
rubbing her upper arms and chafing her hands constantly. Her teeth
chattered. Sister Nishakant gave her some large pieces of heavy cardboard and told her to put it on the floor as covering and not to burn
it for fuel in the stove. I remembered that Eudora Welty story where
the sharecropper couple, on a freezing morning, put a chair into the
fire to feel the warmth, and in a fit of madness feed every stick of
furniture they own into the flames. Then, of course, the fire dies and
the cold returns.

Next we visited a two-room cottage, and a slightly older housewife, whose husband had abandoned her. Carlo had loaded the back
with 18-inch squares of scrap linoleum for her, although, being frozen, some of it shattered in our hands when we took it out to give
her. Some children helped carry it to her house. The rear room was
windowless and used for storage. In the dark I could make out half a
dozen cabbages on the floor—semispoiled, judging from the smell—
onions, and some unidentifiable vegetables in jars of tea-colored
brine. This house as well as the first had no decoration beyond a picture of the Sacred Heart and a smaller one of Mother Teresa.

We returned to the Land Rover and visited three or four houses
in other neighborhoods. One was headed, at least provisionally, by
a 13-year-old boy, who took care of a younger sister and brother. I
was told that his mother had been in an overloaded bus that tumbled down a mountainside, as a result of which she'd lost a leg. Her
husband had left her and his children and skipped town, and she was
presently in the state hospital for more surgery. They too got soap
and cereal and some Christmas candy.

On the way home Sister Nishakant stopped at a grocery to buy
flour. The store was small and crowded; I saw bananas and dates and a
30-pound smoked carp and rings of untempting sausage that smelled

like Deep Woods Off. Above the heads of the grocers were rows of vodka and brandy; also the unfortunately named "lemon BARF detergent powder".

Home for lunch, and an hour of adoration. Afterward I visited the children's playroom. Hovanes, whose legs are paralyzed and who muscles himself from chair to chair with his arms, was completing a jigsaw puzzle he had laid out on the table—which I was pleased to see was a 750-piece panorama of the Cleveland skyline. How this particular puzzle ended up in Spitak is a mystery, but it seemed appropriate somehow. When the boys found out where I was from they said, "America—drive big auto!" and made the steering-wheel motion with their hands. When I said I didn't have an auto they grew quiet and appeared baffled, gripping the air more diffidently, convinced I must be mistaken about my car ownership or my nationality but unsure which.

4:30: Heard the sisters' confessions.

I found Sister Romana and Hilde in the nursery, taking turns holding and feeding bottles to the five babies. The youngest, I believe they said, is five weeks old. Two of them were Down syndrome babies, and another two had hydrocephaly, which had given their heads that characteristic inverted-leek-shaped deformity. Romana explained to me that the sisters were engaged in a more or less continual struggle with the surgeons in Yerevan, urging them to perform reparative surgery on the defective children. Sometimes they were able to pay for it with money given by foreign benefactors.

After Vespers, a supper of soup and bread. The heater in my room (which can't be moved above the lowest setting without tripping the breaker) has taken the chill out of air but it's not exactly snug yet. At least I no longer read my breviary with gloves on. Compline and early to bed.

December 24

Up at 4:50: Office of Readings and Lauds. Still no water, so another blitz bath in a plastic bucket. Four or five drowned earwigs found in the water barrel. A spectacular sky walking over for Mass: moonless, cold and perfectly clear, the Milky Way so distinct that the edges looked to be torn out of paper. Mass at 6:00, a quick breakfast, a Holy Hour beginning at 7:00. I noticed the sky begin to lighten at 7:40.

I was asked to help pin up some of the harder-to-reach Christmas decorations in the boys' corridors. Gaik caught my shirt cuff and yanked me into the room he shares with three others. He's about 15 and big for his age, physically coordinated but mentally well below par. He was keen to show me a chess set he had under his bed, and was entranced by the plastic pieces, which he played with like toy soldiers. I started to point out to him where the pieces went on the board but saw the lights go out almost instantly. "America!" he said to me. "Drive car?" At least he thinks I'm still teachable.

In the afternoon I heard the children's confessions. I was given a chair in one of the playrooms, with the lighted candle on a table at my elbow. The sisters brought the children in one by one, reminded them to kneel down, and then left. In the case of the three or four most severely defective children—those incapable of speaking and understanding where they were—I simply gave them a blessing at the sister's prompting and they were led out again. For the most part I was pleased at how well they confessed, even those with Down syndrome; they took some liberties with the order of the ritual, but they knew right from wrong, knew what to confess. For penitents whose English was shaky or nil Sister Anne Marie knelt beside them and served as interpreter—of course, she gets put "under the seal" too.

10:00 P.M., the Christmas vigil Mass. The children were dressed in their best for Christmas; a somewhat shocking change—not that they were scruffy earlier, but in aggregate they'd outshine any congregation in a U.S. church I'd seen in the past 20 years. I was touched by the care they took with Gargarin, who is perhaps the most severely retarded of all; he looked almost natty in sweater and slacks, seated on a bench smiling at the palm of his left hand, which he held continually four inches from his nose. All the children received Communion—again by intinction, according to the Armenian usage. They sang the hymns lustily and grossly off-key; it may well be the first occasion on which the congregation's singing was worse than my own. Compline, and to bed at 12:30.

Christmas Day

Up at 5:50, read my breviary with a flashlight. There's an Italian water heater in the bathroom, but as there's still no running water it's useless. Bathing is unpleasant, but it's the shaving in cold water I really detest. At breakfast, because it was Christmas, the sisters gave me a fried egg.

Christmas Mass at 9:30, Father Harvey presiding.

The temperature outside has risen to about 20°. I was surprised to see students arriving for class at the state-run school to the west of the sisters' house, but was told that December 25 has no particular meaning for Armenians; New Year's Day is the major holiday, and Christians celebrate the Epiphany as well.

That said, the sisters were not going to let the desperately poor go hungry on Christmas Day, and Nishakant loaded the Land Rover with warm food, and Jevgenia and I rode along to help deliver it. We made fifteen stops or so, often feeding two or more households at a time. The sisters had prepared stewed chicken, boiled potatoes, and a salad of peas and grated carrot. There was also an apple and a tangerine for every person in the house. One complication—which, I'm ashamed to say, hadn't occurred to me—was that food containers were scarce, and people sometimes brought out buckets and wash-basins, into which Nishakant and Jevgenia carefully ladled the meal. I'd help carry it into the homes, say a blessing prayer with Nishakant, and sprinkle the room with Holy Water. Looking around for other food I usually saw nothing. Most people gave no sign of gratitude or resentment. One woman scolded Nishakant ("She asks for clothes, Father"). Another woman wept.

Slowly it dawned on me that nearly all the most wretched folks we visited were mentally deficient, and that in addition to being destitute they were imperfectly capable of keeping house and taking care of themselves generally. I mentioned this to Nishakant and she nodded, and explained that depression was an even greater problem; sometimes the hardship became overwhelming and people just quit. She told me that "Ripsy" (Hripsime, one of their wards) was found as a baby, black with filth, lying in a dirty bed with her head crawling with lice.

Back at the compound, I followed the spry Father Harvey down a concrete conduit into a well pit to try to prime the pump that services his bungalow. Water flowed for five minutes and quit.

After lunch there was a Christmas pageant, which had been in rehearsal for several days. With the help of some creative gender-bending, everybody had a part. The infant Jesus was convincingly played by a 3-week-old girl whom the sisters laid in a bassinette.

Those confined to wheelchairs, for the most part the most severely retarded, served as the angels, wearing white robes with tinsel haloes and cardboard wings fastened behind. As they slumped in their chairs, cross-eyed and drooling, it came home to me that few persons who played the part would be likely to pass more of their lives in the state of grace. A two-man pantomime donkey genuflected in the general direction of the manger, next to four of the Three Kings.

Afterward, Santa Claus made an appearance and gave each child a gift from his sack, for which the recipient performed a dance or sang a song. I sat on a folding chair helping with hard-to-open presents, etc., caught unawares several times by slobbery kisses on the temple and neck from overexcited children.

Vespers, a bowl of soup, and to bed before 9:00.

DIOGENES: THE EARLY DAYS

Father Mankowski often observed that liberal thought is characterized by inter-nal contradictions and double standards, if not outright hypocrisy. But since the purveyors of liberal ideology are not embarrassed by their inconsistencies, he argued in these blog posts that the most effective response is not solemn rebuttal but satire and ridicule—the handiest weapons in the armory of Diogenes. At times, his parody would take the form of an imaginary news story, issued by a nonexistent wire service. In the final piece in this section, he explains why this approach is appropriate—even (or perhaps especially?) for ecclesiastical affairs.

Twilight in Camelot

July 25, 2003

Uh-oh. You know there's trouble in the Kingdom of Eagle's Wings when the *U.S. Catholic* urges us *not* to shop for worship outside our own parish boundaries. This from an article by Peter Feuerhard:

> Jesuit Father Walter J. Burghardt writes that "some Catholics refuse to worship with other Catholics save on their own narrow terms." Those terms can include all sorts of factors—a similar social class, ideological temperament, ethnicity, and age—yet imposing these conditions are stabs to the heart of the unity of the Body of Christ. It's not that parish shoppers are evil. However, they might be establishing an alterna-tive structure of church without thinking through what is being lost, namely the vitality of the neighborhood parish.

Understood at face value, outside of its real-world context, Fr. Burghardt's rebuke is entirely on target. We shouldn't flit from church to church in search of designer liturgies that gratify some idiosyncratic and spiritually irrelevant caprice. Yet many orthodox Catholics will feel their throats tighten at the unfairness of the sug-gestion. Why? Because too often they are made to feel that the desire

41

to have a Mass "by the book" is as self-serving and "ideological" as the motives of those who change the words and actions on their own authority to conform to feminist or New Age fashions. "You prefer 'Peace to His people on earth,'" the pastor explains patronizingly. "Others prefer 'Peace to God's people on earth.' I can't please everybody."

Which option wins out nineteen times out of twenty? You guessed it. And that is why the orthodox often flock to churches with a reputation for Masses celebrated as the Church requires they be celebrated. The liberal response? Well, dialogue, and patient renegotiation, one might think.

Not so. Just as liberals rediscovered the liturgical sovereignty of the local bishop once the Holy See began restoring order across national and diocesan boundaries, so they've rediscovered the virtue of the geographical parish now that Catholics (and those disproportionately young and committed) are packing out the trad Masses and ritually kosher liturgies. When libs are reduced to the expedient of deploring "an alternative structure of church"—precisely the cause they've been beating the drums for these thirty years past—you know they're running scared.

Unpleasantness at the Vatican

December 15, 2003

"I'm not here to celebrate, like you, the birth of Christ, but to ask you why you are not in mourning for his death in this place. God has been a witness to the corruption of his leadership, of the exploitation and abuses by the clergy."

That's hip-hop artist Lauryn Hill scolding the audience at the Vatican's Christmas concert held Saturday evening in the Paul VI Auditorium. Her *j'accuse* was a not-entirely-coherent mixture of old-style Protestant polemic ("I don't believe in God's representatives on earth") and contemporary invective against the corruption exemplified by the clergy abuse scandal.

It's impossible to gauge the sincerity of Hill's admonishment, but it's clear that the publicity thereby gained will sell lots of albums and cost her zero customers. Moreover, a person engaged in the pop music business at any level is in an extraordinarily poor position to criticize others for sexual exploitation of youth. Ask yourself whether the entertainment industry helps teenagers make choices in favor of purity, rationality, sobriety, and thrift.

That said, there's a sense in which Hill's Vatican hosts got what was coming to them. I'm referring not to her reprimand on sexual abuse but to the ill-focused worldliness of senior clergy who wish to nuzzle up to the rich and famous of whatever stripe, including those who exult in contempt for Christianity. The Italian daily *La Repubblica* says a rapper named Shaggy was not allowed to perform a number called "Hey Sexy Lady" before the assembled bishops, but clearly the stuff that makes the cut is pretty gamy.

Are Vatican photo ops with pop stars expressly designed to show the world that Catholic clergy are no longer ingenuous and unworldly mystics locked away in monastic libraries? If so, many of us will wish to say: "Gentlemen, *you've proved your point.* Rembert Weakland and Robert Lynch have convinced us more thoroughly than many thousands of acoustic guitars could have. If you're missing, we won't go looking for you in the adoration chapel—a point you made by inviting Lauryn Hill to amuse you in the first place. Now can we move on?"

The Young Prospectors; or,
Nemo restaurat quod non habet

January 15, 2004

Several bloggers have commented on Fr. Andrew Greeley's "Young Fogeys" piece in the current *Atlantic*, in which he retails the unsurprising news that

> a generation of conservative young priests is on the rise in the U.S. Church. These are newly ordained men who seem in many ways intent on restoring the pre-Vatican II Church, and who, reversing the classic generational roles, define themselves in direct opposition to the liberal priests who came of age in the 1960s and 1970s.

Greeley is not alone among aging liberals in viewing the future with dismay. "I haven't attended more than once any church," admits the NCR's [*National Catholic Reporter*'s] Arthur Jones, "where the altar is home to the new-style soutaned papal marionettes." (In "soutaned papal marionettes" one hears the ecclesial counterpart of Rush Limbaugh's "mind-numbed robots"—minus the jocularity.)

Though characteristically tendentious in presentation, Greeley's portrait of the generational divide corresponds in rough outline to my own experience and hunches—including the finding that "only about 40 percent of the younger generation believe that birth control is always wrong" and the conclusion that it represents a "failure of the Restoration efforts of the past thirty years." Greeley seems smugly pleased with this failure, though most of what he reports he considers bad news on his own terms.

Where Greeley is hopelessly wrong is in his conviction (repeated six times) that the conservative ideas of young priests represent a *restoration*. To restore something, it needs to have been there in the first place, and for the newer priests the Catholic life they're trying to bring into existence is as remote from their juvenile experience as "Blowin' in the Wind" was foreign to the childhood of Andrew Greeley. If a 35-year-old Catholic opts for Gregorian chant or the doctrine of *Humanae Vitae*, he's not replicating the cozy ambience of his own years as an altar boy—remember, for him a priest is a mysteriously angry man in Docksiders haranguing the assembly that Lent is no longer a penitential season—no, the orthodox priest had to work to discover the tradition and he had to work to hang on to it through hostile years in the seminary.

There are of course seminarians today who are timid, unimaginative, intellectually passive, and overly eager to ingratiate themselves with the faculty. The irony is that, in 2004, the brain-dead sycophant who parrots his profs holds the opinions of ... Arthur Jones. And Andrew Greeley.

A Sign of Contradiction

March 9, 2004

A friend of a friend who teaches at Smith College in Massachusetts said that jewelry salesmen often come onto the campus and display their wares on a blanket spread out on the grass. As he was walking to class one day he passed a woman student checking out silver crosses (of the kind used as necklace pendants) and heard her ask the sales-man, "How much are the ones with the little man on them?"

The controversy surrounding *The Passion of the Christ*—even if it serves no other purpose—should have the wholesome effect of shocking Christians back into a recognition that the Cross was an instrument of torture and execution, and that "the little man" sol-dered onto the bit of metal and worn as a pin or brooch or charm represents the corpse of a Jew executed as a criminal—or at least the last agonies of his execution. The point is not that the Cross shouldn't be used as a sign of victory, but that it's a paradoxical sign, and we need to keep before us both aspects of the paradox. Helen Hitchcock once asked how we'd view the entrance rite at Mass if the lead altar girl paraded down the main aisle holding aloft a processional noose.

As Chesterton never tired of pointing out, a cross is also a cross-roads, a "sign of contradiction" that requires a decision of us—the most important decision we will ever make. Hence the cross has always been a source of uneasiness to those for whom no parting of the ways is ever required by their convictions and for whom religion is a kind of cotton candy. During the 1998 controversy at George-town over whether or not crucifixes should be removed from the classrooms, university campus minister Adam Bunnell, O.F.M.Conv., proposed that a pitcher and towel (representing Jesus' washing of His apostles' feet) would be a better symbol for Christianity, since Christ taught us to serve others. No crossroads there.

Repositioning Religious Practice

March 29, 2004

From a Jerry Filteau CNS [Catholic News Service] story on a sym-posium on confession held at Catholic U:

> [Boston College Prof. James] O'Toole contrasted a New York City parish in 1896–97, where the seven priests on staff heard 78,000 con-fessions a year, with the typical parish today, where the bulletin may list a half-hour or 15-minute weekly time for confessions, or perhaps offer them "anytime by appointment." "Between 1965 and 1975, the numbers of American Catholics going to confession fell through the floor," he said.

OK, OK. It's a Legion of Mary–caliber mistake to see this as BAD news. We're in CTSA [Catholic Theological Society of America] country here, and that means before the end of the article our Brylcreemed heads are going to be patted by the union theologians while they explain how spending Saturday afternoons watching *That Girl* reruns is really a sign of vibrant spiritual health. Scapulars tucked away? Drool wiped off your chins? Right then. Here's Joseph Chinnici, O.F.M., dean of the Franciscan School of Theology in Berkeley, California:

"Are we seeing a decline in confession or an expansion of forgiveness?" he asked. "What was happening was that the religious practice of auricular confession was being repositioned in relationship to multiple expressions of penance now occurring in church life."

That's why folks don't budge from the couch on Saturdays: they sense an "expansion of forgiveness"—it's so expansive, in fact, that they stay home Sunday mornings too. (I speak only of the spiritually mature, of course.)

To the extent that the gap has been filled at all, it is General Absolution that has taken its place. And when you think about the folks for whom the sacramental "resolution of amendment" is a particularly sticky issue, you can understand why they want auricular confession to die and the bullhorn model ("I absolve you *all* ...") to proliferate.

In its bell-bottom days, the CTSA crowd inveighed against the *ex opere operato* nature of "laundry list" confessions—the mechanical, putatively unspiritual recital of sins and the rote (bad word) act of contrition. All the more ironic that today's "thinking Catholic" has embraced *ex opere operato* theology in its most extreme sacramental form: simply by being in this particular lighted room at this particular time the penitent is absolved of his sins. Progress.

Matthew 18:15–17 (corrected)

May 10, 2004

If thy brother shall trespass against thee, go and tell him his fault between thee and him alone: if he shall hear thee, thou hast gained thy brother. But if he will not hear thee, then take with thee one or two more, that in the mouth of two or three witnesses every word may be established. And if he shall neglect to hear them, tell it unto the church. But if he neglect to hear the church ... well ... let him remain to thee as a brother while thou settest up a blue-ribbon committee to study the appropriate response mechanisms. With any luck, by the time the committee doth issue a report, thy brother shall have finished his second term and the church will be a Muslim day care facility anyway.

Can't We All Just Get Along?

October 9, 2004

Good news from this week's *America*: the editors are calling for a return to "charity in intellectual life". When the playground bully starts pleading for Queensbury Rules, he fears he's in for a thrashing. Check this out:

> The ferment produced by the Second Vatican Council has been stilled. Perhaps the last great Catholic contribution to American culture came with the bishops' pastoral letters of the 1980's. *The Challenge of Peace*, in particular, had significant impact on the wider society, educating the public and politicians to debate issues of peace and war in a disciplined way.

Sorry, lads, but anyone who believes *The Challenge of Peace* had "significant impact" on anyone outside of the bishops' print shop is delusional, and seriously so. Exactly whose mind was changed—changed in favor of Catholic teaching, I mean—by this document? Of course it may well have been a high-water mark for the Jesuits of 56th Street, when the bishops and the Catholic academy were safe and snug in the embrace of the Democratic Party, but things began to slip soon thereafter:

> In the intervening years, deep fissures have appeared in the U.S. church. On the public side of American Catholic intellectual life, charity has become hard to find. Intellectual exchange has fallen victim to petty name-calling, *ad hominem* arguments and a "gotcha" politics of denunciation. As Archbishop Harry Flynn of St. Paul-Minneapolis wrote last month, "This uncharitable, biased and reckless substitute for what formerly was fair-minded commentary and fact-based dialogue has found its venomous way into our Catholic family."

Translation: "Having been shielded from criticism for our entire adult lives by the enjoyment of a virtual monopoly on communications media, we now find ourselves obliged to operate on what is nearly a level playing field, where we find our noses rubbed in the same stuff we have heretofore dished out to our adversaries with impunity. It is unpleasant."

Since when is the " 'gotcha' politics of denunciation" foul play? Since when are *ad hominem* arguments out of court? Remember Rembert Weakland's crack (cited in a fawning *New Yorker* profile) that pro-lifers "basically need a hug and a laxative"? Did *America* ever rebuke the archbishop for petty name-calling? Did Harry Flynn take him to task for his reckless substitute for fact-based dialogue? They did not. Why bother? After all, anyone with such poor breeding as to find Weakland's quip uncharitable was in no position to make his complaint heard anyway, and besides, Susan Sarandon is calling on line 3.

It is characteristic of moral imbeciles to be incapable of seeing things from the other man's point of view. Hannah Arendt tells how Adolf Eichmann, after his capture, lamented the fact that he advanced in the SS no further than lieutenant colonel, expecting his Israeli interrogators to sympathize with his hard luck. In the same way it argues for shocking obtuseness on the part of *America* in imagining that Catholic conflicts, until recently, were marked by equilateral charity. The fact that the alarm should be sounded today is a recognition, however confused, that the old order is coming to an end.

No Easter for 2008, Bishops Say

November 17, 2004

WASHINGTON, November 17, 2007 (XIS)—Citing increased awareness of pastoral responsibilities, the U.S. Catholic bishops decided yesterday to drop Easter in 2008 from the roster of Christian feasts. By a vote of 184–28, the recommendation of the USCCB Task Force on Kerygma for "strategic pruning of liturgical deadwood" was adopted by the assembled prelates.

The resolution proposed by the committee expressed concern that the Easter date of April 11 in 2008 would "materially distract

Americans" from their civil obligation of preparing income taxes before the April 15 filing deadline. It was further noted that the NBC miniseries *Dead Ball Foul,* which concerns the HIV infection of former Los Angeles Lakers star Magic Johnson, is scheduled to climax on the evening of Holy Saturday, causing a "potential conflict" for Catholics who could feel "caught between a sentimental attachment to the beauties of tradition and their Christian duty to stay fully informed about the premier health care issue of our time."

Anticipating grumblings from traditionalist factions within the U.S. church, the resolution conceded that "the symbol of the dead and rising god was and remains a cherished part of our heritage" but insisted that "quality scriptural and theological scholarship reminds us that even the first Resurrection Event was not a 'holy day of obligation' but a reaffirmation of what is best and noblest in the human experience."

Objections by some bishops that dropping the feast would reduce revenue on a prime collection weekend provoked sharp responses from many of their brothers. "We are an Easter People!" said Delbert Popp, the Archbishop of Muncie. "Easter is an affair of the heart, not of the calendar." Popp suggested that opponents of the resolution were trying to "box God in a paper time frame" and to "frighten Catholics out of the faith by telling them 'Don't think of God unless we say so!'"

Medford auxiliary Tod Malcomune concurred. "My priests are already stressed to the limit and beyond," he insisted. "They're presiding at three or four liturgies a week, not to mention their breviary. Even without this Easter business many have had to give up *Desperate Housewives* and *E.R.,* and one of my best men is considering dropping his aerobics class. How are we going to be available to God's people if we keep the church's past as an obstacle in our path?"

We've Had It Worse, Boys

April 1, 2005

For the ecclesiastically despondent Catholic, few forms of self-medication are as effective as a careful read through Owen Chadwick's *The Popes and European Revolution* (Oxford, 1981). When one realizes just how grim the situation looked from the vantage point of the late 18th century, our current woes, and the woefully inadequate leaders arrayed against them, appear comparatively manageable—not illusory, but less than lethal.

In 1768, for example, after a series of defeats and political humiliations, Pope Clement XIII issued a threatening edict against the Duke of Parma that was impossible to enforce, and the Englishman Horace Walpole, writing to gloat over the disaster to his friend Horace Mann in Florence, said, "This is a crisis for the Court of Rome from which it will be impossible to recover." And again, after the death of Clement the following year, Walpole wrote Mann asking when the cardinals would elect "the last Pope".

Walpole was not without grounds for his belief. The man elected as Clement XIV was Lorenzo Ganganelli, whose papacy is best known for the suppression of the Jesuits, and who seems eerily contemporary in his style of churchmanship:

> He remained for hours at his desk but he found it difficult to be responsible for even minor decisions, and was confronted with one of the most agonizing decisions which ever faced a Pope. He liked to be liked, shrank from displeasing, and therefore suffered temptation to say pleasant things to both sides and to procrastinate lest decision be unpleasant.

Sound familiar?

Walpole and similar-minded despisers of Catholicism rejoiced in the disarray in which the Church found herself in the early 19th century, but didn't and couldn't predict a Pope Pius IX, nor imagine how loss of temporal power could correlate with an increase of moral authority. So too it's worrisome, in our own time—when pride, sodomy, and the love of compromise have softened the episcopacy to a Ganganelli-like level of timidity—to contemplate the way forward. That's why it's nourishing, as Catholics, to have the consolation of history. Been there. Done that. Bought the hair shirt.

Shell Game

May 23, 2005

The *Boston Globe* has a story on a lay push for a probe into the handling of donated monies on the part of the Archdiocese of Boston:

The heart of the complaint is the accusation that the archdiocese diverted about $4.5 million donated annually by parishioners over 16 years for the priests' pension fund, which is now badly underfunded.

So the question, lads, is this: Did you divert the $4.5 million?

"The Archdiocese takes up special collections for many purposes including support for our clergy," Chancellor David W. Smith said in a statement released by the archdiocese.

Great. We believe you. But did you divert the $4.5 million?

"Each one of those collections is remitted exactly as we represent it will be."

Wonderful. We believe you. But did you divert the $4.5 million?

"Both the Archdiocese of Boston and the clergy funds are audited on an annual basis ..."

Outstanding. We believe you. But did you divert the $4.5 million?

"... and at no time have any of the audit firms raised any questions whatsoever about our handling of these funds."

I repeat the question.

Today's Church, Tomorrow's Treasure

August 29, 2005

XPQwire (August 29)—"WE'RE BUILDING for the future," claims Los Angeles Archdiocesan Projects Manager Msgr. Bud Bradelstad. The man who directs its long-range planning explained that California's largest Catholic diocese designs its churches with a view to future use—as warehouses, fast-food outlets, or even skating rinks.

"We estimate between 40 and 70 percent of our properties will be sold in ten years' time," said Bradelstad, "just to pay the buggery bill. So resale value is hugely important to us. Now if you sell a church that can be easily converted into a Wendy's, say, or a Jiffy Lube, you're getting maybe 80 cents back on your construction cost dollar, compared with 15 cents for a Gothic-style building."

Bradelstad has little patience with critics who prefer traditional church architecture. "It's like marrying a dumb fashion model," he snorted. "Sure she's pretty, but can she cook? And brother, we NEED buildings that can cook—probably $200 million worth of cooking all told. I mean, what can you do with a traditional church except use it for another traditional church?

"Look," he continued. "I like the old-style buildings myself. They're cute. But to build a nave-and-sanctuary prayer-machine in today's world is grossly irresponsible, pastorally speaking. It's a dog. And in the end it's the seller who pays for the makeover."

Recent bankruptcy court decisions in Oregon and Washington have made diocesan real estate more fungible and increased the need for a functional "turnover strategy", according to Bradelstad.

"Take our new cathedral. We could've gone the ritual and worship route and got stuck with an old maid. Instead we went with maximum second-owner flexibility: a poured-concrete megabox that'll bring in big bucks come market time. I'm thinking frozen foods, I'm thinking cineplex, I'm thinking long-term storage, I'm thinking foundry or medium-industry manufacturing. Hey, we've already had interest expressed by General Motors and Lockheed. It's a winner."

Msgr. Bud expressed the hope that the archdiocesan laity would eventually become reconciled to reality and accept the fact that massive legal payouts were part of the "price to be paid" for the advantage of being served by a fully renewed clergy. "You can't keep the lads away from the candy," he said, "and candy costs plenty in the courts. Figure a million three for every Fr. Hollywood on the job. All I'm trying to do is ensure that there'll be a Fr. Hollywood in your future."

Mention of the aesthetic value of European Catholic churches is something of a sore spot with Bradelstad, goading him to exasperation: "Everybody comes whining to me: Look at Chartres Cathedral! Look at Chartres Cathedral! It's so beautiful, so prayerful, so lovely, blah, blah, blah. Well, let me tell you, I've BEEN to Chartres Cathedral. There isn't even a place to park!"

Renewal Pays Off

September 8, 2005

How many priestly ordinations did the Archdiocese of Dublin have this year?

Zero.

That's right, folks. This year was "the first in the history of the diocese," according to Archbishop Diarmuid Martin, "that we have not had a priestly ordination."

Of course we have to take into consideration the *quality* of our newly ordained and not simply the quantity. We are an Easter People.

P.S. No good asking the archbishop if something needs to change; he's already on record: "I am surprised at the superficiality and the anecdotal evidence I am presented with when I ask about concrete pastoral options and about the situation of the faith in Ireland."

You got me there, Your Excellency. No priests. Doesn't get more superficial than that.

Tidings of Comfort and Joy

December 14, 2005

Yet another bold, transgressive artist dares to speak truth to power—in this case, as far as I can see, the power that last resided in the Holy Roman Empire.

> In the Yuletide yukfest, the "Rescue Me" star has a skit about lesbian nuns and a song by "Our Lady of Perpetual Suffering Church Choir" about a hooker. But what really has the Catholic League ready to launch a holy war is Denis [Leary's] take on the origins of Christmas.
>
> "Merry Christmas," says Denis. "Tonight we celebrate the birth of the baby Jesus, whose mom, Mary, just happens to be a virgin—even after she apparently gave birth to Jesus. At least that is what the Catholic Church would have you believe."

As Mark Steyn writes of self-righteously "transgressive" artists: "If you're going to be provocative, it's best to do it with people who can't be provoked." In this case, the worst that could happen to our intrepid social critic already has: a complaint issued by Bill Donohue. Had Leary "transgressed" Shiite pieties with the same breezy contempt he brings to Christian ones, his mom would be pacing Tremont Street in elbow-length rubber gloves, putting his remains into a one-quart Ziploc bag.

So, Leary scores zero points as a critic. But note that he got his catechism right.

It may be said, paradoxically, that blasphemy is the tribute that demons pay to divinity. No one goes out of his way to commit sacrilege unless he implicitly recognizes there's something sacred about the target of his profanity. Leary's tirade—bogus though it is as an act of artistic boldness—concedes in spite of itself that the Church has gotten under his skin—and, presumably, that of his audience as well. This means that the teaching Church is still teaching, her many shonky ministers notwithstanding. Should the Learys and their personal trainers ever decide to lay off the Church and put another moral authority in their crosshairs—*that*, boys and girls, will be the time to start worrying.

Ever Vigilant

July 6, 2006

The USCCB uses a six-element classification of film ratings, ranging from A-1 (general patronage) at one end of the spectrum, to O (morally offensive) at the other. The rating L is explained as "limited adult audience, films whose problematic content many adults would find troubling." Troubling how? To one's taste, conscience, digestive system? Maybe we're not meant to ask.

Check out the explanation offered for the L rating assigned the movie *Loverboy* in the USCCB review:

> Promiscuity, some brief sexual encounters, artificial insemination, partial rear and upper female nudity, breastfeeding, some crude language, an act of animal cruelty, suicide, and murder attempt.

Well. I'm glad they warned us about the breastfeeding.

On Rounding Up to Two

August 7, 2006

Rereading J. Budziszewski's excellent essay in the July 2005 *Touchstone*, I knocked up against the following line: "Sociologists Sara S. McLanahan and Gary Sandefur remark in their book *Growing Up with a Single Parent* that 'if we were asked to design a system for making sure that children's basic needs were met, we would probably come up with something quite similar to the two-parent ideal.'"

It's hard to pack more academic cowardice into thirty words. Put aside the patronizing absurdity of the hypothesis and the pseudo-modest qualifier "probably". What can "something *quite similar* to the two-parent *ideal*" possibly mean? Do experiments show that two parents score slightly beyond the optimum, that the actual asymptote is reached at 1.888 parents?

As this wonderfully deadpan quote illustrates, the "soft sciences" are soft all over. In that world, it is clearly intolerable to assert the obvious truth that children are meant to have a mother and father; the best one can do is suggest that the best theoretical child-rearing design *approximates* the mom-and-pop arrangement.

An institution's inability to state an obvious truth means that institution is seriously deranged. It's not that McLanahan and Sandefur have tumbled into falsehood; the academy is indicted by their mandarin extravagance of apology for daring to dance around the vicinity of an unspeakable fact. Traditional marriage and child rearing serve as a rebuke to those academics who have departed therefrom in their personal lives, and objective attribution of rightness to this "design model" has the sting of moral rebuke. Whence it's unmentionable.

N.B. When the day arrives on which your ophthalmic surgeon assures you he's striving for "something quite similar to the two-eye ideal," ask him, gently, to put down his grapefruit knife while you make for the door. It's time to change doctors.

Five Years On

March 24, 2008

Off the Record has now been in existence for a span of five years and to the extent of 4,600 postings, and it may be opportune to do what we've heretofore left undone, namely, to explain what we think we're up to.

Though subtagged "Notes from the Newsroom", OTR had its beginnings in an ongoing exchange of e-mails among half a dozen correspondents wryly exasperated by the failures of senior ecclesiastics to conduct themselves as Catholics, and by their even more distressing failures to permit others access to the Church's spiritual bounty. Many of our exchanges took the form of routine grousing about the flakiness of this or that homily or pastoral letter or interview, but underneath there was a deeper sense of unease. Bad churchmen are a vexation, but an understandable and probably unavoidable vexation. Harder to explain—and progressively harder to deny—was The Void at the center of the Church's activity: the absence of concern for souls in jeopardy.

"Work out your salvation with fear and trembling," said St. Paul, "for it is God who is at work in you." OTR was created to grapple with the problem (never articulated as such by the contributors): How does a Catholic work out his salvation when his pastors don't believe there is any damnation to be saved from?

Perhaps no Catholic bishop or religious superior has publicly stated his disbelief in the possibility that a soul might be lost. Yet it is so rare for a churchman to affirm this doctrine that it's stunning when it does occur—think of the amazed indignation in response to the disciplinary actions of Bishops Bruskewitz and Burke.

More disquieting than the bishops' silence, however, is their "performative" repudiation of a salvific component to their ministry. Whatever their personal opinions may be, they don't *act as if* it were possible for a man to lose his soul by making a spiritually lethal choice.

Imagine a mother whose toddlers crawl past her legs under the kitchen sink, open various bottles marked with the skull and crossbones, pour the contents into sippy cups, and then trot off drinking the contents while she shakes her head in bemused resignation. Either the woman is criminally negligent, or she doesn't believe the marked bottles really contain poison. There is no third possibility.

The eerie but incontestable fact is that most Catholic pastors behave like this unnaturally nonchalant mother. The Church still labels certain bottles with the skull and crossbones—i.e., she still professes a belief in mortal (soul-destroying) sins, but even those of her clergy who give verbal assent to Church doctrine seldom conduct their office in a way that is intelligible if the doctrine were true.

Take a simple example: weekly participation in the Sunday Eucharist is a precept of the Church, failure at which the *Catechism of the Catholic Church* calls a grave sin (no. 2181). Less than a third of U.S. Catholics abide by this precept. That means more than 60 percent of the laity are at grave spiritual risk. Yet perhaps one clergyman in a thousand displays the concern toward the 60 percent he'd show toward someone in danger of bodily death. It's likely that many among that 60 percent are too poorly catechized to commit a deliberate mortal sin by skipping Mass, but inasmuch as this compounds the failure of the clergy, it should increase their alarm rather than allay it. By their insouciant inaction they announce they don't take damnation—theirs or their flock's—as a serious possibility.

Or again, think of the Church's missionary outreach to the unevangelized: once a prime concern for Catholics everywhere, now emptied of urgency by the sentimentalism that surrounds the Anonymous Christian and his exotic spiritualities. Missionaries return to give us glad news of wells dug or dances learned, rarely of pagans baptized.

One can examine ecclesiastical endeavor along any axis of Catholic teaching and find further performative confirmation of The Void. But it was the crisis of clergy sexual abuse that changed unease to outrage. Shocking as the abuse was in and of itself, the truly unsettling aspect of the scandal was the reaction to the abuse on the part of bishops, religious superiors, and other clergy in positions of responsibility. The official denials, the cover-ups, the silent transfers of offenders, the hardball tactics with victims pointed to a moral callousness that appalled even civil agencies. Still worse, and immeasurably harder to reconcile with the Faith, was the near-total absence of concern for the spiritual destiny of the victims, the perpetrators, and (in view of their lying under oath) the bishops themselves. OTR was born out of our stammering attempts to make sense out of a Church governed by churchmen drowsily indifferent to her supernatural ministry. Either they are malign, or they don't really believe anything important is at stake. There is no third possibility.

OTR has permitted itself disparagement of "empty suit" clergymen, especially senior ecclesiastics, disparagement that many goodwilled Catholics find repellent in itself and contrary to Christian discipleship. We do not doubt the good faith of their objections; we hope our critics are right and hope that it is we who have misread the situation; we wish them success at proving us wrong. But the key sticking point is that these critics deny what we find undeniable: the bishops indulgently beaming at the little ones with Liquid-Plumr in their sippy cups.

Unlike the liberals or the factionalist Right, OTR is not calling for "structural change" or some newfangled system of accountability. Individually we've each written numberless letters of appeal to numberless ecclesiastics, but OTR does not circulate manifestos or canvass for signatures for petitions. We want the clergy to do today what the Church has called them to do from her beginnings. If our dismay sometimes takes a sardonic form of expression, it should be remembered that we're measuring our pastors not against an idiosyncratic standard of our own devising, but against the promises they themselves made on taking office. The goal is to alert high clergy and low that some Catholics still count on these promises, and to remind them—in terms they're likely to remember—that their spiritual duty is not optional.

In the course of the next month OTR will be reposting some blog entries from the first half of its existence, by way of providing some background for new readers and a kind of synthesis for others. Feedback in the comboxes, especially critical comment, is always welcome.

THE USE AND ABUSE OF LANGUAGE

Because he was an expert on biblical languages, as well as a priest who sought to preserve the beauty of the Catholic liturgy, Father Mankowski took a special interest in the debates over liturgical translations. He took a dim view of "inclusive" language and of translations that deliberately lowered the solemn tone of the liturgical texts.

Lord, Who Sinned?

April 1, 2003

Ecclesiam tuam, Domine, miseratio continuata mundet et muniat, reads last Monday's collect.

"God of mercy, free your Church from sin, and protect it from evil," says the Sacramentary.

Odd. Why should the ICEL [International Commission on English in the Liturgy] translators want to suggest that it's the *Church* that is enchained by sin?

Coming Soon to a Pulpit Near You

May 11, 2003

Call to Action listed the following presentation in the brochure for one of its national conferences:

Jesus Christ as Cognitive Behavioral Therapist

Patrick Brennan discusses how Jesus tried and tries to change how we think and feel, as well as how we act. Using scripture and the principles of cognitive behavioral therapy, he looks at how Jesus would respond to anxiety, depression, anger, and troubled relationships. Fr.

Brennan is pastor of Holy Family Parish in Inverness, Ill., in Chicago's northwest suburbs, and speaks out of the ongoing experience in that parish. He founded the National Center for Evangelization and Renewal, and teaches at Loyola U.'s Institute for Pastoral Studies. *Re-Imagining the Parish* is one of his many books.

Fr. Brennan's Soft Toy Messiah puts one in mind of H. Richard Niebuhr's sardonic observation on the nature of liberal Protestantism: "We want a God without wrath who took man without sin into a kingdom without justice through the ministrations of a Christ without a cross."

THEN COMETH Jesus to a city of Samaria, which is called Sychar, and a woman of Samaria cometh to draw water, and he saith unto her, Go, call thy partner, and come hither. The woman answered and said, I have no partner. Jesus said unto her, Thou hast well said, I have no partner: For thou hast had five partners; and he whom thou now hast is a troubled relationship: in that thou spakest truly. The woman saith unto him, Sir, I perceive that thou art a cognitive behavioral therapist. Jesus saith unto her, Woman, believe me, the hour cometh, and indeed now is, when Blue Cross shall no more pick up outpatient counseling, neither in this mountain nor in Jerusalem. The woman saith unto him, I know that universal health care cometh; when it is come, it will pay for all things. Jesus saith unto her, Greater faith than this I have not seen. Thirty shekels, please.

And, behold, there cometh one of the rulers of the synagogue; and when he saw Jesus, he fell at his feet, and besought him greatly, saying, My little daughter lieth at the point of death: I pray thee, come and lay thy trip on her, that she may be healed and live. And there came from the ruler's house a certain man which said, Thy daughter is dead: why troublest thou the master any further? And Jesus spake unto him and said, Why callest thou me master? I've got a doctorate from Georgetown. And he cometh to the house of the ruler of the synagogue, and seeth the tumult, and them that wept and wailed greatly. And when he was come in, he saith unto them, Why make ye this ado, and weep? the damsel is not dead, but dysfunctional. And they laughed at him. And he took the damsel by the hand, and said unto her father, Calitha tumi; that is, VISA number and expiration date, please. And they were astonished with a great astonishment, and said to one another, Who is this man, that the rulers of the earth prepay him?

Documentary Find Wows Scholars

January 26, 2004

A partially damaged papyrus manuscript recently discovered in Bethsaida sheds new light on first-century epistolary practice. The translation is still provisional.

162 Via Media
Jerusalem

7th Abib, 0033

Dear Rabbi Bar-Joseph,

Thank you for your letter of the 3rd inst. regarding the Greater Palestine Common Ground Initiative. As always we welcome your input. I must say, however, that your comments reflect a serious misreading of the document "Called to be Canaanite" and neglect the efforts of those thinking women and men who are, in a very real sense, desirous to embrace the full richness and diversity of contemporary Yahwism.

None of us, we must admit, has a monopoly on the truth. Great damage to the spirit of unity has been caused in recent years by individuals who stigmatize those with whom they disagree as "hypocrites". Labeling others risks aggravating rather than healing the divisions among us.

Regarding your own ministry, I want to affirm you in your valuable theological insights. Yet I do not hear in your letter a respect for those who have theologies different from your own. Is it not meet, after all, that one doctrine should die for the sake of the people? That a prominent member of your own congregation has requested a copy of our Pastoral Implementation Plan (30 shekels + SASE) is, I must say, a sign of hope. Praying that this coming Passover will be a truly special one for you and yours, I remain

Seamlessly yours,
+Caiaphas Bar Nun

P.S. Our records show that we are not in receipt of your tithes on mint and cumin for the week of Nisan 12–19. Kindly rectify the anomaly.

Say It Ain't So

September 11, 2004

> Pope John Paul has asked an Austrian bishop at the center of a sex scandal involving his seminary to resign from his office, according to the Kathpress news agency on Friday. "Church sources in Rome said on Friday that the Vatican has suggested to St. Poelten Bishop Kurt Krenn, who is in Rome this week for talks, that he retire due to health reasons," the Kathpress news agency reported. Bishop Krenn's spokesman declined to comment to the Austrian news agency APA.

I *hope* this story is false—well, half-false, anyway. It's good news that Bishop "Kiss Me Kurt" Krenn will get the hook. The bad news is the heartbreaking dishonesty of the words the Austrian Catholic news agency attributes to the Pope. Why the official fiction of retirement "due to health reasons" when health, as commonly understood, had nothing whatever to do with it?

To be fair, we don't have the Holy Father's exact statement in its original language, and there's still room for pious maneuver. Following the *praesupponendum* of St. Ignatius Loyola, let's try to come up with a favorable spin:

- Best Case: The Pope spoke in Latin, whence *propter salutem* can mean "for the sake of [Krenn's] salvation"—a spiritual purpose—as well as "for reasons of health".
- Next Best Case: The Pope spoke in Italian, whence *per motivi sanitari* can mean "for the sake of hygiene"—a prudential purpose—as well as "for reasons of health".
- Third Best Case: The Pope was sending a message in the Mafia mode, delivered by a thick-necked goon meaningfully hefting a length of pipe: "If you value your health, Eccellenza, you will retire at the earliest possible opportunity." This explanation has, at least, the virtue of pastoral solicitude toward the diocese.

The remaining possible interpretation of the words is: a flat-out lie.

We might yet hope the Holy See's "suggestion" came not from the Pope's own pen but from the office of some midlevel apparatchik.

Most of us have become accustomed to government agencies' issuing (in the Soviet fashion) transparent lies that aren't meant to be taken at face value but must be decoded by experts who sift official falsehoods for crumbs of truth. Still, it's discouraging to have to resort to such measures in straining to understand the man that Christ left us as the prime Evangelist of His Church.

The motto of this pontificate is "Be Not Afraid!"—implemented to so much good in so many ways. So why do they seem afraid to trust us with the truth?

Pasting in the Footnotes

June 25, 2005

Anybody else fouled out by the translation of this morning's first Mass reading? Here's the traditional RSV rendering of Genesis 18:11–12.

> Now Abraham and Sarah were old, advanced in age; it had ceased to be with Sarah after the manner of women. So Sarah laughed to herself, saying, "After I have grown old, and my husband is old, shall I have pleasure?"

Here's what we heard at Mass today:

> Now Abraham and Sarah were old, advanced in years, and Sarah had stopped having her womanly periods. So Sarah laughed to herself and said, Now that I am so withered and my husband is so old, am I still to have sexual pleasure?

The RNAB Lectionary is notorious for this kind of patronizing help to the hearer, using the idiom of a sophomore high school health teacher to expand what it regards as vague expressions in the biblical text. Last Thursday we got "He had intercourse with her, and she became pregnant" for the standard "And he went in to Hagar, and she conceived." Is anyone old enough to understand the situation in doubt about the meaning of the traditional literal translation?

A Case for Hate Speech

August 16, 2005

British PM Tony Blair has asked for new legal muscle in order to deport those he calls "preachers of hate". We all understand the pressures that make it an attractive political temptation to silence hate speech, but I think it's a temptation that should be resisted. Speaking from within the citizenship of a democratic state—as opposed to, say, membership in a Catholic parish—I'd want to defend the right of other citizens to give voice to their hatreds, including hatred of Catholics in general and of this individual Catholic in particular.

Isn't spreading hatred a sin? It is. But how many of the sins you admit in confession are, or should be, crimes under civil law? Western democracies happily tolerate greed speech, lust speech, envy speech, sloth speech, pride speech—in fact, it's a rare specimen of advertising, entertainment, or political oratory that doesn't urge us to embrace one deadly sin or another. Why should "hate speech" be singled out for banishment?

One obvious reason is that civil peace requires a minimum level of mutual toleration, and by definition hatred is intolerant. But all democracies have laws against "incitement to riot"—public encouragement to break the laws already in place. So it's not persons or property that are defended by laws prohibiting hate speech. What is?

Laws against hate speech protect and fortify the ideological worldview of those who enforce them—and here I don't mean cops, but the politicians, the law profs, the prosecutors, the judges, and (most importantly) the media elites who beam the spotlight of their antagonism on some groups they find noxious while giving others a pass. What makes hate speech a crime is not what the perp actually does or intends to do, but what the victim claims to *feel*—and, de facto, only certain groups are accredited as victim groups. If your target doesn't qualify as an approved victim, it doesn't matter how much heat is in your hatred; if it does qualify, the goodwill that motivates your discourse is equally beside the point. Do we trust Harvard Law School, CNN, and the Cook County Democratic Committee to decide what speech is hate speech and what isn't?

Earlier I linked a photo from the March for Women's Lives showing a gal holding a sign that reads "Euthanize Christians". Sure smells like hatred to me. On the other hand, it's pretty much par for the course among pro-aborts and only slightly more edgy than the discourse common in gender studies departments and the journalism of "alternative" weeklies. Dawn Eden's example of the Planned Parenthood snuff cartoons belongs in the same category. Has any law prof or prestige-media editor suggested this verges on the criminal? Even those whom it targets have largely become inured to the venom. Sure they hate us, so what's new?

If the tables were turned, and the material splashed in public read "Euthanize [*insert accredited victim group here*]"—we can imagine all too clearly the consequent outrage, and if that outrage were equipped with the power to punish with criminal sanctions, it would not be slow to use it. But within the last five years we've seen the "hatred threshold" ratcheted down dramatically. It's no longer a matter of spray-painting tombstones or shattering windows—public reading of the Book of Leviticus can count as hatred. Remember, what matters is what the victim wants to matter. The Episcopal bishops of Massachusetts linked hate crimes to a notice from the CDW [Congregation for Divine Worship] on admission to Holy Orders. If our prisons become (even in part) reeducation camps on the Chinese model, do we want to give these guys the power of the keys?

For Christians, hate speech laws are a lose-lose proposition. We have excellent reason to doubt the elites will accord us victim status, and excellent reason to believe the same elites will find crimes in our ordinary evangelical discourse. I admit I don't like it when some red-fanged imam gloats over the torment awaiting the infidels, but it's a price we should be willing to pay for the liberty to speak the truth ourselves. "Blessed are you when men hate you," Jesus said. He commanded us to pray for those who wish us ill, but did not tell us to gag them.

Samuel, Samuel!

January 11, 2006

In the current *First Things*, Fr. Richard Neuhaus takes on the needlessly, perversely clumsy Bible translation that serves as the base for our Lectionary, the Revised New American Bible (RNAB). Massgoers often cringe in anticipation as the lector climbs onto the podium, since it's a rare reading that doesn't contain at least one clunker. This morning's offering was no exception.

> Samuel grew up, and the LORD was with him,
> not permitting any word of his to be without effect.
> Thus all Israel from Dan to Beersheba came to know
> that Samuel was an accredited prophet of the LORD.

An *accredited* prophet?

One would be inclined to write this down as another random RNAB infelicity, were it not for the mindset that "full-time ministry" does, in fact, require a master's degree and a cursus of qualification workshops. It's hard to allay the suspicion that, in rendering the Hebrew so as to make Samuel into an Accredited Visionary, the translators thought they were paying the lad a compliment.

Prayers at the Foot of the Altar

February 20, 2006

From the Missale Nonoxynolense *(Redondo Beach, 2009), translated from the demotic Californian by Sr. Marie-Eugénie de l'Assomption, S.L.*

> I come to the coffee table of the Lord
>   To God who gives joy to my youth.
> Plows are tacky, but I *love* a beaten sword;
>   So strum the harp, and pour the sweet vermouth!
>
> Let us rise, uproot our oaken pews,
>   And cast them in the Lake of Innisfree:
> Then build (in def'rence to a younger Muse)
>   Unstructured space for worship/ministry.
>
> O hang the walls with beadwork from Malaya,
>   Beneath my feet a lilac carpet lay.
> *Lava a romanitate mea*
>   *Et a machismo meo munda me!*
>
> Put a watch before my lips, O Lord,
>   A Rolex by the gatehouse of my mouth,

That we might hymn (in liberal accord)
   The macroeconomics of the South.

Incline thy ear to this my tongue's oblation;
   Spurn not inclusive liturgy resoúrces;
For I sing a song of human maturation
   In words our campus Worship Team endorses.

A polyester ephod weave for me
   To grace thy courts on ferials and festals.
And might we laud thy Domesticity
   With earthen-ware, and more-than-earthen Vestals.

Deliver us from Krakows and from Galways—
   Benighted ghettos blind to their mistake;
Enlightened minds cry, "Give us *this* bread, always—
   And let the peasants starve, for pita's sake!"

Semper fi, Sometimes

January 13, 2009

"Cornerback Pollard Decommits from Irish" announces an article about a Notre Dame football prospect who decided to play for UCLA. I confess the verb "decommit" was new to me. Linguists tell us that languages spontaneously produce the words required to deal with new needs, and contemporary life has produced plenty of gaps for this verb to fill. I saw just the other day that Georgetown University decommitted from Leviticus 20, again.

ASSAULTS ON THE DIGNITY OF LIFE

Abortion, the most divisive topic on the American political agenda for decades, was constantly in the headlines during the early years of the twenty-first century. Diogenes was a stalwart defender of the right to life—and wondered aloud why Catholic prelates were not as anxious to join in the battle.

NOW Objects to Peterson Double-Murder Charge

April 20, 2003

The head of the National Organization for Women's Morris County chapter is opposing a double-murder charge in the Laci Peterson case, saying it could provide ammunition to the pro-life lobby. "If this is murder, well, then any time a late-term fetus is aborted, they could call it murder," Morris County NOW President Mavra Stark said on Saturday.

Got it in one, Mavra. Congratulations.

The Futility of Euphemism

April 22, 2003

An arresting paragraph from a CNN story on the Peterson murder case:

> Regarding the killing of the unborn child, the complaint states, under the heading Termination of Pregnancy: "During the commission of the murder of Laci Denise Peterson, the defendant with knowledge that [she] was pregnant did inflict injury on [her] resulting in the termination of her pregnancy."

Why is this interesting? Because nobody believes that Scott Peterson [Laci's husband, the defendant] is being charged with practicing medicine without a license. *Killing the baby* begat *abortion; abortion* begat *termination of pregnancy.* Now the semantic chain has circled upon itself, so that a murder committed with malice aforethought is reflexively called termination of pregnancy.

George Orwell's famous essay on language proposed that politically expedient equivocations are not really semantically ambiguous; they're used to ask and extend permission to do things whose true motives cannot be spoken out loud:

> The inflated style is itself a kind of euphemism. A mass of Latin words falls upon the facts like soft snow, blurring the outlines and covering up all the details. The great enemy of clear language is insincerity. When there is a gap between one's real and one's declared aims, one turns as it were instinctively to long words and exhausted idioms, like a cuttlefish squirting out ink.

Does it work? Only in the short term, and even then only when backed by force. In charging him with termination of pregnancy, the Modesto police and the Stanislaus County District Attorney's Office understand perfectly, and want us to understand, the *motive* of the accused. That means for the past 30 years the women's health clinic surgeon, in his white lab coat and with his diplomas and grave, solicitous manner, has been up to the same thing as (allegedly) Scott Peterson. No one was ever fooled.

Coals to Newcastle

May 20, 2004

According to the *Washington Post*, 48 Democratic congressmen wrote Cardinal McCarrick warning him that withholding Communion from politicians who support abortion rights will increase anti-Catholic bigotry. In case you were wondering, the *Post* mentions that the signers "include at least three House members with strong antiabortion voting records."

> One of the signers with a solidly antiabortion voting record, Rep. Bart Stupak (Mich.), said in an interview that bishops "are making

these statements thinking they're undermining the candidacy of John Kerry, when what they're really undermining is the Catholic church."

Stupak added that he has been surprised by the partisanship of some bishops.

"I've had some threaten not to give Communion to me, even though they don't know my position, just because I'm a Democrat," he said. "I've had cardinals refuse to shake my hand because I'm a Democrat, and then somebody whispers to them that, 'No, no, he's a good guy.'"

WwweeeeEEERP!

You just heard my tauroscatometer blow a fuse. It's conceivable, barely, that an infielder for the St. Louis Cardinals might refuse to shake a congressman's hand "just because he's a Democrat"—but anyone who thinks there are cardinal archbishops (plural!) inclined to snub Dems *quâ* Dems is stark drooling mad. Stupak should be ashamed of himself for not being able to concoct a more plausible lie.

This letter is fishy is several respects. For starters, writing to McCarrick to be openhanded with Communion is like pleading with Barbra Streisand not to succumb to the blandishments of the Christian Right. Clearly the manifesto serves no purpose in convincing the already convinced, but it has great leakability in the Washington area and hence greater news value. Moreover, the bits quoted are suspiciously similar to the song sung by Fr. Thomas Reese, S.J., editor of the Jesuit magazine *America*, who is constantly warning bishops that their credibility will suffer if they get mixed up in religion.

The Church's disastrous record in implementing her teaching in the public arena ought to be obvious in the *Post*'s deadpan admission that, of 48 signatories, "at least three" had "strong antiabortion voting records", by which they mean "at most three" have any antiabortion votes at all. The degree to which Catholic congressmen let themselves be instructed by *Lumen Gentium* is perhaps more easily discerned in the last sentence of the article: "Other signers included House Minority Leader Nancy Pelosi, presidential candidate Dennis J. Kucinich (Ohio) and Rep. James P. Moran Jr. of Virginia."

Think! Does the Church really want to put the careers of these fine Catholic public servants at risk?

Didn't Inhale

January 25, 2005

The following cite, which I am not making up, comes from the *New York Times'* account of Hillary Clinton's speech in which she pokes an olive branch into the eye of the pro-life movement: "Several audience members inhaled sharply, for instance, when Mrs. Clinton said that 7 percent of American women who do not use contraception make up 53 percent of all unintended pregnancies."

Well, boys and girls, which fact is more astonishing? That 7 percent of American women have unintended pregnancies in the old-fashioned, pre-Copernican way of having an unintended pregnancy? Or that 47 percent of the unintended pregnancies occur in women who use 21st-century contraceptive devices but conceive all the same?

Sister Joan Explains It All for You

February 18, 2005

A ~~disappointing shoddy~~ breathtakingly stupid essay this week from Joan Chittister in the NCR [*National Catholic Reporter*]:

> Obviously, the whole question of the morality of abortion is a serious and an imperative one, as is birth control for some denominations and alcohol for others, for instance. Just as obvious, however, is the question of whether or not the government of a pluralistic state ought to be legislating for any of those things according to the tenets of any one particular religious tradition. Those are questions of faith, not of politics. That's how we got the Taliban in the first place. Someone somewhere decided that their religion had to be everybody's religion.

Bracket for the nonce Sister's insinuation that opposition to abortion belongs to the same moral category as, say, the Muslim prohibition of alcohol. Obtuseness is the kindest explanation for this frippery.

No one who has read the real arguments—especially those made by Catholics—could pretend that the pro-life movement was an attempt to make "my religion everybody's religion". The Catholic Church insists that the truths of morality, even those that have also been revealed to man by God in Scripture, are of themselves "accessible to reason alone" (*Catechism*, no. 2171). That means the wrongness of abortion (like the wrongness of lying or oath breaking) can be reliably grasped by the unaided human intellect. It often happens that Sacred Scripture helps Christians see the truth that abortion is murder exercised against a particular class of victims, but the public arguments put forward in defense of this truth are no more "denominational" than the multiplication table.

Where do you hear the opposite claim? Why, from NARAL and Planned Parenthood and the abortion industry itself. These groups have a huge interest in shouting down the pro-life arguments for the obvious reason that, in the arena of argument, they lose. They survive by means of a nonstop torrent of high-decibel mendacity, including the lie that it's theology, not biology, which teaches us that unborn children are human beings. Now that the new ultrasound images are daily corroding the plausibility of that lie, they have cranked up the volume even more.

It's ironic that elsewhere in the NCR, a liberal Catholic academic is quoted as lamenting the "new ugliness" he finds in the in-house culture wars: "We do not even know how to talk to each other—to have responsible adult conversations—in areas where there is serious disagreement."

Adult conversations? Well, my progressive siblings-in-Christ, if you want dialogue, it's a good idea to start by making a pretense of listening to the other guys when it's their turn to do the talking. If you want to know what pro-lifers think, you have to switch off the television (you won't learn it there), switch off NPR (you won't learn it there), and actually pick up a book. The Chittister trick—by which you ignore pro-lifers and instead read what Kate Michelman says about pro-lifers—has served you well for these thirty years. But dialogue it ain't.

Operation Rescue: Why It's Important

July 2, 2005

Imagine a new religion, whose devotees call themselves Sciuridans. The most distinctive characteristic of Sciuridans is their belief that the creatures the rest of us call "squirrels" are, in reality, abandoned human children. Sciuridans are convinced that there is a witch who casts a spell on abandoned children that turns them into squirrels for a period of nine months, after which the spell loses its potency and the squirrels turn back into human children (who have no awareness of the experience).

Not surprisingly, Sciuridans are resolutely opposed to squirrel hunting, since they believe it is a human life, not a rodent's, that is at stake. They are energetic campaigners for a change in hunting laws.

Yet the laws aren't changed, and every season untold thousands of squirrels are killed by hunters.

Now here's my question. Most of us would find the Sciuridans' religious beliefs preposterous—but even so, wouldn't we expect them, in virtue of their own principles, to go beyond merely legal and educational maneuvering and to take active measures against squirrel hunting—e.g., shooing away the quarry, sabotaging the firearms, perhaps in extreme cases even tackling the hunters at the point of firing? In fact, if the Sciuridans took no interdictive action and simply deplored the activities of the regrettably deluded hunters, wouldn't we be inclined to doubt that they *really* believed squirrels were human beings in the ordinary sense of the term?

So Who Decides?

September 27, 2005

Pro-abort Amy Sullivan has an interesting article in the *Boston Globe* explaining how NARAL and NOW imperil the future of abortion by harming the electability of Democrats. I'd like to pick up on one phrase mentioned in passing: "The issue, for people like me, isn't certitude—we don't question that the decision to end a pregnancy should be left up to a woman and her doctor."

As John Wauck once wrote in the *Human Life Review*, the phrase "a woman and her doctor" is little more than an outdated figure of speech, like "a boy and his dog." For most women who undergo an abortion, by the time they first see a doctor they're already sedated and in the stirrups.

But let's take Sullivan's language at face value: "The decision to end a pregnancy should be left up to a woman *and her doctor*." This, of course, is a deviation from the strict feminist orthodoxy, according to which the woman and only the woman decides to abort. But if we include the doctor in the decision-making process, it's obvious that there are two persons, hence two wills, hence four possible scenarios regarding the choice to abort: woman pro, doctor pro; woman con, doctor con; woman pro, doctor con; woman con, doctor pro.

Where woman and doctor concur there is no problem from Sullivan's perspective. But what if they disagree?

Now it might be the case that Sullivan is simply saying that a woman should solicit medical advice and then do what she damn well pleases; if so, her view reduces to the standard feminist position, and the doctor's advice is just one more datum that goes into her equation (like the data provided by her banker, her boyfriend, her employer, etc.). My hunch is that if, for example, the woman wanted to abort but her doctor advised against it—on the grounds, say, that it might aggravate her depression—99 percent of NARAL/NOW feminists would uphold the woman's will against the doctor's advice, regardless of how well qualified the doctor was and how ill-suited the woman was to make the decision.

But take the last possibility: woman con, doctor pro. Imagine a pro-choice woman who manages to conceive a much-desired child late in life. Testing shows the fetus is defective, and the mother's desire to continue the pregnancy is no longer clear, changing from day to day. During in utero surgery to correct the abnormality, the doctor decides the fetus is beyond repair and aborts it, let's say, based on his own medical judgment. To make the example more interesting, let's imagine that the woman is cognitively impaired and that whatever consent she gave to the surgeon's prerogatives was founded on gross misunderstanding of the medical reality. When she awakes from the anesthesia she is devastated by the news of what the surgeon has done and sues. Well, Ms. Sullivan, Ms. Gandy, Ms. Michelman: who wins—the woman or her doctor?

Make That Medium Rare

February 25, 2006

There's no such thing as a bad abortion, in the view of the *über-*feminist Katha Pollitt, and she doesn't hide her alarm and disgust with those of her comrades who are sweetening their language for reasons of political expediency: "The trouble with thinking in terms of zero abortions is that you make abortion so hateful you do the antichoicers' work for them. You accept that the zygote/embryo/fetus has some kind of claim to be born. You start making madonna-whore distinctions."

Pollitt is canny enough to realize how the logic works: concede that abortion is—or could ever be—regrettable in a way that removing a tumor is not, and they've lost game, set, and match. The intermediate steps in the moral reasoning may take some time to unfold in public, but once the key pass is sold, the move to invest the unborn child with human rights has to follow. Therefore Pollitt insists on an extreme moral solipsism: the woman is the *only* party whose will matters in a pregnancy. She allows no half measures. Admit that even a subsidiary interest might be accorded the father, the state, or the fetus itself, and you've "obliterated" the woman.

Not even Mordor is buying—at least, there are signs that hard-core pro-aborts are abandoning Pollitt's rhetoric, if not her goals. NARAL President Nancy Keenan is outraged that South Dakota passed a bill outlawing abortion last week, but the statement she issued in protest uses the "let's make abortions rare" language:

"Rather than continuing these unconstitutional assaults that threaten to endanger women's lives and imprison doctors, these legislators should commit to enacting commonsense legislation to prevent unintended pregnancy." ...

Keenan continued, "South Dakotans who cherish the fundamental American values of freedom and personal responsibility must call on Gov. Rounds to veto this egregious legislation. We should work to reduce the need for abortion, not continue to battle about *Roe v. Wade*."

Compared with the standard NARAL line of even five years past, Keenan's approach shows considerable softening. She realizes that the old magic no longer works. And while Pollitt is overly pessimistic about the immediate future—it'll be a long time before the blue states and the prestige institutions relinquish abortion—her political allies understand that the terms of the debate have shifted. Even Frances Kissling said

that it is more expedient to be morally incoherent (and visibly uncomfortable with incoherence) than to appear heartless:

> As a prochoice advocate, I want my movement to help shape this strug-
> gle, *which includes living with public discomfort*, as we discuss how to bal-
> ance women's predominant right to make decisions about their lives
> and society's right to be involved in questions of respect for human life,
> even for life that is not yet a person and properly is not accorded rights.

"In the war of ideas," wrote Kissling last year, "not every hill is
worth climbing." She's got it exactly backwards. It's in the realm of
ideas that one's philosophy is obliged to take on every challenge; in
the realm of politics one can work instead for what is possible. Thus
she's prepared to support laws requiring late-term babies to be anesthetized prior to abortion because the contrary position doesn't play
well in public, even though such support is at odds with her own
contention that "women have a basic human right to decide what
to do about a pregnancy" and that "the human rights community is
moving steadily towards recognizing a woman's right to choose and
there is no countervailing view in this community that even considers the question of whether or not fetuses are rights-bearing entities."

C. S. Lewis wrote that a long face is not a moral disinfectant. It
can, however, be an effective piece of stagecraft. In defiance of Pollitt's exasperation at their hypocrisy, NARAL and CFFC [Catholics
for Free Choice] and even Hillary are pulling a long face for the
benefit of the "persuadables"—those voters in the middle who want
the option to eliminate inconvenient persons but feel queasy at the
glee displayed by the Wavers of the Bloody Coat Hanger: a killing
can't be so bad, after all, if the killer pretends it's a morally serious act.
However unconvincing the hand-wringing itself, the very fact that it
fills a need tells us the momentum is changing.

The Right to Lose

September 8, 2006

South Dakota's abortion ban will be put to a referendum this November. In the September 11 issue of *America*, Rapid City Bishop Blase

Cupich calls for "civility and depth" in the upcoming debates on the issue. "Let us recognize," he says, "that in public discourse moral passion must walk hand in hand with mutual respect."

Most pro-lifers will feel their stomachs tighten at this language. Because it's false? No, it's perfectly true, even platitudinous. Yet we only see this kind of episcopal finger wagging when conservatives get within striking distance of the goal line. Other instances of "moral passion" go unrebuked. Perhaps Cardinal Mahony has warned the United Farm Workers to preserve civility and depth in their agitation, but if so I've missed it.

Cupich squarely positions himself as pro-life, but he frames the issue in precisely the wrong way, i.e., in terms of the "competing interests" one is taught to identify in those weekend conflict-resolution workshops for business execs. Here's the second of Cupich's three "conditions for discussion":

> There should be agreement that any discussion of abortion and the law must recognize both the suffering of the unborn children in abortion and the suffering of pregnant women in dire circumstances.

> [Cupich's exposition:] Some pro-life advocates focus almost exclusively on the rights and suffering of the unborn baby, while some pro-choice advocates focus equally exclusively on the rights and suffering of pregnant women. This is a distortion of the moral choice that confronts us as a society. Abortion is a searing and divisive public policy issue precisely because two significant sets of rights are in conflict, and no matter which set of laws it enacts, society must choose between these rights.

Superficially judicious, this call for evenhandedness concedes the only important point to the wrong team before the debate begins.

What "two significant sets of rights" are in conflict? The baby's, certainly, is the right that any innocent human being enjoys not to be murdered. But what *right* of the mother could be *in conflict* with this right of her baby? One can see that certain interests, desires, and projects of the mother, even wholesome ones, could be put at risk by childbirth, and these interests, desires, and projects might be sanctioned by loosely attributed "rights" (the right to the pursuit of happiness, the right to decent health, the right to a career, etc.).

But no one even pretends that these rights "conflict" with the lives of innocent human beings in such a way that homicide is an option that can be licitly contemplated. My right to marry may be frustrated by the highly inconvenient fact that the only person I want to wed is betrothed to someone else, but even those who fully acknowledged my suffering wouldn't see a *conflict of rights* at issue, certainly not one involving my rival's right to life.

He doesn't spell it out, of course, but the only "right" of the mother Cupich could oppose to the baby's right to life is the so-called "right to choose", more precisely, the "right to choose to abort". But the very question at issue is whether such a right obtains, or could ever obtain, and to suggest that it does is not evenhandedness but a silent endorsement of the *conclusion* of the pro-abortionist camp. It means that the conflict—in Cupich's words, the "searing and divisive public policy issue"—is in fact a zero-sum game, no different in principle from the competing interests we find in a wage dispute between employer and employee. The problem is, while General Motors and the UAW can walk away from arbitration with satisfactory, though partial, self-interest intact, what *partial* rights does the aborted child enjoy?

"No matter which set of laws it enacts," writes Cupich, "society must choose between these rights." I don't think he really believes this. At any rate, he insists that even the "terrible dilemmas that pregnant women often face ... do not justify the taking of innocent human life." Yet Cupich could hardly have chosen a worse way of stating the Catholic case, and his notion of rights-in-conflict invites us to sell the pass by negotiating (with civility and mutual respect) a reasonable and decorous defeat.

Healthy and Wealthy and Dead

October 19, 2006

Well, U.S. elections are coming up next month, and that means another crop of voter's guides designed to give Catholics permission to yank the lever for pro-abortion candidates.

The latest to hit the market is called *Voting for the Common Good: A Practical Guide for Conscientious Catholics*. It attempts to disarm

conservative criticism by grabbing its own skirts at the outset and dropping a curtsey to "key themes" that include "Life" and "Family"—
then goes on to explain why they can be safely ignored in the polling
booth.

Voting for the Common Good differs from its predecessors in aim-
ing less to provide rationalizations for Dems to vote the party line,
and more at supplying sound bites for confounding pro-life and pro-
family activists. So, whereas earlier voter's guides cited masters of
Catholic social thought such as Joseph Califano and Saul Alinsky,
the new model quotes Pope John Paul II three times and even Cardinal Ratzinger once. Clearly the heavy names are intended not to
instruct the voter but to silence objections from believing Christians
(renamed, in election years, "the Christian Right"). I got a kick out
of VCG's Ratzinger-for-Rahm [Democrat Rahm Emanuel, candidate for U.S. House, Illinois' Fifth District] ploy:

> Is it okay to vote for a "pro-choice" candidate? When confronted with
> this question in 2004, Cardinal Ratzinger (now Pope Benedict XVI)
> responded that it could be acceptable for a Catholic to vote for a "pro-
> choice" candidate if "proportionate reasons" exist, and if the voter is
> voting based on those reasons and not the candidate's "pro-choice"
> beliefs. It is never acceptable to vote for a "pro-choice" candidate
> merely because of that candidate's position in favor of legal abortion.

The case Ratzinger was addressing in 2004 is that in which ALL the
candidates are pro-abortion (such as obtains in most of Massachusetts,
New York, and Illinois), and in which the Catholic is faced with
the choice of voting for a pro-abort or not voting at all. In such a
predicament the cardinal said it's licit to cast one's vote for the least
pestilential candidate (e.g., the one who's willing to draw the line at
partial birth abortion, if he exists). *Voting for the Common Good* turns
this permission on its head and does a classic Bernardin:

> Many "prolife" candidates talk a good talk on ending abortion but
> don't produce results. On the other hand, there are candidates who
> don't believe in making abortion illegal, but who support effective
> measures to promote healthy families and reduce abortions by provid-
> ing help to pregnant women and young children.

Sure, sure. And in 1943 there were *good* Nazis who, while they didn't believe in outlawing the gassing and cremation of non-Aryans, supported Reich-funded family clinics for hair bleaching and rhinoplasty so as to reduce the need for race-based *Sonderbehandlung*. Back to the text:

> Catholics must look at a candidate's position on other life issues. Can one really claim to be "pro-life" and yet support the death penalty, turn a blind eye to poverty, and not take steps to avoid war? Our Church teaches that the answer to this question is "no."

Seamless garbage.

The point is that homicide is not commensurable with temporal benefits the state may provide for or withhold from its citizens, and it is mischievous to claim the contrary. There are electoral races in which the rival candidates propose radically different and mutually exclusionary public policies on abortion: one policy exposes a disfavored class of human beings to unjust killing, while the rival policy would protect the same class from that fate. In such races, you can use your vote to make a concrete endorsement or rejection of a fundamental human good. You can contribute to a beneficent outcome or contribute to a maleficent one.

But the situation does not obtain in the case of, say, welfare relief. The difference between Republicans and Democrats on ADC [Aid to Dependent Children], school lunches, health care, Social Security, etc., is one of degree, not of kind. Perhaps the Dems want to devote 26 percent of GDP to social relief programs and the Republicans 19 percent of GDP. If their respective place on the spectrum makes the Democratic position the moral choice and the Republican position the immoral one, would a Green Party or Socialist candidate who proposed spending 33 percent of GDP on relief thereby make himself the only licit Catholic option, such that both the Republican and the Dem were immoral? Of course not. Unlike abortion, this kind of spending is a context-conditioned choice, and spending levels for which liberals now condemn Republicans were themselves proposed by the Democrats in the 1950s, for which they received the endorsement of bishops and moral theologians.

The choice before voters may determine whether a single mother gets only $320 per month in relief, as opposed to $400 per month.

But abortion doesn't admit of this kind of sliding-scale alternative. It's not as if Nancy Pelosi wants to excise 80 percent of the fetus and Henry Hyde only 64 percent. It's a thumbs-up/thumbs-down acey-deucey decision. Moreover, the baby that doesn't make it out of womb in the first place—thanks to the options the law lets her mother exercise—is in no condition to receive any of the wonderful "pro-family" benefits provided by voting for ~~Barney Frank~~ the common good. Again, think of the happy Jews who were able to take their family picnics in the Black Forest in 1946 thanks to Hitler's *marvelous* autobahns; if you can swallow that, you can swallow VCG's moral equivalency line. Not otherwise.

In case the readers of VCG didn't pick up the hint before, the veil drops in the discussion of *true* Catholicism.

> In recent years we have witnessed an unfortunate trend of religious leaders abusing their positions by using politics to impose their faith on others. True Catholicism, however, calls us to propose policies that work to better the common good of all humanity.

Think they're referring to Mario Cuomo's veto (on religious grounds) of New York's legislation reinstating capital punishment? Neither do I.

Let me sum up *Voting for the Common Good* for the use of Sunday homilists: "Sam Brownback may hold the Catholic position on abortion, but Hillary Clinton embraces the U.S. bishops' policy on wetlands reclamation. So go with your heart." You have to wonder why they even bother to fake it at this stage. You'll be edified to learn that the Association of Jesuit Colleges and Universities has distributed VCG to its 28 American campuses, but in the long run it would be simpler to pass around a bag of Valium-flavored Tootsie Pops on election morning. The purpose, after all, is to numb the conscience, not to quicken it.

Moral Absolutes

November 2, 2006

Check out this ad from Catholics in Alliance for the Common Good:

Some things ARE as simple as RIGHT and WRONG

Abandoning the poor is WRONG
45 million Americans without health insurance is WRONG
Torture is WRONG
Government corruption is WRONG
War without a plan for peace is WRONG

Notice anything missing?

It's always sad when people feign an interest in subjects that bore them. Think of the progressive Christians you know: is there a single one of them who doesn't convey the attitude that religion is an irritating interruption of more important business?

What a Week

May 9, 2007

From time to time, when I happen to come upon the fairly well-known photo of the Carpathian Jewish woman and her children walking toward the Auschwitz gas chambers in 1944, I've been moved to wonder how the persons who "selected" them for death (having determined they were unfit for labor), and how the persons who so carefully recorded the event on film, would have given voice to their feelings at the time. My hunch is that their dominant emotion—at least the emotion that would find expression—would be *self*-pity, perhaps tinged with self-congratulation.

Take a look at this recent posting on the *Abortion Clinic Days* blog—a blog that fascinates me precisely because it lets us hear—in real time, so to speak—the resentments and satisfactions and defensiveness of persons engaged today, in our own community, in putting the innocent to death. "What a week it has been!" exclaims the blogger-in-chief; "a number of the counselors i work with and i, too, have had some really challenging cases to deal with." She gives us a long recitation of on-the-job hardships:

> a third patient is fighting for custody of her three kids. she recently had a preliminary hearing in which she and her attorney assumed

that the case would be dismissed since the ex-husband has a criminal record, an alcohol problem and had not been the best dad when they were married. but the judge is allowing the battle to continue. this woman, cindy, said that she is now so scared that her ex can outfight her because she does not have the money for an extended legal battle and so is tempted to continue this pregnancy (conceived through a birth control failure) so she'd at least have one child with her. but she fears the pregnancy could also cause the judge to rule against her. another tough choice.

the ability to work with women in crisis, to allow them to voice their fears, grief, and weaknesses is a true gift. not every one could do what we do. and i say that not to brag about what we do, but rather in humility that we were given this ability to "walk with women and men in their darkest hours". we do not judge, we do not run away, we do not fear to hear the unspeakable. this is the work we do. some divine power has allowed us to be present in others' lives and bear their burdens for a bit, yet still have our own lives, our own joys. it can not have been an accident that we were granted this ability.

See the twist? "We"—the abortion providers—"do not fear to hear the unspeakable." And note the implied conclusion: because we have the courage to hear the unspeakable, we are blameless (or even enno- bled) when we make the unspeakable into the fait accompli, when we turn horror into a reality.

I've had occasion before to mention Hannah Arendt's book *Eich- mann in Jerusalem,* and her penetrating insight into the mind of Reichs- führer Heinrich Himmler, especially regarding his success in getting ordinary men to do—how can we put it?—extraordinary things:

Hence the problem was to overcome not so much their conscience as the animal pity by which all normal men are affected in the presence of physical suffering. The trick used by Himmler—who apparently was rather strongly afflicted with these instinctive reactions himself— was very simple and probably very effective; it consisted in turning these instincts around, as it were, in directing them toward the self. So that instead of saying: What horrible things I did to people!, the murderers would be able to say: What horrible things I had to watch in the pursuance of my duties, how heavily the task weighed upon my shoulders!

All too effective. You watch Carpathian Jews heading off to be gassed, you help Cindy overcome the "temptation" to continue her pregnancy, and you write home to your loved ones: "What a week it has been!" Tough on *you*. Taxing for *you*. Your self-esteem not only stays intact, but buoys a little.

But it doesn't end there, does it? Take careful note of our abortionist's admission that "*some divine power* has allowed us to be present in others' lives and bear their burdens for a bit." That ought to make the hair on your neck prickle. The Bible too knows of a spiritual power that helps its host bear the burden of *inflicting* homicide. Its name is Legion. "It can not have been an accident," muses our diarist, "that we were granted this ability."

It almost certainly wasn't.

THE POLITICAL WORLD

Why have American bishops not disciplined prominent Catholics who defend and promote abortion? Why has the bishops' conference embraced advocacy of other issues, on which loyal Catholics differ? Once again Diogenes saved his most trenchant criticism for the Catholic leaders who failed to uphold the fundamental moral teachings of the Church in this realm.

A God That Knows His Place ...

August 2, 2003

Massachusetts Sen. John Kerry is incensed that Leviticus completely disregards the writings of Thomas Jefferson:

> A fuming Kerry, taking on his own Catholic Church in the midst of a campaign for president, said Rome should have more respect for America's long-held separation of church and state.... The Democrat said political concerns are secondary to his moral outrage over Thursday's Vatican statement on gay marriage. "Our founding fathers separated church and state in America. It is an important separation," he said. "It is part of what makes America different and special, and we need to honor that as we go forward and I'm going to fight to do that."

The Church's teaching on sexuality is universal and immutable, and addressed to citizens of all nations. Does Kerry think the Holy See, before issuing a statement on public order, should study the political and legal history of Albania, Uzbekistan, and Burkina Faso to make sure that *their* understanding of church–state relations is not offended by its teaching?

Another Uncertain Trumpet

October 14, 2003

The U.S. bishops' Office of Social Development and World Peace has released another worthless pre-election document to aid Catholics at the polls. Even the bishops' own news service, combing the text for a paragraph thematic enough to quote from, couldn't come up with anything better than this:

> Faithful citizenship calls Catholics to see civic and political responsibilities through the eyes of faith and to bring our moral convictions to public life. People of good will and sound faith can disagree about specific applications of Catholic principles. However, Catholics in public life have a particular responsibility to bring together consistently their faith, moral principles, and public responsibilities.

Right. And Catholics should floss at least once a day. Substitute "Calvinist" or "Mennonite" for "Catholic" in the text (at least, the prescriptive parts) and see if you can find a glitch. You can't. You're not meant to. There are parents who send their teenagers out the door with the admonition "Be good!" in a tone of voice that gives permission to do the opposite. This document, by urging Catholics to bring their faith to public life even though they may "disagree about specific applications", in effect gives them permission to ignore unpopular teachings (provided some pretense of hand-wringing takes place). Savor this fine specimen of fluff peeled out of the episcopal lint trap:

> The Catholic community is large and diverse. We are Republicans, Democrats, and Independents. We are members of every race, come from every ethnic background, and live in urban, rural, and suburban communities in all fifty states. We are CEOs and migrant farm workers, senators and persons on public assistance, business owners and union members. But all Catholics are called to a common commitment to protect human life and stand with those who are poor and vulnerable. We are all called to provide a moral leaven for our democracy, to be the salt of the earth.

What the right hand giveth, the left hand taketh away. "We need," the bishops say, "to support gun safety measures and reasonable restrictions on access to assault weapons and hand guns, and to oppose the use of the death penalty." I don't remember an instruction from the CDF on assault weapons, or a national debate on religious dogma and gun safety legislation, but let that pass. The issue of same-sex unions, by contrast, is a huge and hot topic, occupying talk shows wall-to-wall and focusing sharply on the role of religion in public life. Yet the document makes no explicit reference to same-sex unions, preferring to state, briefly and delicately, the positive case: "Marriage must be protected as a lifelong commitment between a man and a woman and our laws should reflect this principle."

What the right hand giveth, the left hand taketh away. A truly conscientious Catholic citizen, one sincerely looking for guidance, will find no more help than that which Bucky Badger provides at halftime of the Wisconsin-Iowa game, when he exhorts the specta-tors to "get out and vote."

Unfair? Think back to last summer, to the press photos accompa-nying pro-life Priscilla Owens' failed candidacy for a federal judge-ship. There was Sen. Orrin Hatch, heatedly defending her; there was Sen. Patrick Leahy, not only gloating over her defeat but warn-ing Bush not to send any more "ideological appointments" to the Judiciary Committee. Remember the white-hot telegram of remon-strance from the U.S. bishops' Office of Social Development and World Peace? Neither do I. The sad fact of the matter is, if every Catholic elected official in the U.S. were to drop dead tomorrow and be replaced by a Mormon, we'd see more, not less, Catholic teaching become law.

We are the salt of the earth.

Burke Borked

January 21, 2004

St. Louis–bound Bishop Burke put the cat amongst the pigeons in a big way by announcing that pro-abort pols would be denied Com-munion. Clever folks at the *Post-Dispatch* phoned around the country to Burke's brethren to see if his spokespersons-in-Christ might help cut the ground out beneath him. They were not disappointed:

The Rev. Christopher Coyne, the Boston Archdiocese spokesman, has no expectation that O'Malley would ever direct his priests to refuse communion to pro-abortion rights officials, he said. Unless a person is clearly deranged or saying things against the church at that moment, the archdiocese's policy is that no priest or lay communion minister should ever refuse communion, he said.

"A priest or a Eucharistic minister is not a policeman or police-woman," Coyne said. "The proper place for a conversation (about church doctrine) is not in the communion line, but before or after."

Three points: First, Coyne's "... or policewoman" line signals which moral imperatives the archdiocese is *really* prepared to take seriously. Second, it's nonsense to imply that a bishop's responsibilities regarding admission to Communion are no different from those of a lay extraordinary minister faced with an on-the-spot decision. Third, Coyne's suggestion that "a conversation" about doctrine should take place outside of Mass would be reasonable if he were saying this: it is a bishop's duty to confront public dissenters, and, should they prove obdurate, only then must he deny them Communion.

Well, [Ted] Kennedy and Kerry are famously obdurate. That means either the confrontations have never taken place, or they took place and the bishop backed down. Well, Fr. Coyne, which would you have us believe? More to the point, which of the two paths—hiding or caving—should Bishop Burke pursue if he is to move the Archdiocese of St. Louis forward?

Burke gets tweaked as well by Cardinal McCarrick's flak, who sniffs that, in Washington at any rate, the church doors are open to absolutely anyone with half a trillion in public funds to disburse:

Cardinal Theodore McCarrick, archbishop of Washington, D.C., works with pro-abortion rights Catholic politicians on a spectrum of moral issues. McCarrick deals with the morality of their action and their relationship to God in private conversations, never publicly, said McCarrick spokesman Susan Gibbs.

"In this diocese, priests and Eucharistic ministers don't refuse communion," she said. "We keep the doors open."

How sweet. It must be said about these "private conversations" that the bishops have certainly managed to impress on their interlocutors the importance of the privacy aspect. So much so, in fact, that it's hard to name a single example of a pro-abortion Catholic pol who changed his mind or who, having refused to change it, left either his office or his Church.

Election Time Again

February 14, 2004

Every four years the USCCB puts out a voting guide which, in nervous and indirect language, invites U.S. Catholics to wring their hands for ten minutes outside the polling booth before voting Democratic. Not surprisingly the guides tend to be light on theology and big on the importance of daily flossing, say, or responsible lawn care. Check out the following focus question from the latest specimen: "How will we address the tragic fact that more than 30,000 children die every day as a result of hunger, international debt, and lack of development around the world, as well as the fact that the younger you are, the more likely you are to be poor here in the richest nation on Earth?"

Can a child really die *as a result* of international debt the way his brother dies *as a result* of hunger? Has any child ever died as a result of lack of development? Why is it a tragic fact that "the younger you are, the more likely you are to be poor here in the richest nation on Earth"? How is this a worse scenario than "the *older* you are, the more likely you are to be poor"?

To raise such objections to *Faithful Citizenship* is in deplorable taste, obviously, but also beside the point. The document is by design morally frivolous: its purpose is anesthetic, not educative. If a high school girl offers a prayer at a youth retreat that we forgive Zambia's debt, it's unsporting to ask her to explain the consequences for foreign investment and for the rural economy. The USCCB, like this globally aware sophomore, is out to teach us neither moral theology nor economics but to help numb the conscience as we yank the lever for Ted Kennedy or Barney Frank. If famine were truly a moral concern to a bishop, instead of an onion hidden in his political hanky, he couldn't write this kind of blather.

Well, then, what might he write?

When I ponder the thousands of children who will die of famine
before this day is out, and when I consider the millions of dollars
my diocese has spent simply to keep its priests out of the prison that
their crimes deserve, and when I realize that this same money might
not only feed many of these children but help them make a down
payment on a Buick, I confess I tremble for the salvation of my soul.
Accordingly I have decided, by way of penance and reparation, to
halve my annual salary, sell my beach house, fast two days a week, and
donate the difference to the Missionaries of Charity. May God in His
infinite mercy spare me at the Last Assize.

Hint: Don't look for many changes in the 2008 edition.

Just Curious

November 9, 2004

Can anybody give me a link to a story or photo of Sen. Kerry attend-
ing Mass the Sunday *after* the election? His religion, after all, is very
important to him.

Your Collection Plate Dollars at Work

January 22, 2006

The Catholic Campaign for Human Development claims to have
provided more than $280 million in grants, over the 35 years of its
existence, to sponsor projects such as Poverty Awareness Month. It
recently announced the results of its Poverty Pulse survey:

WASHINGTON (January 19, 2006)—Nearly two-thirds of Americans—
65 percent—fear that poverty will increase in the United States in 2006
while seven in 10 (71 percent) believe there are more poor people
today than a year ago and 63 percent worry that they could themselves
become poor, according to the latest Poverty Pulse survey by the Catholic Campaign for Human Development.

I don't get it. What's the point—given the USCCB's responsibilities—of gauging the man-in-the-street's fears about poverty? Who benefits? What action are we, or the bishops, supposed to take as a result? We're not told whether the poll respondents were given a working definition of poverty (e.g., a certain family income level) on which to base their replies, or whether "poverty" was just a bogey-word, left for the respondent to interpret on his own. The fact that 63 percent of the respondents "worry that they could themselves become poor" indicates a pretty elastic understanding of poverty (and of worry, for that matter).

Unlike Salvadoran or Sudanese poverty, American poverty is overwhelmingly a consequence of family pathology. If your mother's boyfriend is not your father, chances are you're poor. Catholic moral teaching, applied with any pastoral canniness, is an antidote to this disease, yet it seldom rates a mention by the CCHD. The monies paid to conduct the survey neither fed the hungry nor instructed them, but provided more footnote fodder, I suppose, for policy statements. As with everything it touches, it's hard to shake the suspicion that the CCHD's concern here is less for poor folks than for politics.

Our Bishops' Conference Is Deeply Disappointed ...

January 31, 2006

USCCB President Bishop William Skylstad gives Congress a scolding about its budget:

> In December, as President of the United States Conference of Catholic Bishops, I wrote to you expressing serious concerns about provisions in the budget reconciliation bill. The proposed changes in Medicaid, child support enforcement funding, Temporary Assistance for Needy Families (TANF), and agriculture conservation programs, in particular, could have a negative impact upon the most vulnerable in our nation.
>
> Our Bishops' Conference is deeply disappointed that the final budget reconciliation conference agreement coming once again before the House of Representatives includes provisions in these areas which we believe could prove harmful to many low-income children, families,

elderly and people with disabilities who are least able to provide for themselves. Because of these concerns, we ask you to oppose the budget reconciliation conference agreement.

So imagine you're a congressman. How are you going to react to a moral reprimand concerning your budget priorities delivered by a bishop whose own diocese has filed for bankruptcy? Having been upbraided for not demonstrating greater solicitude toward "the most vulnerable in our nation," how will the admonishment strike you— knowing that the bankruptcy in question was brought about, not by imprudently lavish charity on the part of the diocese, but by costs consequent upon the sexual predations of its clergy? With the beam of the Buggery Bill lodged firmly in the eye of the episcopacy, are you going to trust it to remove the budgetary mote from your own?

Pure and Simple

June 7, 2006

Massachusetts' senior Catholic public servant takes a stand: "'A vote for this amendment is a vote for bigotry, pure and simple.' Thus spoke Sen. Ted Kennedy in reference to the Marriage Protection Amendment being debated in the Senate today."

Vexing? Yes. A novelty? On the contrary, it's the world's oldest profession.

Writing about the Roman author Petronius—specifically, about his depiction of the freedman-parvenus of first-century Italy—Erich Auerbach described the mad scramble for riches that attended the break-up of the old regime, "with masters bequeathing large slices of their wealth to slaves who do their sexual bidding." Yesterday, your father carried wood; today, you adjust your morals to your master's caprice; tomorrow, your son will be in a position to buy himself a senatorship.

In the 21st century, as was the case in the 1st, fortunes are to be made by turning catamite. The favors solicited are not always sexual, of course, nor is the payment always monetary. Yet there's no important *moral* difference between the rent boy who accommodates his client for cash and the congressman who agrees to push same-sex marriage in exchange for political endorsement. Perhaps most people go along with the fiction that the stateman's (journalist's, academic's, judge's ...) principles are somehow more sanitary than the catamite's lower intestinal tract, but in doing so they're swayed more by sentiment than by reason. The willingness to sell what shouldn't be sold, to those willing to buy what shouldn't be bought, is common to all harlotry. Some practitioners show more profit than others.

Annoying though it is, it's impossible to take Sen. Kennedy's recent statement seriously. In his world it's a career move: that's to say, business is business. We don't know what his real convictions about the gay agenda might be, just as we don't know the real sexual predilections of Petronius' Roman slaves. In both instances, the Inner Man was bartered away to wealthy homosexuals for sordid purposes of their own devising. We have no positive duty to visit contempt upon the persons who have made this bargain. By the same token, when they ask us for our respect, we're under no obligation to humor them.

That Faith and Values Thing

July 12, 2006

> *Almost all absurdity of conduct arises from the imitation of those whom we cannot resemble.*
>
> —Samuel Johnson

At the Democratic National Convention in 1988, held in Atlanta, the traditional red, white, and blue bunting was replaced by the designer colors salmon, cream, and lilac, because the Dems' media consultants assured them it came off better on television. It came off instead as ridiculous, and in so doing showed the gap between policy-making liberals and the rest of the citizenry. Those for whom patriotism is a distasteful ritual enacted under compulsion only once every four years find it hard to counterfeit, and it's not surprising that when they try to fake it for the cameras they can't get it right. Fr. Neuhaus had some fun the other day spoofing E.J. Dionne's clumsy defense of his fellow libs: "The progressive and the reformer have a problem with what passes for unadulterated patriotism." It's hard to convince others you share a value you sneer at.

We see the same salmon-cream-lilac obtuseness when Lefties try to talk religion. They live and move and have their being in a secular elite culture that has nothing but disdain for Christianity and Christians; at best they regard piety as a childhood disease. Only the coarsest political necessity obliges them to take notice of believers in the first place, and their discomfort at feigning an interest in faith is obvious. Still, like a drooling guy trying to convince a ballerina he "really digs Prokofiev", the liberal lust for votes won't help them get the words right. Mark Tooley reports on Jim Wallis' pathetic teach-in for Dems on the make: "[Howard] Dean shared hope for America as a 'moral nation,' with national health care, an increased minimum wage, and a protected estate tax. 'The folks in this church are ones who live their faith through works—that is the mark of a real Christian,' he assured his audience."

A protected estate tax. *That*'ll impress the Christian voter. But while you're laying this line on her, Howie, try not to stare so hard at her legs.

The sad futility is evident in another column by E.J. Dionne, where the liberal Catholic journo is gushing about the liberal Christian pol Barack Obama: "And if you think this sounds preachy, Mr. Obama has an answer: 'Our fear of getting "preachy" may also lead [progressives] to discount the role that values and culture play in some of our most urgent social problems.'"

They've both got it backwards. Religion is about *ends*, and genuinely religious people are not flattered when you point out how well their religion serves as a *means*. Christian charity may be useful in alleviating homelessness, but to praise its utility is to demean it. A politician not constitutionally allergic to faith might have written, "Our fear of getting 'preachy' may also lead progressives to discount the importance of urgent social problems in the personal decisions that religious persons consider matters of their salvation and damnation." Hint: Don't look for many changes in Campaign 2008.

In the Safe Embrace of the State

April 17, 2007

"What is needed, urgently, is stronger controls over the lethal weapons that cause such wasteful carnage and such unbearable loss." With Pavlovian predictability, the better trained media have displayed the reflex reaction to homicidal madness: increase state control, curtail personal liberty. American intellectuals have become so European-ized over the past fifty years that it may be worth remembering why America severed its European political ties in the first place, and why, having done so, it radically changed the relationship of governors to the governed.

The clearest statement I have ever read of the American theory of government came from Ronald Reagan, speaking on Soviet televi-sion before his 1988 summit meeting with Gorbachev. It came out in response to an interviewer's objection that Reagan seemed to have forgotten that the Soviet Union had a constitution too.

> You have a constitution; we have a constitution. The difference between our two constitutions is very simple. Your constitution says these are the privileges, rights, that the government provides for the people. Our constitution says: we the people will allow the govern-ment to do the following things.

Bull's-eye. That's why a low-to-middle-income American can have a rifle leaning in the corner of his dining room that the local chief of police knows nothing about, while his European counterpart cannot. Also, in part, that's why totalitarian statism has not been a serious threat to Americans. So far.

"We the people will allow the government to do the following things ..." If the coercive power in a given nation belongs exclu-sively to government agencies, the notion of government "by the people" becomes vacuous. The Second Amendment reflects the rat-ifiers' understanding of this grim truth; and the guarantee that "the right to bear arms shall not be infringed" was intended, in part, to diffuse coercive power among as broad a spectrum of the citizenry as possible. It makes a difference. When the state is the only armed party in the state-citizen encounter, it tends to consult its own convenience at the expense of other human goods.

As anyone who has lived abroad can attest, the police and other agents of the state who come onto one's property have one atti-tude when they *know* there's no lethal weapon on the premises, and another attitude entirely when they don't. It's true of friendly visits, and true of not-so-friendly visits. Would the ratifiers have approved the right to bear arms had they foreseen massacres staged by madmen? Almost certainly. Any liberty will be abused. All liberties come at a cost of life. Those who prefer life to freedom are traditionally given the name slaves.

In this vein, I was struck by an argument made some years ago by a constitutional scholar named Robert Cottrol, who gave the following justification for the Second Amendment (a very rough paraphrase): In pre-Enlightenment Europe, the notions of nobility and the right to own weapons were interchangeable. To be noble was to be "armigerous"—a word that means not only to have a coat-of-arms, but more generally to bear weapons. Government was aristocratic, which in theory and in practice meant the government of the commons by the nobles, i.e., the unarmed by the armigerous.

Then two kinds of revolutions shook up the old regime. One was that of the French Revolution and its statist imitations, which obliterated the nobility: all persons were to be *citoyens*. Rule was by a cadre of political managers, in whom resided all powers of violent coercion. This produced the modern European state.

The other kind of revolution was the American. In this revolution (if I have Cottrol right) hereditary classes were abolished by declaring all men intrinsically noble. Thus all men were rightfully armigerous. Thus the right to bear arms was not to be infringed—any more than the right to a trial or the right to free speech was to be infringed. The result was a distinctively American refusal to regard one's governors as one's superiors. An associate at a Washington law firm once told me that a Chinese intern at the same firm confessed her perplexity that many Americans criticized President Clinton so harshly and vocally. When told this was common she replied, "But why does the government *let* them?" Now that's the voice of the statist.

We see the divide very clearly in the way the decisions made by the European Union are enforced in the member countries. When the state has determined that a personal liberty is to be curtailed, the presumption is that the citizen who resists is in the wrong. Even if a reprieve is granted—think of the two years given the Catholic Church in the U.K. to come to terms with gay adoption—that reprieve is viewed not as a right but as a favor bestowed by the state, and at the state's pleasure. In the U.S., though it's becoming yearly less true, government initiatives to curtail freedoms are viewed as wrong until proven otherwise. We the people, to the extent that we still have a say in the matter, are less inclined than statists simply to roll over and take it from the government.

Many people will scoff at the "nobility" of an armigerous Nebraskan farmhand with his gun rack hanging in his pickup. They prefer their nobles more—dare we say it?—European. Like the Europeans, they'll be shaking their heads at the Virginia Tech massacre and sniffing, "If the proper laws and proper enforcement were in place, this never would have happened." In the final analysis there's no reply to this, because it declares a difference of first principles. Sure, we can point to the backpack bombing in gun-free Madrid, and we can ask why a maniac with a match and a coffee can filled with gasoline can't out-Columbine Columbine, but it in the end it's a question of—when civil amity breaks down to the point that coercive force is necessary—which armiger we want on the business end of the arms. I'll take the Nebraskan in the Dodge Ram.

Second Collection

October 27, 2007

The Catholic Campaign for Human Development is the Plymouth Duster of the U.S. bishops' conference, a relic of early 1970s social activism that—except for its value as a fashion statement—was a disappointment when it was launched and hasn't improved with age. Yesterday we were given our official annual spadeful of the 40-year-old rhetoric:

> The Catholic Campaign for Human Development (CCHD) distributed more than $9.5 million in grants to local organizations working to overcome poverty in the United States.
>
> The 2007 grants, totaling $9,578,000, will be used by 314 projects in 46 states, the District of Columbia and Puerto Rico. The average award is $30,500 and will go to local organizations that address the specific concerns of their poor and low-income members. These groups work toward economic justice, fair housing, health care access, living wages, and immigrant and worker rights, among other concerns.

Note the phrase "working *to overcome* poverty"—this is the key element in the CCHD mission and what we're told makes it different from a conventional charity: i.e., poverty relief through almsgiving. Helping the poor overcome their poverty is a noble endeavor, but the CCHD's idea of overcoming poverty seems in every case to be a statist solution: cash disbursements to Left-leaning action groups aimed at redirecting government funds towards their own purposes.

Think of it this way: you'd be pleased to learn your pastor gave your 12-year-old a part-time job; less pleased to discover that what the job consists of is pestering you for a larger allowance. The grantees the CCHD chose to tell us about are the Mississippi Poultry Workers Center, Natural Home Cleaning Professionals (Oakland), the Albany Park Neighborhood Council (Chicago), Women's Community Revitalization (Philadelphia), Families United for Racial and Economic Equality (Brooklyn), and the Disabled Rights Action Committee (Salt Lake City). One notes that organizations aimed at empowering homeschoolers and pregnancy help centers are not much in evidence. A visit to the website of Families United for Racial and Economic Equality (FUREE, get it?) provides a list of "victories" chalked up to the organization—victories at overcoming poverty, I presume. For example:

- We worked with welfare rights groups around the country to influence the debate for TANF Reauthorization in 2002. This included participating in a take over of the ultra-conservative Heritage Foundation, a protest at Hillary Clinton's residence and a historic march on President George W. Bush's ranch in Crawford, Texas.
- As a part of the core organizing coalition of Still We Rise (an alliance of NYC groups fighting to bring the agenda of poor to low income peoples to the forefront) FUREE helped lead the organizing of the march against the Republican National Convention in NYC on August 30th 2004 with thousands of New Yorkers.

A takeover of the Heritage Foundation? *That*'ll feed a lot of hungry children. Try a mirror-image reversal of the party politics and ask yourself how much cash the CCHD would toss at a group that shut down the ACLU or the National Lawyers Guild.

Three points. One: The partisan politics of the CCHD are overwhelmingly lopsided, yet its Leftist bias is never candidly admitted come special collection time. Two: The funded programs don't teach unskilled workers to become welders or encourage men to marry and stay married to the mothers of their children, but rather take social breakdown for granted and seek government monies to make the breakdown less irksome; it can be argued that this approach doesn't overcome poverty but perpetuates it. Three: Even where the funds fought for and won serve a good cause, other good causes will thereby go unfunded; who's to say the net change is for the better?

Almost every social ill in the U.S. has its roots in the breakdown of the family, and, conversely, a healthy family situation gives its members advantages that almost no external misfortune can offset. And the Catholic Church is uniquely well placed to use her teaching to remedy the ills of family life. The irony of the CCHD is that it seems consciously to exclude the Catholic view of the human person from its understanding of poverty and its programs for overcoming it. True, $9 million isn't a huge sum by the standards of contemporary diocesan payouts (barely five creation spirituality convictions, at current rates), but it still seems Catholics could untrouser the cash they have left for purposes closer to their hearts.

WHAT WE BELIEVE

Diogenes had little patience for professional theologians (or amateurs, for that matter) who professed to be Catholic but could not accept the doctrines of the Catholic Church. Women who pretended to be Catholic priests—while organizing their services in non-Catholic churches, and denouncing the Vatican patriarchy—gave him extra scope for satire.

Committed to Scripture

April 5, 2003

"We're Christians—we're Nicene Christians, we're creedal Christians, we're orthodox Christians ..."

Culture war veterans will reflexively stiffen at the words above, recognizing that, whoever this speaker may be, whatever his agenda, he wants to rob us of our inheritance. The verbal chloroform is administered before the larceny takes place.

The setting is the Episcopal Church in the U.S., whose bishops recently commissioned and accepted a report entitled "Gift of Sexuality". By now the moves are familiar ones in all the mainstream churches: a hard teaching becomes a complex issue becomes an object of theological dispute becomes a locus of productive tension becomes a source of diversity becomes a new orthodoxy in which—you guessed it—St. Augustine doesn't qualify as a Christian.

"What we did in the paper on issues of sexuality was, we took the statement about theology that we began with 18 months ago and we reworked that and said this is the framework or the context within which the whole discussion is taking place," [Central Florida Bishop John] Howe added. "We're Christians—we're Nicene Christians, we're creedal Christians, we're orthodox Christians—it restates that and says, within that context, we hold really divergent opinions about matters of sexuality. Our present conclusion is that equally orthodox

Christians who are equally committed to the Scripture can come to very different opinions about these matters," he said.

So, what is it to belong to a Church? It is to choose *this* group of people with which to sing hymns we don't believe. Catholics cannot indulge in sectarian morose delectation here; our own bishops' document "Always Our Children" differs from the Episcopalians' only in the degree to which they were able to push the envelope. Says ECUSA Bishop Robert Ihloff of Maryland: "The experience of thinking and stretching was grace-filled," he said, "with a group of diverse people committed to the church and each other. It took a long time to reach consensus and not everyone will be pleased but *we went as far as we could at this time.*"
Exactly.

Stiff-Necked Conservatives and the NCR

May 2, 2003

> I do not object to bishops being the ones who ordain, if it is understood that they represent the local as well as the universal church. I believe the validity of their act of ordaining is rooted in this relation to the church. It does not flow literally from an apostolic secession [*sic*] that imagines the power to ordain as a "magic touch" passed down from bishop to bishop through two millennia. At the same time, when bishops grow so derelict in carrying out their responsibility to ordain a ministry in adequate numbers and quality to serve the church, then the church as people of God have a right to take back the power to ordain and carry it out themselves. It seems to me that this is the case today in the Catholic church.

That's Rosemary Ruether in this week's *National Catholic Reporter*. Her theology seems to get fuzzier and her antipathies sharper as the years go by. She professes a conventional Baptist understanding of ministry—according to which it is the community that confers on the ordinand whatever there is to confer—then contradicts herself in the notion that the people can "take back the power". But Rosemary, how can the community take back that which it never let go?

I myself have twice been invited to participate in "laying hands" on people being ordained in a Baptist setting. One was a friend being ordained to a social ministry in Washington, D.C. The other was the first woman to be ordained by the Baptist church of Nicaragua.

Ruether, clearly, has no shortage of spiritual homesteads. Why then is she so keen to yank ours from underneath us? Like St. Peter— "Lord, to whom shall we go?"—we have no alternatives, no fall-backs. It would appear that her aim is not to find a place of shelter for herself and her comrades but to make orthodox Catholics homeless.

My interest is less with Ruether's project in itself than with the editors of the *National Catholic Reporter* who keep her on board. Do they really think conservatives are being captious when we doubt the sincerity of the NCR's goodwill toward the Church? We may at times express our suspicions uncharitably, but do they really think we *misunderstand* their motives?

Anybody Home?

April 8, 2003

A Milwaukee parish staged a mock Mass two weeks ago where a sac-ramentally vested woman directed the agitprop as part of a "World Day of Prayer for Women's Ordination". That's only a symptom. Here's the deeper problem:

> St. Matthias agreed to host the prayer service, according to pastor Fr. David Cooper, only after consultation with staff members and parish-ioners. "St. Matthias Parish was only a host for the prayer service," said Cooper. "The parish has no official or unofficial position on the question of the ordination of women."

A parish that has no "official or unofficial position" on defined Cath-olic doctrine is, for this very reason, not a Catholic parish. Once that fatal step is taken, why should it matter whether the parish provides a podium for Cardinal Ratzinger or a stage for Wicca street theater?

(Note that the link and quote come from the *diocesan* newspaper. By a coincidence, one of those gathered for prayer had a camera ready and was able to submit a photo to the editrix.)

Consequences

May 4, 2003

One summer Sunday in 1979:

> She stepped up to the makeshift altar, made a sign of the cross, and began to say the liturgy. She lifted bread and, for the first time in earnest, uttered the words, "This is my body." Afterward, the community's regular priest—whom the Catholic Church had removed from ministry when he married—told her: "Judy, you have been ordained." Any other ceremony would only confirm it. Some in the group had qualms, however. They debated for nine months before voting to permit Heffernan to submit to an ordination ceremony.
>
> On May 11, 1980, a Jesuit priest laid hands on her head before the community, and performed the ordination rite canonically done by Roman Catholic bishops.

No, Judy, you are not ordained. The bread you declaim over remains bread. The sins you shrive still bind the penitent. The Jesuit who laid hands on your head no more effected an ordination than a six-year-old playing Mass in his bedroom confects the Eucharist. This, at any rate, is the Catholic belief about Catholic belief.

You were voted into the job by your "group". Think about what that means. Either they have ceased to believe in consecration and absolution full stop (and simply prefer to take their bread and encouragement from you than from Fr. O'Halloran), or they have ceased to believe that Holy Orders confer any sacramental powers at all—any power, i.e., that can't be ginned up by a half dozen folks with a big red book and a candle.

By your actions you have proclaimed your denial of the infallibility of the Church. Well, is your group fallible or infallible? If infallible, how can you *know* it? If fallible, then think about the responsibility you have taken on yourself: the eternal destiny of souls which, henceforth separated from the Catholic Church and the graces channeled by her, are staking the rightness of every collective decision they take on the rightness of the decision they took in 1980.

Do you really want these men and women to die with *your* wafers on their tongues? Do you really want them to die with their sins hinging on *your* faith, *your* theology, *your* sense of election?

Bishops and the Women Question

June 4, 2003

After the NCCB's women's pastoral fiasco of a decade ago, which resulted in the eminently forgettable "Partners in the Mystery of Redemption", the U.S. bishops have made piecemeal efforts to communicate their sympathies to feminists. Another series of "listening sessions" has just ended. Was any woman you know invited? Exactly.

> Ability and willingness of priests, especially the newly ordained, to work with women. This was a major issue throughout the consultation. Participants felt that a significant number of newly ordained priests are not prepared to work with women as colleagues in ministry. Some had experienced a lack of respect. Others said that some newly ordained priests show an excessive concern for power and authority; some cannot accept women as their supervisors. Participants expressed concern about the psycho-sexual development of newly ordained priests, especially as it affects their ability to relate to women.

There's lots more, but you get the drift. The idea that such an agency can accurately canvass "women's concerns" is as fruitful as a survey of "men's concerns"—that is, not very. But this is a product of the Bishops' Committee on Women, itself a task force of the Secretariat for Family, Laity, Women, and Youth. As the patronizing name itself indicates, "women", for episcopal-bureaucratic purposes at least, are one more special interest group, comparable to Ruthenians or the hearing impaired, who require an occasional pat on the head and a popsicle. Bishop Joseph Imesch of Joliet masterminded the first pastoral, which suggests that the bishops give this kind of job to the guy they don't trust to drive the lawn tractor.

The theme of this round of "breakout sessions" is collaboration between women and clergy. I haven't seen all the documentation yet, but no homeschoolers or pro-lifers seem to have qualified as women—or, if they did, their constitutional bashfulness kept them silent.

Regarding those who voiced "concern about the psycho-sexual development of newly ordained priests, especially as it affects their ability to relate to women"—do you think they were referring to gay clergy whose mannerisms and emotional immaturity were repellent to moms on the parish school board? Neither do I.

Tapeworms

August 7, 2003

The Anglicans' approval of a gay bishop and the Vatican's instruction on opposing same-sex marriage have had the beneficial consequence of flushing many anti-Christians and pseudo-Christians from the high grass where they've been hiding. Latent for decades, the lines of battle are taking shape swiftly across the landscape. Within Catholicism too, waverers are beginning to nail their colors to the mast. Sulky passengers like Andrew "I still love Mum when she's wrong" Sullivan are on the brink of honesty—i.e., of admitting the apostasy that occurred long ago. Caring Priests™ are shrieking the one thing they've ever cared about. And at the *National Catholic Reporter*, where the Barney Frank method of birth control has long held a place of special esteem, publisher Tom Fox has a uniquely revealing editorial:

> Consider something else. Is it possible the Catholic Church still has it wrong on sexual morality and needs to reconsider church attitudes and teachings? This would require admitting the church is, like other institutions, capable of making mistakes, even big ones. It would require becoming a more humble church, perhaps one with less sweeping claims to infallibility.

Cute, isn't it? Our 'umble essayist 'umbly invites the Bride of Christ to admit she has spots and wrinkles like the rest of us 'umble folks. The Church makes mistakes too.

Fraud, and an ugly fraud at that. An honest man does not speak of "less sweeping claims to infallibility." If my calculator gives me a wrong answer for a sum, I don't stroke my chin and suggest that Texas Instruments make "less sweeping claims to accuracy"—I say the calculator's worthless, and throw it away. Dissenters have in fact ignored the teaching Church for years; they occasionally agree with her, they are never taught by her. Indeed, they *can't* be taught by her, any more than I can let myself be informed by a calculator that once gave me a bad answer. It's psychologically impossible. I might keep a worthless calculator as a paperweight; I can only keep a worthless church for private purposes of my own devising.

Dissenters are tapeworms. Both a tapeworm and a fetus may simultaneously draw nourishment from the same woman. But whereas the baby is nourished bloodstream to bloodstream, as it were, and so extends and continues the mother's life, the tapeworm feeds her blood into its gut. The tapeworm is an alien, no matter how intimate and "inside" it may be, no matter how furiously it insists it is feasting at the same table as the baby.

In the Church, at the altar, fetuses and tapeworms share one loaf and one cup. From the outside, it's impossible to tell us apart. And note that what makes a baby and what makes a tapeworm (in this sense) has nothing to do with sinfulness. Many babies fall frequently into grave sins, and many tapeworms lead lives of continence and generosity. Tapeworms are often more likeable and usually more presentable than babies. It's not a question of "we're better than you"; it's an admission that the relation of mother and child and the relation of host and parasite are radically contrary. For us, the Church is *mater et magistra*; for dissenters, she is a source of jobs, or Marty Haugen music, or chances for self-display, or political soapboxes, or hiding places, or access to important people, or opportunities for sabotage.

But isn't the distinction drawn too sharply? Aren't some Catholics part fetus and part tapeworm? Impossible. As Newman said, a thousand difficulties do not make one doubt. In the same way, there's all the difference in the world between the scandalized and anguished Catholic hanging on for dear life and the breezy dismissiveness of the dissenter who chirps about "less sweeping claims to infallibility." It's not our task to start a pogrom—remember the parable of the wheat and the tares—it's our job to drink more deeply than ever from the springs of salvation. To be Catholic.

The Reckoning

April 29, 2005

George Weigel argues that Ratzinger's election signifies the twilight of Catholic progressivism:

It was expected that the Catholic Church would, indeed must, take the path of accommodation: that has been the central assumption of what's typically called "progressive" Catholicism. That assumption has now been decisively and definitively refuted. The "progressive" project is over—not because its intentions were malign, but because it posed an ultimately boring question: how little can I believe, and how little can I do, and still remain a Catholic?

I'm not as sanguine as Weigel regarding the intentions of progressivists. After all, they haven't been low-profile church mice quietly pleading for a live-and-let-live Catholicism. Though the now-comic 1960s culture of flowers and folk music may incline us to view them as harmless sentimentalists, they were and are revolutionaries, out to replace the old order with a new one of their own devising. Think of the way they've taken over most theology departments, some seminaries, some diocesan RE [religious education] offices, and occasionally entire religious congregations. Think of the way they've used the shibboleth issues (contraception, women's ordination, gay rights, inclusive language) to hire and promote ideological allies and torpedo others. Weigel is right that progressivists failed to sell their project to the majority of churchgoers, and right that religious minimalism had much to do with this failure. But most of us probably know a seminarian or grad student or lay volunteer who, in spite of his goodwill and *because* of his orthodoxy, found himself unemployed and unemployable before he knew what hit him.

For the same reasons I don't expect progressivists to shrug and gracefully fade off the scene. What's at stake is not a failed literary review, but the meaning of their entire life. In the Bolshevik revolution, the young firebrands of 1910 did not cede authority to the young firebrands of 1980; once having seized power, they couldn't relinquish it, and kept a white-knuckle grip on the Party until it was loosened by clogged arteries.

So too in the post-Conciliar Catholic putsch, the angry young mustangs of 1968 became the angry middle-aged mustangs of 1988 became the angry old mustangs of today. Only in the case of gay politics have younger men risen to form a wary alliance with the *Humanae Vitae* dissenters. I agree with Weigel that their future is as bright as one would expect for a movement infatuated with sterility.

Remember too that mainstream Catholic liberals, largely through moral weakness, have blood on their hands—at least via political complicity, when not in gruesome fact. Once they threw in their lot with contraception in 1968, the pressure to give a green light to abortion after *Roe v. Wade* in 1973 proved too great to resist. This was a flat contradiction of their professed concern for the voiceless, of course, so, being good revolutionaries, they had to change their ideology to justify retrospectively their own history of bloodletting. That's why Catholic liberals detest any and all mention of abortion: it reminds them of their betrayal of the sole element of nobility in the progressivist project.

"Weak men are apt to be cruel," said Lord Halifax, "because they stick at nothing that may repair the ill effect of their mistakes." The ad hoc acts of injustice perpetrated in seminaries and theology departments—rejections, firings, demotions—were for the most part tactical cruelties necessitated by the dynamics of revolution: with 40 million casualties behind you, there's no stopping, and there's no going back.

Allegiances

May 11, 2005

A couple weeks ago I saw two or three articles with the title "Santorum reconsiders death penalty stance"—or words to that effect. A pro-capital-punishment Republican senator, Santorum was reported to be rethinking his support in the light of recent statements from Pope John Paul II and the U.S. bishops.

I don't know whether or to what extent Santorum shifted. But what struck me is how unthinkable it is that any of our pro-abortion Catholic senators would let himself be taught by the Church on this topic. Would they even let it be known that they were contemplating the possibility of letting the Church form their thinking?

It's true not only of officeholders but of dissenting Catholics generally: if you decide the Church is in error about something—I'm talking about solemnly declared doctrine—you make that judgment according to some standard. That standard, then, replaces the Church as your final arbiter of truth. That means the Church becomes superfluous, redundant, worthless (i.e., as a teacher; you can still use her as a soapbox or music hall). You may sometimes *agree* with her, but so what?

Hence the phoniness of so much of the "let's patch up our differences" rhetoric. The spiritual orientation of the man who has judged the Church wrong isn't and can't be the same as that of him who offers her his obedience—however perplexed or tormented he may find himself. If you think the Church has given you false answers, then even the value of her right answers is provisional. Should you come to doubt the truth of an answer you once thought right—say, about the prohibition of remarriage—what sort of spiritual resistance could you put up? What would such resistance mean?

Polemically it's an effective sound-bite slam to contend that orthodox obedience means checking your brain at the door, refusing to think, etc. But those who let the Church teach them know that's not how it feels from inside. Everyone craves to understand what he loves. If God's word is important to you, you can't help but ponder the difficult or even shocking parts. It's not a matter of closing the mind but of opening up something deeper than the mind, of letting the word speak to you after setting aside your suspicion.

There is a necessary chasm that separates the dissenter from the Catholic, because both intuit that "belonging to the Church" has a radically different meaning for each. We share pews, hymnbooks, potato salad at the parish picnic, but always with the hope (a hope which nearly all churchmen will forbid us to express) that the other guys will eventually amend their lives—not a change of mind, but a change of allegiance.

His Slowliness

May 25, 2005

Doing its best to loosen rivets at key junctural points of orthodoxy, *U.S. Catholic* passes on advice addressed to the Pope by thirteen hostile women, the *least* rancorous of whom is Joan Chittister:

> We will all come to [truth] slowly, with more or less reluctance, with more or less insight into the meaning of it for us in the here

and now because people develop at different rates as a result of different experiences. I want to tell you that in periods such as these, we may all stand at different points on this continuum of growth and development.

Got that? It's not that Pope Benedict is necessarily evil. He's just a slow learner.

Free to Be Me

July 25, 2005

A Boston area innkeeper has declared her intention to be ordained a Catholic priest today in a privately arranged service conducted by apostate women. She is unembarrassed by the act of claiming for herself the authority that the Church invests in the sacrament of Holy Orders, while denying the Church's authority to teach what is and is not valid matter for the same sacrament. "Marie David, who opposes mandatory celibacy for priests and is married to a former priest, shrugs off the possibility of being excommunicated by the church, saying 'there would be a sadness, but I refuse to recognize their authority to tell me that.'" Outstanding.

Your Uncle Diogenes, coincidentally, begs to announce that he will shortly accede to the title of the Duke of Devonshire. It's true, I confess, that neither my father nor any other male antecedent ever held the title, but it's always been my deeply held personal belief that real nobility has less to do with parentage than with attitude.

I fully expect the House of Lords to throw me out on my ear when I attempt to take my seat among other members of the peerage. There will be a sadness, but I refuse to recognize their authority to tell me who I am.

It must be understood that I reject the whole idea of hereditary succession on which the traditional peerage is based. Consider: Who gave *these* people the titles in the first place, and by what right do *they* decide who may and may not inherit them?

Some of my more conservative acquaintances have tried to dissuade me from my purpose. Kind hearts are more than coronets, my mother says, and ermine can be hell in the hot weather. But I pay her no attention. She's just a commoner, poor thing.

Why Can't Women Be Priests?

July 22, 2005

When a puzzled Jewish academic asks me, "Why doesn't the Catholic Church ordain women?" I can give him a pretty satisfactory answer—satisfying, that is, to the historical curiosity behind his question. It's largely a matter of laying out the nature of decision-making authority in the Church, reviewing the relevant tradition, and giving a synopsis of the authoritative decisions made. Within the terms of authority as that authority understands itself, the answer to his question doesn't admit of much doubt.

But very often today another question is asked: "Why can't women be priests?" And almost always the person who poses the question in those terms wants a different kind of answer than that which satisfied our Jewish professor. As the words "can't be" indicate, this questioner is usually asking for a *deductive* proof; he wants an explanation why—given what we believe about the nature of the Trinity and the nature of women—the doctrine on Holy Orders *could not be otherwise* than it is. In effect, he's making this demand: "Prove to me that God could not have included a female priesthood in His plan of redemption without acting contrary to His divine nature."

This challenge is perhaps impossible to answer, and as far as I know hasn't been seriously attempted. Most educated Catholics, including I think the greater number of bishops and priests, are keenly aware of this limitation. Since no deductive proof can be offered in response to the question "Why can't women be priests?" they tend to the belief that there is no valid theological argument at all for excluding women from Holy Orders, and consequently think that, sooner or later, shifts in cultural attitudes combined with new urgency of pastoral needs will bring about a change in the teaching.

But many solemnly defined doctrines are equally "vulnerable". Suppose we ask, "Why can't rye bread become the Body of

Christ?" Is there a deductive proof that will satisfy the questioner? Is the nature of God such that, of all the cereal grains, wheat and only wheat could provide the matter of the sacrament? Such that rye by its nature as rye is ontologically unsuitable? Such that Eucharistic doctrine could not be otherwise without an offense against reason or Trinitarian dogma?

Of course not. You can't put a pistol to the head of the Church and demand a deductive proof for the exclusive validity of wheat. The Church can only answer (1) that her use of wheat is fitting (it is appropriate in itself and doesn't contradict Scripture or other doctrines); (2) that it is consonant with her tradition (we know it has been used in the past and have no reason to believe the orthodox have used anything else); and (3) that every time a doubt has been raised, she has given the same answer. It's a humbler kind of suasion than a deductive proof; it doesn't silence personal doubt with the finality that a syllogism does, but the nature of the wheat-versus-rye question is such that no other kind of considerations could be tendered in reply.

Now when you examine the arguments that the Church proposes for restricting the priesthood to men—laid out in *Inter Insigniores* by Paul VI and reaffirmed by John Paul II in *Ordinatio Sacerdotalis*—you see they're of the "wheat-not-rye" variety:

> [The Church] holds that it is not admissible to ordain women to the priesthood, for very fundamental reasons. These reasons include: the example recorded in the Sacred Scriptures of Christ choosing his Apostles only from among men; the constant practice of the Church, which has imitated Christ in choosing only men; and her living teaching authority which has consistently held that the exclusion of women from the priesthood is in accordance with God's plan for his Church.

Deductively conclusive? No, but it doesn't pretend to be. It's congruent with, but not dictated by, ordinary human reason and the biblical data. You have to trust the Church is preserving God's sovereign freedom here as you have to trust her in the case of Eucharistic matter. Once you suspect she's lying, or hiding a deeper truth that you (or your coterie) can recover, you step out into The Void.

A final word. I mentioned above that many churchmen, impressed by the lack of proof for the traditional doctrine, believe the Church will eventually bow to necessity and change her practice. Of course they're also aware of the feebleness of the culturally conditioned prudential considerations that individual clerics—not infrequently they themselves at an earlier stage of enlightenment—offered against women priests ("Women can't be priests because they don't know Latin", "Women can't be priests because they can't keep a secret", etc.). Often, by a kind of occult compensation, such men erroneously attribute these prejudices to the teaching Church, and then reproach her for irrationalities that she never indulged, though many of her ministers did.

When it comes to doctrine, then, you can either take the Church as a loving teacher, or you can take her as an opponent and reckon her defeated wherever and whenever she doesn't pin your shoulders to the mat. The injustice and unloveliness of her ministers often make the latter the more attractive option, but to those who mistrust her she has no gift to offer at all. None.

Truth or Consequences

July 18, 2005

Yet more Catholic women are attempting to bootstrap themselves into Holy Orders. This time in the waters of the St. Lawrence Seaway.

> All the women being ordained July 25 are members of Roman Catholic Womenpriests, an organization of Catholic women whose goal "is to bring about the full equality of women in the Roman Catholic Church," said the group's Web site. Seven women were ordained in the organization's first ceremony in 2002.... "We consider these ordinations to be valid but illicit," said [Prof. Victoria] Rue, who was ordained as a deacon last year and will move a step up to priest this year.

Here's a thought experiment, notionally addressed to a liberal Catholic who approves of the ordination of women or believes it may take place in the future.

Let's assume that a male Anglican bishop with valid episcopal orders performs the Catholic rite of priestly ordination upon a
woman called Kate. As an orthodox Catholic, I contend Kate has not
been ordained. But you, thinking it possible that women might one
day be ordained, are obliged to acknowledge that some women *have*
already been ordained—viz., those subject like Kate to the conditions
just mentioned. Prof. Rue is correct that an ordination may be illicit
(i.e., contrary to ecclesiastical norms and permissions), but still valid.
However, a future pope's or future council's decision could change
the conditions of liceity for Holy Orders, but not the conditions
of validity. Thus, if it will ever be the case that women are validly
ordained, then it already is the case that women are validly ordained.
I deny the if-clause, of course, but you don't, and so are obliged to
accept the consequent.

Suppose Kate attempts to confect the Eucharist and you and I each
come into possession of the communion wafers. You are obliged to
treat them as you would treat the Blessed Sacrament validly consecrated by a validly ordained priest. (Can you be *sure* they aren't the
Real Thing? You can't.) I would treat them no differently from the
biscuits left behind by my kids after staging a pretend Mass on a shipping crate in the basement. (No Mass took place in either case. For
Kate as for my kids, what was flour before remained flour afterwards.)
Now if I saw you trying to insert Kate's wafers into the ciborium of
our parish tabernacle, I would do everything—not excluding physical
constraint—to prevent you. And if you saw me disposing of Kate's
wafers according to my belief that they are nothing more than stale
bread, you'd be obliged to do everything you could to prevent me.
Please note that these aren't in-your-face demonstrations of personal
bigotry. These are sober and sensible actions directed by conventional Eucharistic doctrine.

Now here's my question. Is it possible that two persons such as
ourselves (1) could be in total agreement about the facts of the case
(i.e., the circumstances of Kate's ordination and her eucharistic action
regarding the wafers), (2) could be in total disagreement about the
ontological reality of the wafers in question, such that one worships
what the other discards, and (3) could both belong to one and the
same Church? If 1 and 2 are true, doesn't it follow that 3 must be
false? Finally, if orthodox and liberal Catholics wouldn't belong to

the same Church under the conditions so specified, do they belong to the same Church *now?*

Second Things

May 3, 2006

From the *Baltimore Catechism* (III), 1891:

> Q. *491. What is the duty of the Teaching Church?*
> A. The duty of the Teaching Church is to continue the work Our Lord began upon earth, namely, to teach revealed truth, to administer the Sacraments and to labor for the salvation of souls.

Listening to "progressive" bishops lecture us on the use of condoms for reducing AIDS infection, I was struck by how far the model of the Church's teaching office has departed from the traditional one stated above. Note that the catechism said the Church's prime duty was to teach *revealed* truth—not psychology, not medicine, not sociology. And the goal of such teaching was not improved hygiene or race relations, but the salvation of souls.

Since the Council we've watched "the salvation of souls" drop out of the vocabulary of the progressivist Catholic majority, while the duty to teach *revealed* truth has been shouldered aside in favor of efforts to engage contemporary secular problems in contemporary secular terms. The thinking behind this shift (fueled by a grotesquely sentimentalist misreading of certain passages in *Gaudium et Spes*) was to revitalize the Church by regaining the attention of the indifferent masses by showing interest in what the masses were interested in. Old liberals deny it today, but back then they gleefully announced from every podium the self-evident truth that, by accommodating herself to cultural and political fashions, the Church would see huge increases in Mass attendance and vocations, a reanimated parish life, and a groundswell of enthusiasm for religion on the part of young people. "Let's engage the Church's worldly mission," the thinking ran, "then we'll be in a stronger position to engage her supernatural one."

Wrong. When the Church tried her hand at psychodrama and economics she dismayed those who loved her, amused those who hated her, and simply bored the rest. Churches, convents, and seminaries emptied, and the young people for whose sake the supernatural duties were abandoned resented being patronized even more than being scolded.

In a 1942 essay called "First and Second Things", C. S. Lewis drew attention to the paradoxical nature of the blunder: "To sacrifice the greater good for the less and then not to get the lesser good after all— that is the surprising folly." He went to generalize the law:

> Every preference of a small good to a great, or a partial good to a total good, involves the loss of the small or partial good for which the sacrifice was made. Apparently the world is made that way. If Esau really got his pottage in return for his birthright, then Esau was a lucky exception. You can't get second things by putting them first; you can get second things only by putting first things first.

The sight of a retired Jesuit archbishop reduced to coaching Africans in marital onanism is sorry enough, but it only recapitulates the trajectory of his own order. Precisely in the measure that it swapped faith for justice, it ended up with neither. And the same is true of post-Conciliar progressives in general: by putting secular prestige before spiritual duty and teaching human sciences instead of revealed truth, they gutted the Church Militant and lost contact with the Church Triumphant. Today, strutting in an empty chapel of their own design, they can neither bless nor heal.

Eagerly Awaiting Your Reply

June 16, 2006

More sacrilegious, and pathetic, Neverland Katholicism, celebrated this time aboard a cruise boat near Pittsburgh. On July 31, says an article in the *Post-Gazette*:

> Three women in vestments will lay their hands on the heads of the 12 women and anoint their hands with oil during an ordination ceremony that will be the first of its kind in the United States. Among the participants is Joan Clark Houk, 65, of McCandless, who with

seven other women are answering a call to be priests; the other four are candidates to be deacons....

In a three-page letter dated May 9, Mrs. Houk, a member of St. Alexis in McCandless, advised Bishop Donald Wuerl of her plans.

The bishop did not respond. Presiding at the ceremony, we're told, will be three women "who live in Germany and are bishops in Roman Catholic Womenpriests, an international group of Catholics who support women's ordination."

You have to wonder whether these gals apply the same Make-Believe Theology to the sacrament of matrimony. Using the logic that battered Bishop Wuerl into silence, one of them may send off a letter to, I don't know, Brad Pitt, informing him that she intends to become his wife; that the theology of marriage is in flux; that consent of the bride (if enthusiastic enough) may supply for a defect of the same on the part of the groom; that the validity of the sacrament is not subject to patriarchal norms of liceity; that his attempts to ignore or deny the spiritual reality of their marriage is a cowardly rearguard action of a discredited monogamism; that her birthday is May 11 and her favorite flowers are carnations.

The analogy, though suggestive, suffers from an obvious and lethal flaw: the proposal to Brad Pitt has a *theoretical* chance of success.

Rigidity Revisited

November 26, 2006

"A Tumultuous World Tests a Rigid Pope" reads a *Wall Street Journal* headline. Well, we've got prelates aplenty who bend. A little rigidity won't come amiss, especially where the truth is at stake. The article ends on an encouraging note:

Last month several dozen top Catholic theologians crowded into a Vatican chapel for 7:30 a.m. mass with Benedict. The pontiff gave pointed marching orders:

"Speaking just to find applause or to tell people what they want to hear ... is like prostitution," he told the theologians, according to a transcript. "Don't look for applause, but look to obey the truth."

Bull's-eye, boss. I've read no small amount of comment about Joseph Ratzinger suggesting that he was traumatized by the student unrest at the University of Tübingen in the late 1960s and that this resulted in a profound temperamental change toward conservatism. There is not one crumb of evidence for this thesis—beyond the fact that Ratzinger didn't follow the trajectory common to his generation of academics, viz., by giving in to pressure and becoming a squishy Leftist. Compare Ratzinger's writing with that of his contemporaries, pre- and post-1968, and the conclusion is pure Kipling: it was Ratzinger who kept his head when all about him were losing theirs.

Some men of the time (including clergyman-scholars) did become true reactionaries; they were psychologically overwhelmed by the turmoil of those years and so retreated into cloisters or rectories to lick their wounds. They typically developed strange crotchets in dress and mannerism. They ceased any patient engagement with their contemporaries, either withdrawing entirely from the academy or lurching into violent polemics. To put Ratzinger in this category is stupid.

I don't believe, though, that the people who claim Ratzinger to be reactionary are themselves stupid. Most are, or were, harlots— harlots precisely in the sense that Pope Benedict describes above: they made careers for themselves by seeking applause and telling people what they wanted to hear, and in so doing they put up for sale what ought not to be sold. Those who are conspicuously successful don't like to be reminded of the way they got started ("I was young and needed the money ..."), and their distinguished professorships make them forgetful of the metaphorical Hershey bars for which they first swapped their virtue. For such persons the existence of a Ratzinger is like a slap on a sunburned back. Small wonder if stung pride tries to make *him* out to be the weakling.

Jesus displayed forbearance and mercy toward prostitutes, however, and his present vicar has likewise shown a remarkable clemency in this regard. Doubtless he remembers how fierce were the pressures to succumb. Nor, to be honest, can your Uncle Di acquit himself of a strain of pharisaism here ("This man welcomes Swiss theologians and eats with them!"). Yet Pope Benedict is not a controversialist out to do down his adversaries, but a pastor of souls. It's easy to get impatient with the sheep that won't hear his voice, but there's not much doubt about whom Benedict is listening to.

Who Really Cares?

October 15, 2007

Most metropolitan areas in the U.S. have a large Catholic church near the city center—perhaps a cathedral, shrine, or basilica—that provides Mass and confessions more or less continually throughout the day.

If you enter such a church while Mass is going on, you'll notice three distinct categories of visitors: worshipers clustered in the pews near the altar, obviously partaking of the Mass; tourists strolling around with their maps and videocams, obviously not partaking; and a third group sitting or kneeling in the gloom at the back of the church or in the side aisles. Their connection with the Eucharistic Action is not clear. They don't want to be seen as participating in the Mass; in fact, they don't want to be seen at all.

This third contingent has a heterogeneous composition. Some are pious Catholics engaged in private prayer. Some are seekers: non-Catholics who find themselves attracted to the Church and her Eucharist and who want to take in as much as they can of the experience without committing themselves. Still others, I surmise, have been estranged from the Church by divorce and remarriage or by a gay entanglement and yet can't shake the spiritual conviction that it's the Church, at bottom, that has it right. They're afraid to get too close, yet they can't tear themselves away entirely. They put me in mind of St. Peter, warming his hands at the fire in the high priest's courtyard.

All the folks in the third contingent make use of the church's "neutral ground" to address a deeply personal spiritual need. Especially with regard to the last-mentioned category, I hope this neutral ground is never done away with; I hope no Ministers of Greeting (out of misguided goodwill) are commissioned to pounce on the loners so as to bind them into "fellowship".

Fellowship is an excellent thing, but if made into a kind of ticket that must be punched before entering church, it can eliminate that particular freedom—the freedom of the publican in the parable—to pray in God's house as an anonymous sinner, as a believer not yet capable of commitment. My hunch is that many souls are gained or regained for the Church simply by her providing this paradoxical conjunction of the holiest of mysteries along with the space to look on those mysteries from a distance: outside, yet not wholly outside.

Remember, there's a light on above the confessional.

His detractors sometimes write of Pope Benedict that he wants a "smaller and purer" Church. Rubbish. Like all popes, he wants a Church that is purer and *larger*. It's true that efforts to make her more virtuously orthodox are in tension with efforts to include the weaker brethren and increase her membership, but this tension has existed in the Church from her beginnings, as a reading of First Corinthians shows beyond question. And as the fifth chapter of that same epistle makes clear, the Church makes room for the weaker brethren not by softening or blurring her hard teachings, but by stating them without apology, "in sincerity and truth".

God gives no command for which he does not give adequate grace to accomplish. Consoling to all of us, this is especially encouraging for those entangled in habitual sin: every man has the possibility of leaving it behind him. Subversive chaplaincies and pseudochurches, such as the recently mentioned Most Holy Redeemer [a parish in San Francisco], are toxic because they preach and reinforce—not consolation—but in its place a kind of moral despair. By exhorting their confederates to befriend the vice that holds them captive—adultery, perjury, sodomy—they communicate the message that the path to true freedom is open only to others (those others whom accidents of biology or circumstance have blessed more abundantly). This is not only false, but lethal to the virtue of hope, and it's a scandal that the bogus ministers who indulge this cruelty are congratulated for their "pastoral" efforts.

The persons in question need the Church's pastoral help, and deserve to get it. But in their case this help is hard to receive and, for different reasons, hard to give. Those loudest in censure of "the institutional Church's failures" in these areas and most extravagant in praise of accommodationist alternatives might remind themselves that, where *authentic* pastoral help is delivered, neither the giver nor the recipient is likely to advertise the fact. They might stop to think that much spiritual assistance will be conveyed anonymously and in secret. They might consider that many of the most effective ministers and many of the most anguished sinners may have public reputations totally at variance with their unseen lives. They might remember that, at times, it's not in the front seats of the synagogues but in the back of the temple where the real action takes place.

Damned If You Don't

March 11, 2008

Several years ago already the Lutheran scholar Martin Marty gave a lecture entitled "Hell Disappeared. No One Noticed." His subject was the remarkably sudden and thorough elimination of a key doctrine from Christian discourse. It wasn't that hell had been formally repudiated by the mainstream denominations, but as if by tacit consent it ceased to have a place in religious thinking.

It must be admitted that, in the past, alongside a sane and proportionate concern with the subject, there was also an unwholesome interest in damnation exhibited by some Christians. These were always a minority, even among revivalists. But the fact is that making your audience's flesh crawl is all too easy to do—even a meagerly talented speaker can succeed at this sport—and many Christians were tormented for much of their lives by the nightmare images branded into their young minds by reckless and cruel preachers who took a sick pleasure in giving pain. The discourses on hell given by James Joyce's fictional Jesuit Fr. Arnall provide a classic example of the genre.

Has the moralist's delight in cruelty disappeared? Not at all. It is still very much with us.

The sickness has simply migrated into areas where it receives an ideologically enthusiastic reception, most notably among environmental activists. How often do we see news footage of an anti-nuke or antipollution rally without protesters costumed as mutants or monsters or corpses and threatening us with hideous torments for our sins of ecological neglect? As with the old-style Christians, such dementia subsists in a minority; most greens are motivated by a positive attraction to a picture of natural harmony, etc. Yet beside the wholesome folks we find the old disease—operating under a new and progressivist flag, of course—more concerned with spreading terror at the threatened doomsday than hope in the rewards of right action. The fearmongers don't seem that interested in recycling or fuel disposal. Like their forerunners, they get their kicks from giving kids nightmares.

Yet the doctrinal point raised by Prof. Marty remains to be addressed. Granted that it was harmfully exploited by cruel preachers in the past, is the Church's teaching on hell intact or not? And if the doctrine is still intact, and if damnation is a real possibility really contingent on the choices we make, how is it that the persons the Church has set apart to minister to our spiritual destiny seem so nonchalant about the matter?

In his preface to *The Screwtape Letters* C. S. Lewis writes:

> There are two equal and opposite errors into which our race can fall about the devils. One is to disbelieve in their existence. The other is to believe, and to feel an excessive and unhealthy interest in them. They themselves are equally pleased by both errors and hail a materialist or a magician with the same delight.

As with devils, so with damnation. Past ages may have been so fascinated with the Inferno part of the Christian triptych that the Paradiso part became all but invisible. Our own age seems to have attached itself to the contrary delusion. Both are destructive. The *Catechism* (no. 1035) reaffirms the reality of hell without extenuation or apology, yet most churchmen are embarrassed to mention it, as if they wished it could be quietly forgotten. I wonder if they've ever asked themselves about the entailments. If hell could "disappear" and damnation could be discarded as a myth, what purpose would a priest or bishop serve? Lacking a way to go wrong, what would the Church be FOR?

Do You Really Think So ...?

April 12, 2008

How to make Benedict blush.

> "He is a person who could easily hold an endowed chair at Notre Dame." Sitting in a spacious office on the top floor of Notre Dame's gold-domed administration building, the university's president, the

Rev. John I. Jenkins, pays Pope Benedict XVI what might be the ultimate compliment around here.

Notre Dame is northern Indiana's premier Catholic university.

Nonnegotiables

April 12, 2008

Back in 1990, Harvard Professor of Judaic Studies Jon Levenson wrote an article in the *Christian Century* entitled "Theological Liberalism Aborting Itself". Himself Jewish, the author had no personal interest in the triumph of any particular strand of Christian thought. Levenson was concerned to show that the progressive divinity schools, in jettisoning the Christian creeds on which they were founded, had failed to emancipate themselves (as they imagined) from dogma, but had instead replaced a coherent doctrinal orthodoxy with a capricious political one. An excerpt:

> At a conference several years ago, I found myself seated at a dinner table with several other Jews but only one Christian—a professor, it turned out, at a prominent liberal seminary. In response to genial questioning from some of his dinner companions, the lone Christian explained that his institution had long ago shed its once vivid ecclesiastical affiliation. The break had occurred over the application of the historical-critical method to the Bible, a prospect that the denomination had found incompatible with its deepest beliefs. "Are there, then, any beliefs or practices required of the faculty or students now?" asked one of the company. "No," replied the seminary professor firmly. But then, as an afterthought and in an undertone, he added, "except the requirement to use inclusive language."

An overstatement? Fast-forward to 2008, and take a look at the student handbook of the Episcopal Divinity School in Cambridge, Massachusetts. This is from the section headed "Corporate Worship":

> Faculty, staff and students work together in teams according to the scheduled rotation to plan and lead worship. As a practice, worship is

on a four-week cycle that includes traditional language and inclusive language liturgies. A week of alternative liturgies is part of this cycle. The cycle of worship is always being revised. *The primary goal of our liturgical practice is to use inclusive human language* [my emphasis]. Unless otherwise designated liturgies are inclusive.

Next time someone tries to make the claim that progressive theological seminaries have abandoned all standards, tell him he doesn't know what he's talking about.

Incidentally, your Uncle Di was routed to the Episcopal Divinity School website by Chris Johnson, whose own attention was snagged by an EDS course offering named Queer Incarnation.

You don't want to ask.

It's Not Your Fault, Koko Bear

April 20, 2008

Emancipation from religious authority produced in its wake a litter of thumb-sucking books ostensibly designed to help children deal with the consequences of their parents' brave quest for self-fulfillment, most notably the anguish of divorce. We are meant to picture the four-year-old nestled in Mommy's lap while she reads from, say, *Dinosaurs Divorce*, and nonjudgmentally explains why it is that Daddy dyed his hair, left home, and is shacking up with his tennis coach. The text communicates two key messages: the comforting truth that the child is not to blame ("It's not YOUR fault, Koko Bear"), and the comforting falsehood that, in spite of their separation, Mommy and Daddy love each other more than ever. The real point of the book is to assuage the parents' guilt, not the child's.

We've all seen self-deception of this kind on display in the reaction of Catholic educators to last Friday's address by Pope Benedict. Having effectively divorced themselves from the Church with the 1967 Land O' Lakes Statement, U.S. Catholic universities are obliged to explain to confused and wounded parties, most notably donors and alumni, how it is that—while they may provide *The Vagina Monologues* for their students but no course in St. Augustine—they love the Catholic Church more than even their founders did.

Benedict's address to educators contained a minimum of happy talk and was in deadly earnest. Fr. Neuhaus is correct in his observation that "there was an edge to some of his remarks." There was also a highly Christocentric and tightly reasoned insistence on respect for objective truth, which, the Holy Father said, "in transcending the particular and the subjective, points to the universal and absolute that enables us to proclaim with confidence the hope which does not disappoint." Conceding that there is a contemporary crisis of truth rooted in a crisis of faith, the Pope said that "fostering personal intimacy with Jesus Christ and communal witness to his loving truth is indispensable in Catholic institutions of learning." Of course it's this communal witness that the Land O' Lakes universities repudiated when they opted for divorce.

Hard words about the crisis of truth, the crisis of faith, and the indispensability of communal witness to Christ are potentially distressing to donors and alumni of Catholic institutions, and the engines of official reassurance have been up and running at full steam. In anticipation of Benedict's address Phil Lawler predicted: "Every word the Pope utters in praise of the Catholic schools will be repeated incessantly; every subtle criticism will be buried beneath a mound of exculpatory prose." Phil was right. Whereas Benedict urged Catholic educators to bear witness to the hope *which is* Christ Jesus, the commonest spin is that the Pope was encouraging the institutions to be hopeful about the trajectory they have already chosen for themselves.

The most shameless contribution to the thumb-sucking list has to be the summary of Benedict's address provided by the Association of Jesuit Colleges and Universities—a summary which would be comically obtuse were it understood as a good-faith synopsis, but which in fact shows a studied inattention to the thrust of the Pope's remarks. Clearly those remarks cut too close to the bone. The whole piece is worth a look as a specimen of Dinosaurs Divorcemanship. Here's an excerpt:

> Benedict's message was one of affirmation and encouragement for the important contributions that Catholic education offers to our country. The Pope emphasized that, with its mission of combining faith and reason and its constant pursuit of the truth, Catholic education will continue to play a vital role in preparing students for lives of

compassionate leadership and service. Just as importantly, it will continue to provide young people with the moral, intellectual, and spiritual foundation that propels them to seek the truth and bring hope to
those who suffer.

Benedict makes no mention of leadership in his address, much less
"compassionate leadership and service". He does make frequent mention of Jesus—and more importantly structures his argument around
Him as its keystone—yet in the AJCU summary Jesus rates no mention. Instead we get the comfortable and familiar bromides about
"preparing students for lives of leadership," etc. Compare the superficial chirpiness of AJCU's prose in the passage above with the following paragraph from Benedict's talk:

> All the Church's activities stem from her awareness that she is the
> bearer of a message which has its origin in God himself: in his good-
> ness and wisdom, God chose to reveal himself and to make known
> the hidden purpose of his will. God's desire to make himself known,
> and the innate desire of all human beings to know the truth, provide
> the context for human inquiry into the meaning of life. This unique
> encounter is sustained within our Christian community: the one who
> seeks the truth becomes the one who lives by faith. It can be described
> as a move from "I" to "we", leading the individual to be numbered
> among God's people.

The intellectual gulch that separates Pope Benedict from your
standard mercenary academic may be expressed in these terms: that
for Benedict the search for truth is a delight because the truth has,
in part, *already been found*. Referring to St. Augustine, he said during
an Angelus address in 2005: "The more we enter into the splendor
of divine love, the more beautiful it is to proceed with the search, so
that *amore crescente inquisitio crescat inventi*—in the measure in which
love grows, let the search for Him who has been found grow the
more." Yet no upwardly mobile American academic—certainly no
administrator with an eye on his career—dares speak of truth in this
way. Safer to discharge some harmless room-temperature Argon
about truth as our unattainable goal and keep up the prattle about
preparing students for lives of service. And just in case you have any

lingering doubts in the matter, Daddy loves Mother Church today more than ever—even though they live apart.

In Emancipation Land, it's not just the kids who are thumb suckers.

How We've Grown

October 5, 2008

Former Notre Dame President Fr. Theodore Hesburgh, that venerable fraud, gave an interview to the *Wall Street Journal* recently in which he expressed himself on questions of topical import. Addressing the "leadership" issue, Hesburgh said, "I have no problem with females or married people as priests, but I realize that the majority of the leadership in the Church would. But what's important is that people get the sacraments."

Did you notice Father's act of debonair apostasy? He un-Catholic'd himself by denying that which belongs to the deposit of faith, viz., Church teaching excluding the ordination of women. He was shrewd enough to couple his heresy with the nondoctrinal issue of married priests—blurring the pertinent theological distinctions—and he was careful to employ the me-jargon of junior high: he has "no problem" with women priests, much as your 13-year-old has "no problem" with her gay music teacher. Of course Hesburgh is such a weighty presence it seems petty to call him an apostate: "Just because he thinks the Church is wrong about the faith business doesn't mean he's disloyal," many will object. "After all, Father Ted always wears the Roman collar."

Hesburgh is an archetype of his postwar generation of clergy: men who were Catholics in the same way they were Yankees fans or Cubs fans—not because there were objective reasons for their allegiance, but because it was expected of nice guys who grew up in such-and-such a neighborhood. Ordained to the priesthood when they weren't paying attention, they broadened their horizons to discover that many virtuous, intelligent people supported the Orioles or the Dodgers, that many virtuous, intelligent people were Lutherans or Methodists or Jews—and this with the same cheerful goodwill they devoted to their own juvenile enthusiasms. Growing up meant putting away childish things, including the creeds and the Church's Petrine claims. Not that they forgot where they came from: the Hesburgh Generation came to wear their Catholicism the way they might wear a Cubs ball cap at a picnic: as a token of affection for the old neighborhood and its folkways. But to insist that the Magisterium is uniquely reliable in the matter of doctrine was, for them, as puerile and parochial as the belief that Ron Santo is the greatest third baseman of all time, on the grounds that the Cubs press office said he was.

Yet the Hesburgh Generation are the men who "implemented" the Second Vatican Council for the rest of us. That explains, in part, why we can't find the tabernacle in our parish church, why our pastor knows more about protease inhibitors than apokatastasis, why the majority of self-identified Catholics will vote for a presidential candidate with a 100 percent approval rating from NARAL.

The Hesburgh Generation get testy and defensive when we point out their apostasy. They correctly rejoin that they are leaders and benefactors of Catholic institutions; that they often pray, make retreats, occasionally go to Mass. In every worldly endeavor (as witness Hesburgh himself) they have been conspicuously successful— unquestionably more so than orthodox believers. They insist that, having made no institutional break with the Church, they ought not be grouped with formal apostates who identify themselves as Protestants, agnostics, or atheists. That the orthodox consider their dissent blameworthy is, in their eyes, as captious as damning, say, the backup singers on the Johnny Mathis Christmas Album because they don't believe in the Virgin Birth.

There's a common type of academic theologian who, when taxed with heterodoxy, replies huffily, "I'm not paid to teach catechism; I'm here to show students how to do theology." In reality—with the rare exception of extraordinary pupils in contact with extraordinary professors—what is transmitted is not the craft of theology but simply a different catechism: most students quickly learn to parrot those answers (antidogmatic formulae, it may be) that win the praise of their betters. By the same token, the clerics of the Hesburgh Generation want us to understand that they left the Catholic ghetto behind; yet the reality is that they still drink in their opinions from the environment—and that as uncritically as they did as second graders. That environment is no longer St. Polycarp's parish school in the Bronx or Back of the Yards, but the faculty lounge of liberal upper-middle-class academe: a better class of ghetto, perhaps, but still a ghetto. It would be as unthinkable for these chameleons to depart from the received opinion on women priests as it would be for them to countenance segregated lunch counters in Mississippi. Catholics in every respect except religion, they just can't understand why the rest of us can't grow beyond belief. Hey, Ted's got no problem with it.

THE ANGLICAN ALTERNATIVE

The Church of England, Diogenes frequently reminded his readers, has over-come doctrinal divisions by embracing them—that is, by proclaiming that Anglicans are united in faith, although the content of that faith cannot be defined. With his insistence on honesty and logical consistency, Uncle Di could not accept that solution.

Utterly Null and Absolutely Void ... Maybe

June 15, 2003

A friend sends me this quote from a London *Times* article of May 24:

> The Vatican's senior ecumenical official has said that a papal bull declaring Anglican orders invalid is ready for "re-evaluation". Cardinal Walter Kasper ... said a "partial recognition" of the Church of England's episcopal ministry was possible, despite Pope Leo XIII's edict *Apostolicae Curae*, describing Anglican orders as "null and void". "We are no longer at the position of Leo XIII with his bull," Dr Kasper told a conference on ecumenism in St Albans. "A partial recognition is there."

Cardinal Kasper, you remember, earlier took issue with Cardinal Ratzinger's interpretation of *Dominus Iesus* on the grounds that it hindered ecumenical initiatives. Now we have another doctrinal rift in the making. Leo XIII's 1896 bull *Apostolicae Curae* said nothing of Anglican orders per se, but declared that ordinations conducted according to the Anglican rite (*ordinationes ritu Anglicano actas*) are utterly null and absolutely void.

I am unable to imagine what a partial recognition of ministry might be. Nor do I understand why a curial cardinal should think it opportune to toss a bouquet to a schismatic episcopacy, especially to one currently in crisis over the question of whether women, divorcees, and sexually active gays have a place in its ranks. Irrespective of the theological difficulties of the cardinal's position, it is hardly likely to reduce confusion among clergy and laity, and that at a time when trust of the episcopacy is extremely shaky. In fact, it would be hard to think of an issue—in the English-speaking Church at least—better calculated to shock, wound, bewilder, and alienate the Catholic faithful.

Another Olive Branch in the Eye

June 25, 2003

A Catholic priest received communion at a Protestant service during the phony Berlin Kirchentag last month, was disciplined by his bishop, was taken up as a martyr by the press, and has been supported by the Catholic Left.

> *Wir sind Kirche* (We are Church), one of the groups who organised the ecumenical service, called for his reinstatement. "Imposing ecclesiastical punishment for accepting eucharistic hospitality in a Protestant service ... is a heavy affront to the ecumenical movement and the Protestant Church," it said.

All (with the exception of the bishop's decisive action) entirely predictable.

Divisions among Christians are a scandal, and Christian unity is imperative. All the more exasperating that ecumenism has effectively become the property of a partisan clique of half-believers. Does anyone seriously doubt that the satisfaction ecumenists get from such agitprop stunts (about which the media are informed ahead of time) derives from the pain they cause the orthodox faithful and has little to do with reconciliation? Though they speak the language of healing, it's the new wounds that seem to delight them.

Many a Tear Has to Fall

December 5, 2003

John Allen's Word from Rome contains some helpful clarifications of the extent of the rupture in Anglican-Catholic dialogue, but also introduces a few new puzzles, including this one:

> Even though both sides appear determined to keep talking, Anglicans should be under no illusion about the depth of Catholic concern. Some Catholics point to the May 2000 "Mississauga Statement," in which Anglicans and Catholics agreed that neither side should make decisions in faith and morals that would put distance between the two. A more dramatic breach of that agreement, one American Catholic theologian recently told me, is hard to imagine.

Wait a minute. Since when are Catholics bound not to make "decisions in faith and morals" that would distance us from schismatic bodies? Granted that no such decision could ever entail a change in doctrine, who would have the authority to make such a deal with the Anglicans? What could it possibly mean in concrete terms?

It turns out that the "Mississauga Statement" was the product of one of those vegetarian lasagna ecumenical potlucks convened by Kasper's predecessor, Cardinal Cassidy. The conclusions seem to have been hortatory rather than juridical. In fact, the Anglican Primate of Ireland made a point of panning *Dominus Iesus* (issued later the same year) precisely on the grounds that it gave the chop to the billings and cooings of Mississauga:

> [The Mississauga Statement] said that those who had participated believe that our two communions had "reached a very significant new place on our journey." There was also reference to a "new stage of communion in mission." This heartening sense of hope for the future seemed to have brought some warmth into what many had felt was an "ecumenical winter." But that hope was not to last for long because of the declaration, *Dominus Iesus*.

So we can feel some relief in the knowledge that the ecumenists haven't mortgaged the Faith when we weren't looking in order to buy smiles from liberal Protestants. Allen records some mildly testy

remarks of Kasper regarding Cardinal Ratzinger that likewise miti-
gate the anxiety caused by Kasper's proposal of an "ecumenical post-
baptismal liturgy."

But they should never let ecumenists play with live ammo, even
with adult supervision.

The Church You Save May Be Your Own

January 5, 2004

Occasionally one still sees roadside crosses marking the site of a fatal
auto accident at a dangerous curve or intersection—a warning that
we take stock of how fast we are traveling and, more importantly, in
what direction. Today's *Telegraph* sets up such a cross in reporting on
the continuing Balkanization of the Church of England:

> The Church of England may have to split in two if women become
> bishops, one with female clergy and one without, an official report
> has concluded. An enclave for opponents of women priests could be
> created to avert a mass exodus when women are consecrated, possibly
> within five years.
>
> The faction, effectively a church within a church, could have its
> own archbishop, bishops, parish clergy and training colleges. But it
> would exclude women clerics. Proposals for a traditionalist "third
> province" have been floated before but this is the first time they have
> received official recognition.

Of course, women's ordination is only a single axis of dispute; if
we throw the hot topic of gay clergy into the pot we need not two
but four churches-within-a-church to accommodate the factions:
pro-priestess, pro-gay; pro-priestess, anti-gay; anti-priestess, pro-
gay; anti-priestess, anti-gay. And while we're at it, why not erect
churchlets tailored to heartfelt differences of opinion on each of the
Thirty-Nine Articles, giving us 2^{40} or 1,099,511,627,776 distinct
Christianities—roughly 175 times greater than the total number of
persons on the face of the planet? Celebrate, as it were, diversity.

The point is not to gloat at the Anglicans' discomfiture but to
remind ourselves that the same chasms of conviction run through the

Catholic Church as well, from the pews right up into the College of
Cardinals. Of course we have ecclesial advantages over the Church
of England. For the Catholic faithful, among whom we include many
clergymen, the Pope provides a reliable benchmark of orthodoxy,
and almost all bishops are still submissive to doctrinal discipline,
which means that when the Holy See holds a pistol to their heads
and cocks the hammer they will repeat that such and such is, at least
at this point in time, the unchangeable teaching of the Church.

Remember that it is in the worst possible taste to ask if Catholic
prelates actually assent (*ex animo*) to the doctrines they are charged
with promulgating. In the lapidary phrase of Cardinal Maida, his aux-
iliaries were made bishops because of their "well-earned reputations
as team players." At present, the game is that the bishops pretend to
profess the Faith and the rest of us pretend to believe them. In the
language of pastoral theology, the technical term for this compromise
is "renewal".

We are 1,099,511,627,776 Easter Peoples, and counting.

Anglicans Incoming!

October 20, 2009

The Holy See took the ecumenical imperative out of the hands of
ecumenists, with the result that the reunion of Christians—at least in
one limited area of schism—ensued. From the Vatican website:

> With the preparation of an Apostolic Constitution, the Catholic
> Church is responding to the many requests that have been submitted
> to the Holy See from groups of Anglican clergy and faithful in dif-
> ferent parts of the world who wish to enter into full visible commu-
> nion. In this Apostolic Constitution the Holy Father has introduced a
> canonical structure that provides for such corporate reunion by estab-
> lishing Personal Ordinariates, which will allow former Anglicans to
> enter full communion with the Catholic Church while preserving
> elements of the distinctive Anglican spiritual and liturgical patrimony.
> Under the terms of the Apostolic Constitution, pastoral oversight and
> guidance will be provided for groups of former Anglicans through a
> Personal Ordinariate, whose Ordinary will usually be appointed from
> among former Anglican clergy.

The *Times* of London, with its dizzyingly reckless Monty Python approach to religion stories, headlines its article "Vatican Moves to Poach Traditional Anglicans", but the "poaching" metaphor is an odd choice of images when the "rabbits" in question have been pleading, sometimes for decades, to jump into the hunter's game bag. After all, the decisions that changed the playing field were made by the Anglican churches, not the Pope. The Vatican's explanatory statement does not hesitate to point to the shattering effect of Anglican capitulations to Left/liberal secularism:

> In the years since the Council, some Anglicans have abandoned the tradition of conferring Holy Orders only on men by calling women to the priesthood and the episcopacy. More recently, some segments of the Anglican Communion have departed from the common biblical teaching on human sexuality—already clearly stated in the ARCIC [Anglican-Roman Catholic International Commission] document "Life in Christ"—by the ordination of openly homosexual clergy and the blessing of homosexual partnerships.

While in recent years the Catholic Church has lost some members to Anglicanism, she has benefited overwhelmingly from the inbound traffic. As your Uncle Di has pointed out before: The dissatisfied Anglican leaves because his Church ain't what she used to be. The dissatisfied Catholic leaves his Church because she is.

Orthodox Catholics deserve to feel satisfaction at today's development. Yet it's easy to exaggerate the advantages. On one hand, the Anglicans coming home to full communion will be active in practice, theologically aware, and proportionately resistant to gay and feminist faddishness. On the other hand, we have to admit that a sizable minority of (nominally) Catholic clergy envy the Church of England for precisely the reasons its orthodox are bolting. Who knows how many of our own ecclesiastics, even unindicted ones, are gazing wistfully at the lighted windows of Gene Robinson's honeymoon suite while Rembert Weakland's autobiography slumbers in their lap?

By the same token, under the earlier dispensation, most Anglican converts found themselves in ordinary Catholic parishes—with the ordinary attendant problems—and they gave a boost to the orthodox cradle Catholics in the customary street-fighting for decent liturgy, decent catechesis, decent clerical deportment, etc. Yet those potential allies who convert under the terms of the Personal Ordinariate will in one sense be in quarantine, hived off with their own clergy and their own bishop, able to help out in the Catholic culture wars only indirectly if at all. Were I a Robert Lynch or a Roger Mahony I'd feel relieved that these new Catholics, even those domiciled in my diocese, were not under my "pastoral care"—which means I'd have no need to respond to their articulate and well-informed pleading for the redress of grievances.

Based on who's sputtering in indignation at the Holy See's move and who's not, the Personal Ordinariate is a score for the right team. The Church is perpetually and perfectly one, holy, Catholic, and apostolic, but by today's action the attributes "one" and "Catholic" are realized that much more visibly. Praise the Lord and pass the ammunition.

Wet Hankies in Tomorrowland

October 25, 2009

The Pope's Apostolic Constitution erecting the Personal Ordinariate for Anglican converts has not been released, yet there's no question but that it's got the right people pouting. Across the board, among Catholics, Anglicans, and neutral spectators, hostility varies inversely with orthodoxy.

Here's a Lefty Catholic having a good cry in the pages of the *Times* of London:

> I was hoping that the Church's antipathy to female and openly gay priests would, in time, weaken and dissolve. Now instead, it seems, a whole lot of bigoted reinforcements are arriving to galvanise those more unpalatable aspects of Roman Catholic doctrine. Should I stay in a club that would welcome these people as members?

Just can't grasp the mindset. These stances that progressivists today denounce as bigotry were stances held universally and invariably by the Catholic Church for two millennia, and indeed until the last forty years or so they were held by all Protestant denominations as well. You could, if you were brainless, argue that the Church and her saints were bigots from the beginning, yet that's not a reason to hope the Catholic Church will correct herself tomorrow but a reason to reject Christianity root and branch. If you believe the Church was a purveyor of evil in the past, you have no grounds for denying she may be a purveyor of evil in the future. Moreover, the criterion by which you judge the Church wrong in condemning sodomy and correct in embracing it must be distinct from and more reliable than the Church herself, whence the Church is superfluous in any case.

But these reasonings are largely beside the point. Orthodox Christians understand God as a being wholly distinct from His creation: eternal, omniscient, omnipotent, unchangeable. Progressives, however, take a mushier view in which "God" is a kind of projection of human sensibility, which the believing community beams inward as a common consciousness. This fuzzy and ephemeral God changes along with changing cultures, and the Church is a human mechanism for giving voice to consciousness of God as it evolves and adapts. The Church's authority is a sociological datum, not a divine endowment, and to let yourself be *taught* by her is infantilism. Progressive churches claim to hearken to "the Spirit" in embracing contraception, abortion, euthanasia, high-fashion onanism, etc., but they are simply making their own the opinions belonging to a particular elite. Since they refuse to see their faddism for what it is, they regard persons who refuse to change as blameworthy: the orthodox are bigots for continuing to hold the views the progressives themselves held in the days before their enlightenment (this is why liberals cultivate amnesia about their past, like hikers who brush out their own tracks in the snow).

Most progressives acknowledge that the Church as a public institution—like the army or judiciary or Teamsters Union—has some inertia to be reckoned with. For this reason those unconcerned for the Church's flourishing feel entitled to rebuke her, even in matters theological. You'll be amused by this editorial in the *Los Angeles Times*:

Under the 1st Amendment, churches in this country can't be forced to alter their doctrine or to stop preaching against the supposed immorality of homosexuality. Even so, supporters of gay rights in particular— many of them Christians—should try to dispel the notion that belief in God is incompatible with full equality for gays and lesbians.

Now as before the pope's action, Christians can be reminded—as they have been by both Anglican and Catholic theologians—that Jesus said nothing about homosexuality and that church leaders, including popes, have changed their thinking over the years about everything from usury to the culpability for the Crucifixion to the desirability of religious tolerance. You don't have to be Catholic (or Anglican) to realize that society as a whole would be better off if the church's views of women and gays underwent a similar evolution.

And to what place are the Church's views of women and gays meant to evolve? Why, to that of the editorial writers of the *Los Angeles Times*, of course!

As Mark Steyn says, "Politics affords few greater pleasures than that of offering one's opponents some friendly but hopefully lethal piece of advice." Though miffed by the Holy See, the editors must have enjoyed the prank of recommending precisely those positions that have emptied every denomination that adopted them. Even within Catholic religious orders, the more "evolved" the opinions of their members, the more angry, ineffective, and aged are the lonely few that remain. Would "society as a whole" be better off if the Holy See went the progressive route? Only if you think we'd be better off with no Church at all.

On the Laff Track

December 20, 2009

Do you ever get the impression that somewhere around the mid-1980s the Church of England quietly repackaged itself as a BBC comedy serial, without letting on to the laity? The increasingly farcical attempts to contrive a basis for "Anglican communion" succeed one another every five months or so, in reaction to which the actors follow a predictable formula: North America does its drag queen hysterics number, the Africans bellow in indignation, while the straight man in Lambeth Palace, bewildered about the reason for the quarrel, comes up with a ream of unreadable chartered accountancy so tediously irrelevant to the issues that all sides agree to accept it as a truce—not because they think it means anything, but because they're too exhausted to keep up the shouting. Until the next episode.

Last week's installment, once the frying pans stopped flying, gave us something called the Anglican Covenant. Ecclesially it will have the half-life of polonium-214, but its real purpose is to keep the skit alive until the next commercial break. Here's Archbishop Rowan Williams explaining to his cat why it doesn't matter that it doesn't matter:

> It's quite important in this process to remember what the Covenant is and what it isn't, what it's meant to achieve, and what it's not going to achieve. It's not going to solve all our problems, it's not going to be a constitution, and it's certainly not going to be a penal code for punishing people who don't comply.
> [*chop*]
> The last bit of the Covenant text is the one that's perhaps been the most controversial, because that's where we spell out what happens if relationships fail or break down. It doesn't set out, as I've already said, a procedure for punishments and sanctions. It does try and sort out how we will discern the nature of our disagreement, how important is it? How divisive does it have to be? Is it a Communion breaking issue that's in question—or is it something we can learn to live with? And so in these sections of the covenant what we're trying to do is simply to give a practical, sensible and Christian way of dealing with our conflicts, recognising that they're always going to be there.

If we were to read this seriously we'd be flabbergasted at Williams' suggestion that what counts as a "Communion breaking issue" is a matter of after-the-fact empirical observation: "Let's drop the Sixth Commandment and see if the organism gains weight or loses ..." Yet once again the sentences are not supposed to mean anything individually but rather to generate a familiar noise of reassurance.

One Episcopalian at least pretending not to see the joke is (former Catholic) Jim Naughton, whose blog reaction to the Covenant is cited in the *Telegraph* article: "Who needs it? The bureaucratisation of the bonds of affection is an oxymoronic exercise. On the other hand, if getting disinvited from meetings is the stiffest penalty a church would face for following its conscience, I can live with that."

But Jimmy, my man, don't you see that "bureaucratising" the bonds of affection spares you guys the nuisance of actually "theologising" about them—a venture in which your team will unquestionably end up the loser? Williams' gamesmanship has bought you another eighteen months in which to tease the opposition with lesbian bishops while continuing to sing "Once in Royal David's City" on PBS. From your perspective, what's not to like?

A delightful (and gratuitous) footnote: One of the sponsored ads accompanying the *Telegraph* article on the Covenant betrays a bland professional cynicism towards Rowan Williams' assurances that surpasses even Uncle Di's. It reads simply: "Church Split Attorneys: Helping You Honor God in the Midst of Church Splits and Conflict". *Helping you honor God* ... now there's a law firm with a sense of humor.

ABUSING THE LITURGY

The first piece below originally appeared in Catholic World Report *in June 1994 and elated some readers who did not recognize that it was satirical. Diogenes loathed abuses of all kinds. In an earlier section we saw his deft handling of abuses in language and in translations; later we will encounter his scathing and emotional treatment of the sexual abuse scandal. Here he pinpoints abuses in the Church's liturgy. Notice how, in the following "interview" and in the subsequent blog posts in this section, he persistently highlights the failure of Catholic bishops to curb these abuses. The bishops' negligence was another key theme of Uncle Di's work and will be highlighted in the next section.*

The Compleat Liberal Pastor

Trixie Bonvivante

In 1992 veteran journalist Trixie Bonvivante interviewed Fr. Robert Smiley, then a newly installed pastor of St. Pius X Church in Cinder Block, Illinois, for Catholics Are Us *magazine, questioning him about his unusual administrative style. After reading the transcript—and noticing the extraordinary effect that the interview had on Ms. Bonvivante's lifestyle—the editors of* Catholics Are Us *announced their decision that "publishing Father Smiley's thoughts might not be helpful at this point in time."* Catholic World Report *has subsequently obtained the rights to print the interview.*

BONVIVANTE: Fr. Smiley, congratulations on your assignment. You have moved very quickly in the past few weeks, and I feel it is noteworthy that you changed the name of your parish back to St. Pius X.

SMILEY: Thank you, Ms. Bonvivante. Yes, I did restore the parish name to St. Pius X. When I was a boy, I remember reading a lot of encyclical letters issued by Pope Pius X early in this century.

I'm dealing with many happy emotions with his name restored and with the removal of the Community of Pius banners. I attribute my happy face to the change. I feel that the parishioners are entitled to a pastor with a happy face, not a sad one.

BONVIVANTE: Some of the parishioners wore sad faces when you removed the felt and burlap banners. How did that make you feel?

SMILEY: I felt their pain. I really did. I didn't want to remove the banners. But I simply could not tolerate animal abuse. Let's look at the facts. Wool was brutally removed from sheep, processed into felt, and pasted on the burlap. Now, I don't judge the motives of those involved, but I simply could not bear to be reminded of sheep shivering in the wind by gazing on those banners every day.

BONVIVANTE: But the women religious you brought in to staff the school—the Sisters of Perpetual Adoration—they wear wool habits which surround everything but their faces. How do you explain that?

SMILEY: The Church has always taught that when one is presented with two evils, one is to choose the lesser of the two. The sisters wear habits in order to express their concern over the slaughter of baby seals. They enwrap themselves with the symbolic equivalent of baby seal pelts. Now, I couldn't tolerate actual pelts. So I chose the lesser evil and allowed them to use wool. It's a social-consciousness thing.

BONVIVANTE: Many of the young people are attracted to your liturgies. But others say that you are nothing but a rubricist. How would you respond?

SMILEY: I consider myself a real individualist. I know that I'm pretty much on my own when I stick closely to the rubrics. Recent studies in your magazine show that only 5 percent of Catholic priests in America take the rubrics in the liturgy seriously. But I feel that we are a growing minority.

BONVIVANTE: I understand you say Mass in Latin, not English. Why is this?

SMILEY: The most repressive regimes in history have been English-speaking. Look at the conduct of the United States over the last 45 years. We need a more pastoral and politically sensitive language with which to celebrate liturgy. I mean, Romans haven't oppressed nations in over 1,600 years. I feel we must recognize the sinfulness of English-speaking peoples by refusing to use the language of oppression, persecution, and blood. It's a social-justice thing.

BONVIVANTE: Yet your chalice and candlesticks are studded with jewels.

SMILEY: I consider myself somewhat of an ecclesiastical Robin Hood. I take from the rich and make it available for the common use of the poor. My ministry is one of redistribution of wealth. It's an important part of my outreach. The jewels say something important to me. I'm affirmed by them. They say, "Hey, I care."

BONVIVANTE: You are one of the few pastors who do not permit Communion in the hand. How come?

SMILEY: My feeling is that we dare not ignore the symbolism associated with the liturgical gestures connected with Communion in the hand. As long as American hands are red with the blood of exploitation and imperialism in the Third World, I will not give Communion in this way. The unjust social structures here in the United States make it abundantly clear that we have blood on our societal hands. We all share symbolically in the oppression.

BONVIVANTE: Last month you refused Communion to Congressman Malcolm Quisling, who has taken a "pro-choice" stance on the abortion issue. Yet many theologians suggest that the Church is too rigid on the issue. Do you feel that you are being used by the long arm of Vatican oppression?

SMILEY: The media don't understand the Quisling thing. They even missed an important issue. Congressman Quisling has a House of Representatives bank account. So he has plenty of money to toss about. Have you seen the diamonds he and his wife wear? Normally that would not be an area of my pastoral concern. But the diamonds come from South Africa—if you know what I mean.

BONVIVANTE: I've noticed that you never have guitars used in the liturgy. Are your liturgies up-to-date enough to satisfy fans of folk music?

SMILEY: I share your concern. The last pastor did experiment with liturgical music selections from Guns N' Roses melodies. I don't feel he was successful. After considerable dialogue within the Liturgy

Committee, we've come to the painful conclusion that folk music during the liturgy simply gives the impression that we have really entered a new era in the Church. This simply isn't so.

Despite the progress in microchurch here in America, macro-church simply has not caught up with us. We still struggle with macrochurch's rule banning contraception. We still need to come to grips with the whole myriad of woman-church concerns. No, to continue to permit guitars would simply leave us with the feeling that we're beyond where we really are called to be. We risk a certain lethargy, if you know what I mean. The doleful Gregorian chant should remind us that much work remains for the global Church.

BONVIVANTE: What did your Liturgy Committee think about your changing Eucharistic bread from the substantial bread back to the traditional hosts?

SMILEY: Studies show that if parishes across the country used traditional hosts instead of substantial bread for their liturgies, the United States would save 5 million tons of wheat surplus for export to poor countries. That's 5 million tons! I simply couldn't justify that kind of insensitivity and lack of social concern.

BONVIVANTE: Father, I understand that there is a plan to move the altar up to the back wall of the church. Does this mean that you will offer liturgy with your back to the people?

SMILEY: You know, I've always considered myself a liberal. I've always done liturgy facing the people. But when I realized that the altar separated me from the people, I felt I just had to take action. And I also feel—more than anyone can know—the concerns of the women in the church. We need to listen to the women who come to church on weekdays. How do you suppose they feel when they see a male celebrating liturgy day after day? Need we thrust this kind of sexism in their faces time and again? I feel that women need a break. The time has come to be sensitive to their needs and to celebrate liturgy as one of them. This can best be done by celebrating the liturgy by all—men, women, children, and full-time minister—facing the same direction. It would be a mistake to suggest that the full-time minister is "turning his back on the people." On the contrary, by facing the same direction, we will be able to celebrate our oneness and wholeness.

BONVIVANTE: You are introducing many devotions, including nove-
nas. Are you going back to pre–Vatican II days?

SMILEY: No. We can't go back. But the Church is big. It can handle
all sorts of devotions and practices. The real challenge to the
pastor is to remain open to all forms of piety and being flexible
enough to meet the needs of the people. That's where I'm at.

BONVIVANTE: Aren't we beyond Eucharistic devotion?

SMILEY: I'm glad you brought that up. You know, I like to think
of Eucharistic devotion as my own special kind of "centering
prayer". The only difference is, I feel like centering on the
Eucharist and not on myself. I feel better that way.

BONVIVANTE: You have plans to restore the Communion rail?

SMILEY: Yes. The documents of Vatican II are quite clear. We are
called to share and build community. Now, what better way
to share and care than to receive Communion in community
shoulder to shoulder at the altar rail? We are the world.

BONVIVANTE: The sisters you brought to Pius X removed the *New
Dutch Catechism* from the classrooms and are now using the *Baltimore Catechism*. Are you concerned?

SMILEY: I hear you. You know, Trixie, this is a union town. I wouldn't
think of driving about in a foreign car. Can you imagine the
impact on the American economy if every priest purchased a
Toyota or a Mercedes? I'm an American priest. I buy American.
This is the American Church. We don't need Dutch catechisms
or German catechisms here.

BONVIVANTE: I sense a certain militarism in your attitude.

SMILEY: I perceive a certain hostility in that comment, Trixie. I want
you to know that I am feeling real anger right now. I guess what
I've learned is that we all have our hang-ups, Trixie. Care to
talk about some of yours?

BONVIVANTE: It's just that I feel uncomfortable with your biretta. It
brings back pre–Vatican II memories ...

SMILEY: I hear you saying that you are uncomfortable with my biretta.
Maybe you should understand a little bit about me and my
needs, Trixie. When I was a child, I used to fear change. I also
feared the changes that came with Vatican II. I had a narrow
outlook and wasn't concerned with the ozone layer, the rights
of animals, and the need to bring back Gregorian chant in the
liturgy. It took me a long time to admit that. But now I'm

comfortable with change. And I really feel you can be too, if you put your mind to it. What do you say?

The interview ended with a good cry and a warm embrace. Two years after this interview, Fr. Smiley remains pastor of St. Pius X Catholic Church. Ms. Trixie Bonvivante has grown considerably as a person, and recently entered a convent of cloistered nuns. She is now Sr. Mary Pius X.

Eucharistic Sabotage and You

March 8, 2005

"I have determined that there is no need to make any significant changes in our liturgical practice at this time.... Most of the abuses mentioned in *Redemptionis Sacramentum* do not pertain to the celebration of the Eucharist in our Archdiocese."

That's Cardinal Mahony, writing last September.

Fragging the rubrics is a win-win game for saboteurs—not only the deviant liturgists, but anyone with a doctrinal grudge who wants a fractured, enfeebled Church at the end of the day. No matter how trivial a stunt you pull, you put the orthodox Catholics in a bind. If, out of a desire not to offend, they go along with the innovation, great, you've nudged them a little further away from the Roman Rite and from Catholic discipline. If they object, great, you spin it so that they appear the aggressors—rubricists, whose obsession with formalist conformity to detail eclipses the central spiritual significance and majesty of the liturgy, etc., etc.

The Roman Rite is universally, eminently, easily *doable*. That means—apart from inadvertence—deviations occur for the sake of deviance. When the faithful pretend to believe your motives are innocent, they know at some level they're party to a lie. It adds hugely to the fun of this cruelest of all liberal blood sports. If old Aunt Florence doesn't protest your pouring the Precious Blood from a Bloomingdale's carafe into goblets, she's ever so slightly complicit in the act. If she does protest, she either wants to spread dissension and division, or she must be operating under the delusion, poor thing, that it's the most important part of the Eucharistic Action.

Game. Set. Mass.

War against the Working Male

April 30, 2005

When you go to Mass tomorrow, take a look around you and notice what group is most conspicuously absent. Regardless of where on the face of the globe you are, the answer is obvious: missing are blue-collar heterosexual males between the ages of 18 and 28.

Of itself that fact is unremarkable. It's probably true of most Christian denominations in every epoch—spontaneous inclinations to communal worship are rarest among rambunctious young men without families. But let's do a thought experiment. Suppose you were a bishop, and suppose that you felt it your pastoral duty to REPEL such broncos as happened to stray into Mass on Sunday morning. Suppose your crusade demanded lowering blue-collar male attendance from, say, 4 percent to less than 1 percent. How would you go about it?

You'd go in for full court stripe-to-stripe buzzer-to-buzzer gender-bending. You'd choose your presiders from among swish counter-tenors. You'd coach them in theatrical prancing and homiletics. You'd pack the sanctuary with testy, power-suited women reading inclusive language in scolding voices. You'd choose the most sugary musical dreck you could find, and make sure it was performed in an unsingable register. You'd eliminate private space, forcing everyone into lots of touching and interpersonal contact. In short, you'd do exactly what our betters have done over the past 40 years to "renew" the liturgy, for which they ceaselessly congratulate themselves on their pastoral sensibility.

Now, perhaps the Church believes it's a good thing that working men feel unwelcome. Perhaps bishops are possessed of some mystical intuition that welders and truck drivers and sheet metal workers—should they be insolent enough to slip into Mass in the first place—*deserve* to be firehosed with music they find repellent, language they find repellent, camp theatrics that make their skin crawl. Is the idea that, since roofers or firemen tend to be sexist, their discomfort is a salutary penance? Is the idea that, if they can't accept Marty Haugen, they don't belong in our Easter People anyway? Whatever the reason, we must admit that the "threshold of distaste" a normal working man must overcome in order to turn up at church and endure a parish Mass is almost conspiratorially high.

This week's *Commonweal* has two articles by Catholic academics entreating Pope Benedict to listen to his flock. And whom should he listen to? Catholic academics. We get the standard roster of upper-middle-class grievances. But in fact, if you consider the changes to Catholic life effected since the Council—bracketing the documents themselves—you see that almost exceptionlessly these changes have been made in response to the same constituency: prosperous Western liberals. Look at it this way. Take two non-Catholics on the fringes of their respective churches in 1965: a homosexual, Beemer-driving Episcopalian dentist, and a Baptist heavy equipment operator with a gun rack in the back of his pickup. Which of the two is more likely to have found his way into the Catholic Church in the meantime as a result of her "pastoral" initiatives? Which of the two is more likely to hear himself described as marginalized? Which of the two is more likely to find a hearing were the Pope to accede to our *Commonweal* authors?

Progressives would have us think they're being egalitarian in crying up an indisputably elitist agenda. Like the Cambridge matron who strikes a blow for world peace by putting an "Abolish Apartheid" bumper sticker on her Volvo, the rhetoric of inclusiveness allows one to mask self-indulgence as an imperative of justice. In fact, it's a dishonest yet socially acceptable way of excluding undesirables. It's not in doubt what the preferences of hourly wage earners are. We know Pentecostals have made huge inroads among blue-collar Catholics; we know miners and steamfitters aren't flocking into the liberal churches; we know these churches have made zero accommodations in response. Let's call a spade a spade: the project of "Pastoral Inclusiveness" is designed to repulse all but the enlightened elite.

One prefers, after all, to celebrate diversity among one's own.

No One Asked Us, But ...

July 4, 2005

I sympathize with [the blog] *L.A. Catholic*'s suggestion of introducing a "How Am I Presiding?" 800 number to be prominently displayed on the back of every polyester chasuble. The problem, of course, is that the phone would never be answered at the other end. Still, it would sometimes be a relief to leave a really candid report on the Diocesan Liturgy Office answering machine, even in the knowledge that the gal who empties the ashtrays and wastebaskets was instructed to delete all messages unheard.

If your pastor put the question to you, what would you tell him?

The Good Catholic

November 1, 2005

> *It is the right of all of Christ's faithful that the Liturgy, and in particular the celebration of Holy Mass, should truly be as the Church wishes, according to her stipulations as prescribed in the liturgical books and in the other laws and norms. Likewise, the Catholic people have the right that the Sacrifice of the Holy Mass should be celebrated for them in an integral manner, according to the entire doctrine of the Church's Magisterium.*
>
> —Redemptionis Sacramentum, 2004

> *"Are we lost, daddy?" I arsked tenderly.*
> *"Shut up," he explained.*
>
> —Ring Lardner, *The Young Immigrunts*, 1920

Of course we know it never happens in reality, but suppose, just suppose, that your pastor were to depart from the words or rubrics of the Roman Rite in his celebration of Mass. Suppose further that, after approaching your pastor personally, the chancery by phone, and your bishop by letter, you received no substantive explanation and no amendment took place. As a devout and committed Catholic, how do you account for the circumstances?

Account A. You reason that the designated provider of the Eucharistic liturgy is your pastor, that your pastor wouldn't be in the position he is unless your bishop wanted him there, and that your bishop wouldn't be your bishop unless the Pope wanted him to be. Ergo, you have the Mass the Church wants you to have. Call this the Nuremberger with Fries Approach.

Account B. You reason that, appearances notwithstanding, the liturgy as conducted by your pastor—being at least passively ratified by your bishop—*is* in actuality the Mass according to the Roman Rite, but that you yourself are too sinful to see it. Ergo, in the eyes of the saints, you have the Mass the Church wants you to have. Call this the Rex Mottram Approach.

Account C. You reason that, even though your parish Mass is not the Mass the Church *says* she wants you to have, she is the supreme and ultimate guarantor of your rights. Ergo, the Mass the Church wants you to have is a Mass the Church doesn't want you to have. Call this the I Guess It Was None of My Business in the First Place Sorry to Have Bothered You Approach.

Don't be bashful. Tell your Uncle Di: Which line of thinking is most in keeping with our authentic ecclesial maturation and the kind of churchmanship the recently concluded Synod of Bishops wants us to have? I can imagine other possibilities beyond the three mentioned, but alas, they all entail the imputation of discreditable motives to others. Far be it from us to take that path.

ICEL Agonistes

December 1, 2005

Former *Tablet* editor John Wilkins has a shoddy and tendentious article in the current *Commonweal* on the fortunes of ICEL, the International Commission on English in the Liturgy. We get the conventional Four Legs Good, Two Legs Bad storyline, with the Vatican playing its customary role of villain. Wilkins deplores John Paul II's use of his "iron will" to enforce doctrinal conformity—somewhat ungraciously, in view of his acceptance of a knighthood from the palsied hands of the same bigoted Pope.

Controversial since its inception, ICEL became a focus of serious alarm among the orthodox in the 1980s, when it embarked on a revised translation of the Roman Missal. Feminist ideology had made its deepest inroads into English-speaking hierarchies at this time, and Wilkins continues to put forth the party line in his account of the conflict:

> Any commission charged with English translations at that time would have felt the need to use inclusive language. By the 1980s it was hardly possible in ordinary speech or writing to continue to use the words "men" or "man" as applying also to women. The ICEL translators

felt their way forward, both on the horizontal level, where masculine collective nouns, pronouns, and adjectives described groups including both women and men, and on the vertical level, where references to God were wholly masculine. Women religious, concerned that they should not yet again be marginalized by terms that excluded them, lobbied powerfully and effectively.

Effectively indeed. It has never been satisfactorily explained how masculine references to God "exclude" women, nor how *translators* can be licensed to "correct" their originals in this regard. But correct them they did. The first segments of ICEL's revised Missal declared war on the overly masculine deity which feminists found in the Latin *editio typica* (official text). You'd never guess it from Wilkins' superficial treatment, but ICEL engaged in a wholesale transformation of divine imagery, dropping masculine pronouns for God, changing third-person texts to second-person (genderless) addresses, and inserting supposedly feminine attributes to counterbalance masculine ones.

In ICEL's revised Proper of Seasons, for example, the following titles were substituted for the simple vocative *Deus* (God)—i.e., without any qualifier:

God of mystery
God of life
God of blessings
God of majesty
God of mercy
God of our salvation
God of nations
God of hope
God our Creator
God our Creator and Preserver
God ever-faithful
Ever-faithful God
All-provident
Compassionate God
Merciful God
Gracious God
Just and gracious God

Likewise, the title "Lord" was deemed too sexist, and got the gelding treatment. This is what ICEL gave us in place of simple (unqualified) vocative *Domine*. I'm not making this up, folks:

God of light
God of wisdom
God of majesty
God of forgiveness
God of mercy
God of mercy and compassion
God our Creator
All-provident God

To make it clear: ICEL was not commissioned to create a renewed liturgy but to translate Latin originals. The Church understands that the renewal process the Council called for *produced* the Latin originals, whence the Latin *editio typica* was itself the renewed text. But ICEL felt the renewal didn't go far enough, and sent to Rome a gender-titrated, androgynous, 1980s-style God/dess for its *recognitio*.

Dead on arrival. Somebody in the Holy See was paying attention, understood that "merciful and faithful God" did not translate *omnipotens Deus*, and sent it back to ICEL with a "What have you guys been smoking?" letter.

The ICELites are understandably bitter. After all, they were one rubber stamp away from a grand slam. We shouldn't forget, however, that the controversy was not a controversy over methods of translation. They were out to give us a different deity.

The Strange Case of the Missing Mass

December 19, 2005

In his 1981 book *From Bauhaus to Our House*, Tom Wolfe mused on the compound ironies in the fact that America's leading capitalists were headquartered in "glass box" buildings that derived, ideologically, from radical socialist designs for proletarian worker housing. The very folks who could afford to build themselves Buckingham Palace knockoffs built low-ceilinged stack-a-prole chicken crates instead. As Wolfe writes of the flummoxed plutocrats: "It makes their heads hurt. They *just can't understand it.*"

A similar sense of dislocation afflicts Roman Catholics in contemplating the liturgy they experience. They have an unsurpassably rich liturgical tradition. They have Joseph Ratzinger as their Pope. They have Francis Arinze as Prefect of the Congregation for Divine Worship. Yet these heavyweights and that tradition seem strangely powerless to provide the faithful with the Mass the Church intends them to have. In a speech last year in Milwaukee, John Allen said even the Vatican's Office for the Celebration of Papal Liturgies is solidly in the hands of the *Cage aux Folles* crowd: "[Allen] joked that the liturgical office staff try to set a record for how many liturgical rules they can break in one papal Mass. These things usually have dance numbers that rival *Cats.*"

If such things take place in the greenwood, what shall be done in the dry?

An oblique but telling indication of the sorry state of the Roman Rite is the interest in blogdom generated by the new Secretary, or number two man, at the Congregation for Divine Worship. It's an interest I share. But if the Eucharistic liturgy as we presently experience it were in good shape, there'd be no reason for ordinary folks to care who held the Vatican job. Why should they? Yet the rule breaking that Allen cheerfully reports is at the heart of the problem: it deprives us not only of the Roman Rite, but of the possibility of ritual full stop.

C. S. Lewis once discussed the problem in terms I here paraphrase: During Mass I can exercise either a critical or a devotional faculty, and the two are mutually exclusive. If my critical faculty is alert, it interferes with worshiping God, and has to be "lulled to sleep" as it were. The Eucharistic *rite*, when enacted properly, is precisely the instrument by which this faculty can be quieted and the devotional faculty engaged. However, this is dependent upon the expectation of participation in the *Church's* liturgy, not Fr. So-and-so's adaptation of it. For if I have reason to believe that the celebrant will depart from the text or the rubrics, my critical faculty is switched on whether I want it to be or not, because the celebrant's departures may be tendentious or heretical or imbecile or all three. And even if the celebrant's changes turn out to be within the bounds of orthodoxy and good taste, I still would have been forced, against my will, to engage in an activity of criticism rather than of worship. I will have been cheated of a Mass.

Characteristic of a *rite* is that it's uniform in such a way that the human variables, where they exist at all, become inconsequential. Yet Massgoers know that the contrary experience is all too common, and most of us—at the announcement of a new pastor or bishop or CDF Secretary—find ourselves groping for the handle of a (figurative) revolver: "OK, what's *this* clown going to take away from us ... ?" Sometimes we're pleasantly surprised, sometimes unpleasantly. But few Catholics are indifferent.

The young woman who blogs at *But I Digress* has a post titled "It's never a good sign when you go to Mass and ..."—completing the sentence amply from her own experience:

> ... the words of the Great Amen are interspersed with little tinkly piano riffs which build to a full-blown song in the "background" before Father's done.
> ... the Eucharistic Minister doesn't know what to do when you don't want to receive Communion in the hand.
> ... Father adds little phrases into the Eucharistic prayer. Nothing big enough to be a big deal, just stuff like "And then, *we know* that Jesus took the cup ..."

Can you relate? I knew you could. Add to the list? I know you can. What's important to grasp is that these minor deviations are not random; they're of an entirely different order from the inadvertent blunders elderly or spacey priests commit—rather, in each case an element of the self-consciously personal is used to intrude between the worshiper and his anticipated experience of worship, i.e., the experience anyone gets when the celebrant simply opens the Roman Missal, says the black words, and does the red ones. The problem, ultimately, is not what the liturgists want to give us, but what they want to keep us from getting.

So how is it that we, heirs at law of two millennia of authentic Catholic ritual, with every external circumstance in our favor, are still read out of the will? In Tom Wolfe's words, it makes our heads hurt. We just can't understand it.

Benign Neglect—or, Saved by the Bell

April 1, 2006

Fr. Raniero Cantalamessa, the preacher of the Pontifical Household, made this noteworthy observation in his first Lenten sermon two weeks ago.

> It has been written that the Gospels are "accounts of the Passion preceded by a long Introduction." But sadly the latter, which is the most important part of the Gospels, is also the least appreciated in the course of the liturgical year, as it is read only once a year, in Holy Week, when, because of the duration of the rites, it is moreover impossible to pause to comment and explain it.

Cantalamessa, unsurprisingly, focuses on the negative aspects of this neglect: "There was a time when preaching on the Passion occupied a place of honor in all popular missions. Today, when these occasions have become rare, many Christians reach the end of their lives without ever having experienced Calvary."

He's right, of course: when the Passion is read in its entirety there isn't room for a homily.

If that's a misfortune, however, it's a mixed misfortune. Much of the wallop that the Passion still delivers is due to the fact that the gospels have been allowed to speak for themselves. Is this a bad thing? Call to mind your standard Gumbletonian[1] homily—in which any spiritual teeth the readings might have are yanked by his hermeneutic pliers—and imagine the same treatment applied to the Agony in the Garden and the Way of the Cross and multiplied by 40,000. It doesn't bear thinking about.

In fact, we can congratulate ourselves on the present dispensation. The summer school Bultmannians[2] and subscription homily services and Liturgy Training Publications schoolmarms haven't gotten their vandal's paws on the Passion—with the result that the gospels in question have been spared forty years of spiritual corrosion. During the proclamation of the Passion, when we kneel in silence after the

---

[1] Referring to Bishop Thomas John Gumbleton.
[2] Referring to German Lutheran theologian Rudolf Karl Bultmann.

death of Jesus, we still feel what we were meant to feel. For a few moments, the two intervening millennia have ceased to matter.

Perhaps God has preserved for his children this one block of Scripture until the LTP-OCP-FDLC [Liturgy Training Publications–Oregon Catholic Press–Federation of Diocesan Liturgical Commissions] brigade has definitively retired from the field, whereupon (as Cantalamessa suggests) the preached parish mission may allow a new and less destructive generation to appropriate the Passion more fully.

Autocratic Autocorrect: Sanitized for Your Protection

May 26, 2006

"Know that the LORD is God!" reads Psalm 100:3f. "It is he that made us, and we are his; we are his people, and the sheep of his pasture. Enter his gates with thanksgiving, and his courts with praise!" Sound all right? It should: that's the literal RSV [Revised Standard Version] translation. Note that there are six masculine references to God, not counting the token word LORD for the divine name. The U.S. bishops' 1991 translation (RNAB [Revised New American Bible]) feeds it through their standard de-gendering software: "Know that the LORD is God, our maker to whom we belong, whose people we are, God's well-tended flock. Enter the temple gates with praise, its courts with thanksgiving." Bingo: all six masculine references are zapped into nonexistence, with no harm except to the original text.

To men so trained, God's revelation was a pretty slipshod affair, and stands in dire need of improvement. God's Church, moreover, faithfully transmits some of the Bible's greatest blunders in her liturgy, falling short in several respects of the guidelines stipulated by the Task Force on Bias-Free Language of the Association of American University Presses. Hence they see "translation"—whether biblical or liturgical—as first and foremost an opportunity for *correction*.

The Holy See and the U.S. bishops' Committee on the Liturgy are at loggerheads. Cardinal Arinze has insisted that the text to be translated already reflects the desired renewal and stands in no need of a makeover. The BCL's chairman Bishop Trautman maintains he can, and should, find the better liturgy that exists somehow behind and beyond the Latin text and turn *that* into English for our benefit.

They can't both be right. And neither is backing down. In a recent statement, Trautman chose to treat Arinze's latest communication as a mere suggestion, saying that it "offers additional input for the deliberation of the bishops." I detect an equivocation—or better, perhaps, the influence of God's well-tended macro.

Warning: Not for Children or the Squeamish

May 28, 2006

Did you hear the words "mortal sin" from the pulpit this Sunday? Bet you didn't.

Contumacious parishioners, however, at St. Mary's by the Sea in Huntington Beach found themselves charged with mortal sin by their pastor, in a message communicated via the church bulletin. So, boys and girls, what filth, what abomination, what unprintable extravagance of Southern Californian turpitude—so great as to deserve "exclusion from Christ's kingdom and the eternal death of hell," according to the *Catechism*—have the wretched souls indulged in?

Kneeling.

We're talking about kneeling at Mass, after the Agnus Dei. According to the *L.A. Times* article, Orange Bishop Tod Brown is backing the pastor against the kneelers. Helen Hitchcock, who is quoted in the *Times* story, points out that it's telling that a prelate of the "Let a hundred flowers bloom" school should bring the hammer down *against* diversity:

> "It's hard to understand why any bishop would prohibit his people from expressing reverence in the way they have done for centuries," said Helen Hull Hitchcock, a founder of the conservative Adoremus Society for the Renewal of Sacred Liturgy in St. Louis.

Tactful reticence apart, *is* it so hard to understand? If you were one of the folks Tim Radcliffe calls "Kingdom Catholics", and you had the power to enforce your own will in the matter, would you want to see Catholics on their knees before the Blessed Sacrament?

Spiritual Liberty and the Language of Ritual

June 3, 2006

A couple of weeks ago I tried to show how Bishop Donald Traut-man's objections to the language of the new translation of the Roman Missal were misplaced. In a word, he blamed the translators for not giving us the Bible, when their job was to give us the Mass. Allyson Smith's recap of the L.A. Religious Education Congress includes fur-ther remarks by Trautman that deserve comment:

> Trautman addressed another proposed change to the first Eucharistic Prayer—from "cup" to "precious chalice." Said Trautman: "'pre-cious chalice'—when I hear those words, I think of a gold vessel with diamonds on it. Did Jesus, at the Last Supper, use a precious chalice or a cup? The gospels clearly say 'cup,' but even in the lectionary from Rome we have the word 'chalice' imposed on the inspired text to carry out this 'sacred language.'"

When the Church, in her Missal, says "taking this precious chalice into his holy and venerable hands" (*accipiens et hunc praeclarum calicem in sanctas et venerabiles manus suas*), is she really inviting us to imagine that Jesus used a gem-encrusted goblet at the Last Supper?

Of course not. The chalice Jesus used is "precious" not because it was bejeweled or made of gold but because it contained the Blood of our Redemption. It is the Church's contemplative understanding of the unique value of this redemption that prompts her, in awe and thanksgiving, to call the chalice *praeclarus*. It holds, and allows us to partake of, that blood by which our redemption was achieved.

The Institution Narrative recounted at Mass is not a mere tran-scription or bare-bones synthesis of the Bible. Rather, the narrative has been given a ritual form expressed in ritual language, and as such reflects the biblical accounts as they have been reshaped by traditions of prayer, worship, spiritual converse, and theological reflection.

Does this ritual language differ from the language of the New Tes-tament? It does. It should. The Bible gives us the story in stark nar-rative terms. The Eucharistic liturgy retells that story in a way that foregrounds its spiritual meanings—yet not all spiritual meanings, only those proper to one particular ritual of sacrifice and thanksgiving.

Though rooted in the Last Supper narrative in the narrow sense, its diction, imagery, and emphasis ultimately derive from the *whole* of Scripture, New Testament and Old. Prophecy, history, psalmody, and proverbial wisdom—all appropriated and transfigured by the worshiping Church—are among its tributaries.

Think of a newspaper story telling how, by a fluke, a soldier's dog tags deflected a bullet aimed at his heart and so saved his life. Think of how the same soldier, thirty years later, might speak of the dog tags when he shows them off to his grandchildren: "Take a look at these beauties: best body armor ever made." He's not deluded about the cheap stamped metal in his hand. He's not denying or correcting or imposing an agenda on the original newspaper account. He's giving voice to "emotion recollected in tranquillity" [William Wordsworth, *Lyrical Ballads*]. Yet the Church's language reflects not one man's private contemplation but the spiritual patrimony of centuries of believers, guided and shaped by the Holy Spirit into a public and ecclesial form.

The fact is that many people, including some Catholic clergy, don't understand rite, and are put off by ritual action and language. In the years following the Council many were enraptured by the image of the Protestant minister, seated on the lawn with a Bible open on her lap, reading and expounding God's word in Pauline simplicity. By contrast, incense and Gothic vaulting and liturgy itself seemed, to them, impure and pointless *impositions* on the real thing (whence "imposed" is a frequent term in their polemics). Many dealt with their distaste for rite by enacting the Eucharist as if it were theater, or Bible study, or a family picnic: occasions more friendly and familiar to their training and sensibilities.

But we can also see lingering traces of an antipathy to rite that goes beyond distaste and becomes active resentment. Many churchmen find noxious that character of the Roman Ritual which Cardinal Ratzinger, in his book *Feast of Faith*, singles out for esteem: "The obligatory character of the essential parts of the Liturgy also guarantees the true freedom of the faithful: it makes sure that they are not victims of something fabricated by an individual or a group, that they are sharing in the same Liturgy that binds the priest, the bishop and the pope." As no one is above the law, no one is above the liturgy. And that's bad news for a lot of professional Catholics convinced they have a clearer idea than the Church herself of how the Church should pray, should teach, should worship. Authentic liturgy, as the document of that name makes plain, lets the Church speak in her own voice and protects the faithful from the self-credentialed sophists. No wonder they detest it.

Qui omnem sanctificationem compleret

November 9, 2006

Last weekend I heard the Fourth Eucharistic Prayer for the first time in a while. It struck me forcefully that, read together with its preface, it's an almost unimprovably succinct narrative of Catholic faith. In fact, if a curious Buddhist or Muslim were to ask, "What do you Catholics believe about God?" you could hardly do better than hand them that preface and prayer in response. It's all there: divine sublimity, creation, adoration, disobedience, covenant, prophecy, incarnation, redemption, resurrection, ascension, the gift of the Spirit, Eucharistic vigil in expectation of the second coming of Christ. The Creed is also an epitome of Catholic faith, but as is proper to its purpose its affirmations are responses to doctrinal controversies. In the Fourth Eucharistic Prayer the Faith is presented as the simple unfolding of salvation history: no bushfires or ice storms have left their mark on the tree.

It's a hope-illumined prayer. It keeps its gaze fixed on our sanctification: the sacramental business going on now as well as its consummation at the end of history. There's a monastic tranquillity and recollectedness about it, taking in human, angelic, and divine activity in a single glance *sub specie aeternitatis*. If I were a monk I'd see it as a vocational Magna Carta.

For some years we used to hear the Fourth Eucharistic Prayer pretty frequently, then a more politically fastidious clergy choked on all the masculine generics ("Even when HE disobeyed you and lost your friendship you did not abandon HIM to the power of death, but helped all MEN to seek and find you ...") and it fell into disuse. I'm not certain it works perfectly in the Mass myself; there's a lot of sacred history crammed into second-person discourse, and that history seems more fittingly narrated to the people than addressed to God the Father. Yet something would be lost if it were to vanish in the combat to come. Most of the 1970s liturgical gimcrack deserves to end in the bonfire, but I hope this brand is plucked from the burning.

Vine and Branches

November 20, 2006

In his book of memoirs titled *Milestones*, Pope Benedict tells of his having received, in his childhood years, a series of Latin-German missals called the *Schott Messbuch*, which were annotated with progressively detailed "age-appropriate" explanations of the Mass. The following passage gives articulate voice to an intuition that, while often "prediscursive" in itself, will be recognized by those who have shared it: an awareness that the liturgy is something both human and larger than human:

> Each new book I was given was something precious to me, and I could not dream of anything more beautiful. It was a riveting adventure to move by degrees into the mysterious world of the liturgy, which was being enacted before us and for us there on the altar. It was becoming more and more clear to me that here I was encountering a reality that no one had simply thought up, a reality that no official authority or great individual had created. This mysterious fabric of texts and actions had grown from the faith of the Church over the centuries. It bore the whole weight of history within itself, and yet, at the same time, it was much more than the product of human history. Every century had left its mark upon it. The introductory notes informed us about what came from the early Church, what from the Middle Ages, and what from modern times. Not everything was logical. Things sometimes got complicated, and it was not always easy to find one's way. But precisely this is what made the whole edifice wonderful, like one's own home. Naturally, the child I was then did not grasp every aspect of this, but I started down the road of the liturgy, and this became a continuous process of growth into a grand reality transcending all particular individuals and generations, a reality that became an occasion for me of ever-new amazement and discovery. The inexhaustible reality of Catholic liturgy has accompanied me through all phases of life.

Ronald Knox's autobiography likewise describes his encounter, as a boy, with a book called *The Ritual Reason Why*, whereupon he too became fascinated by the way an ordinary object (a cup, a piece of colored cloth) remains what it is while pointing to something more important, something beyond itself—because it is part of the liturgy. Neither for Knox nor for Ratzinger was this intuition part of a passing juvenile enchantment that was later outgrown: both *knew* that the stairway led upwards.

"The fathers have eaten sour grapes," says Jeremiah, "and the children's teeth are set on edge." The technicians arrived. Dom Alcuin Reid, O.S.B., in a lecture given last April called "Looking Again at the Liturgical Reform", cited the Ratzinger passage above, along with several sober observations on the extent to which the post-Conciliar liturgical reformers neglected the slow-growing ritual in favor of university-hatched theories. Reid quotes a 1978 remark of Dame Felicitas Corrigan: "The new Missal is not so satisfactory. It has an artificial ring about it, as if scholars had first mapped it out in the abstract, and then gone to work with scissors and paste in a Roman parlour to produce a live organism. But do living organisms ever follow a neat scientific pattern?"

Those familiar with Tom Wolfe's *From Bauhaus to Our House* may recognize the parallel with the modern architects for whom "Starting from Zero" was the revolutionary motto. They were angry men, men on a mission—and their mission was precisely to purge themselves of any memory of tradition so as to design from scratch a new world in their own minds. They saw themselves as *engineers* of the human soul.

The men who came up with the Novus Ordo were not so thoroughgoing as the Bauhaus iconoclasts, but they brought much of the same abstract academic fervor to the task. They were Big Idea guys. Of course they didn't get all they wanted—some compromises with the tradition were necessary—but the new Mass clearly has that "mapped-out" quality that Corrigan refers to. It's a wordy rite: discursive in form and aimed principally at adults with well-developed language skills. Young children, new immigrants, and mentally impaired adults will (in contrast with the older Mass) miss most of the intended wallop. The sacramental dimension, which fascinated Knox and Ratzinger even as children, gave way to the didactic. There are still sporadic moments of contact with the Holy, that *mysterium tremendum et fascinans*, but the didacticism and stress on the here-and-now-ness of the liturgical action means fascination is rare, and awe rarer still. As Thomas Day laconically remarks, "Not many boys today will put a chair behind their bureaus and pretend to be presiders."

Recent adjustments in the liturgy—such as the restoration of *pro multis* and the broader scope for Latin—are I believe part of an effort to reconnect with that older, organically developing rootstock of which Ratzinger spoke. Progressive fears of a systematic counterrevolution misjudge the situation. What's happening is not retro-engineering, but a move away from engineering full stop, in favor of a cautious return to vinedressing. It's impossible to predict how many Catholics will be going to Mass fifty years from now, but it's almost certain that those who do won't be stuck with the 1974-model-year Novus Ordo. Incremental husbandry, of course, will have its own mixture of failures and successes. Not all grafts are sure to take. Some will.

Can't We All Just Get Along?

April 14, 2008

What is it about "faithful orthodox Catholics" that makes so many of them talk as though despair and anger are the first and only characteristics of the Truly Christian life?

Several blogs have recently raised the question of why orthodox Catholics so often froth at the mouth when the subject of liturgical abuse is raised, why so many of us stumble out of Mass nearly sick with rage, so that we shock and repel those around us.

As a man who very often prays to be distracted during Mass so as not to take a machete to the celebrant, and as one who spreads alarm and despondency among nearly all he meets after leaving church, I feel I'm qualified to speak to the question.

What exasperates and maddens me about liturgical abuses is that the Mass given to us by the Church is so supremely, eminently DOABLE. Almost any priest not in a concentration camp or on a battlefield can do what the Church asks him to do with perfect compliance. It's all there: wear this; say that; bow here; now elevate the host—the dimmest clergyman in the poorest parish on earth can score 100 percent every time, and thereby offer a pleasing sacrifice to God.

That means that the departures happen for a *reason*. The innovator wants to jack us around for motives of his own, which he does not "covenant" with us. We almost never hear complaints about inadvertent omissions by celebrants trying to do it right; it's the deliberate changes that infuriate.

I once read an article in a Lefty newsletter called *Miriam's Song* that laid out the campaign very neatly. The author noted how, on the campus of Ohio State, students would not keep to the sidewalks but would take the most direct route between buildings, thereby wearing out a footpath in the grass. Eventually the grounds crew would acknowledge the fait accompli and lay a concrete sidewalk over the course already marked out by pedestrians who didn't stick to the "approved" ways. The author used this as an analogy to encourage her readers to "make a path by walking on it" in the liturgy—i.e., to start doing at Mass what they want it to become, confident that sooner or later the Church will bow to necessity and declare officially that the innovation (joining in the priest's prayers, say, or having a lay minister communicate the celebrant) is liturgically licit. The Mass becomes an exercise in agitprop.

It's not as if the Mass established by the Church—the standard Mass in the Missal—just happened to coincide with my personal idiosyncratic tastes. I didn't choose *this particular ritual* as I might choose *this particular necktie* out of a hundred possibilities. The Church simply gave it to us. Some parts I find pleasing, others not. But I value it precisely because it's not mine. I value it because we (bishops, priests, layfolk) received it from the Church.

Hence the unfairness of it when the celebrant himself departs from the rubrics, even quite peripheral ones, to "make a path by walking on it." When Father suggests in the vestibule that I'm guilty of pushing a private agenda by asking for a kosher Mass I had no part in making; when he tells me the Mass of the Missal is "not good liturgy" or "not the tradition of our local faith community"; when my only alternative is to keep silent and let him score out his path a little more securely—then, brothers and sisters, I want to jam his *Gather* hymnal down his throat.

And that's not conducive to spiritual repose.

HOLDING THE HIERARCHY ACCOUNTABLE

Theological dissent and dishonesty; pastoral abuse and corruption; foolishness and apostasy: these provided the grist for Uncle Di's mill. But couldn't those problems have been eliminated by clear teaching and effective discipline within the Church? Yes indeed. But our bishops were neither clear nor effective, leaving Diogenes to comment frequently on their negligence. Long before the McCarrick scandal broke, he pinpointed the problem and argued that the only practical solution was for bishops to hold each other accountable—something that they were evidently reluctant to do.

His Grace Is Napping Now, Please Don't Interrupt

April 9, 2003

A poll of 1,482 Catholic priests in Britain indicates widespread disagreement with the Church's moral teaching—surprising, perhaps, to someone recently awakened from a 40-year coma, but to no one else. Forty-three percent of the respondents, e.g., actively oppose the orthodox teaching on contraception, and another 19 percent are "unsure" whether they support it. We are told, utterly predictably, that "a spokesman for the Catholic Bishops' Conference of England and Wales questioned the methodology of the survey," and that he maintained, "The statistical findings of this book must be treated with great caution and cannot be seen as a true reflection of the current beliefs of priests in England and Wales."

This makes no sense whatever. If the findings are wrong, then you don't treat them "with great caution"; you reject them full stop. The spokesman doesn't say this (the libel laws in England have serious teeth to them), which prompts the question, if the stats don't give the true picture, do they err by overstating the problem or understating it?

It makes no difference. If the truth *mattered* to someone, his first cry wouldn't be "Defective methodology!" He'd get on the phone, ask tough questions, and start taking names—hoping the numbers were wrong, but understanding the need to act swiftly and decisively. If a poll claimed to show that 43 percent of surgeons opposed the board-sanctioned standards of antisepsis, would the director of the National Health Service sleepily dismiss the numbers and return to *Oprah*?

Probably not, but then surgery is sometimes a life-and-death matter.

Outrageous?

April 22, 2003

The background: Sally Beres claims she lost her job as parish secretary 20 years ago after she reported her pastor's use of kiddie porn to the then Bishop of Erie, Michael Murphy. The same pastor was arrested in 1999 for—don't be shocked—possession of kiddie porn. Sally Beres (and two friends who were in on the initial whistle-blowing) recently accused Bishop Murphy (now 87 and retired) of a cover-up. Last week the current bishop, Donald Trautman, issued a statement criticizing the women. This from the pertinent news article:

> Trautman in his April 21 statement said the women's account of their conversation with Murphy lacked "corroborating evidence." "The entire treatment of this supposed conversation is one-sided and prejudiced, even though it has been totally denied," Trautman said. "The impression created by this one-sided prejudicial treatment says the Diocese of Erie in the person of Bishop Michael J. Murphy fired a woman who was a whistle-blower. There is no evidence to support such an outrageous claim."

But what exactly is the claim that Trautman damns as outrageous? Is it outrageous to assert that a Catholic bishop—qua Catholic bishop—would act unjustly? Is it outrageous to assert that the Diocese of Erie would act unjustly? Is it outrageous to assert that Bishop Murphy in particular would act unjustly? Lacking knowledge of the persons involved it's impossible to judge whether these women are wrong *in fact* or whether they are ill-disposed toward the Church, but even if their claim were false it's hard to see what canon of decency it outrages.

Let's be clear. Trautman is not to be faulted for defending his predecessor's reputation, *provided he knows beyond doubt that Murphy is innocent.* What is mind-boggling, after fifteen consecutive months of revelations of self-serving episcopal lies in matters concerning sexual mischief by priests, is the suggestion that a bishop's word of honor is worth more than a layman's.

We'll do our best to follow this story. Suppose—just suppose—that Sally Beres and her friends are able to provide materials that refresh Bishop Murphy's memory (let's call it "the institutional memory") of the meeting. In that case, will we read an apology from Bishop Trautman calling his own statement an outrageous violation of justice? Stay tuned.

THAT Should Teach 'Em!

May 22, 2003

Today's *Boston Globe* has an article with this lead ...

> The Catholic bishop of Worcester said yesterday that he will not attend commencement tomorrow at the College of the Holy Cross because the Catholic university is awarding an honorary degree to a television talk-show host, Chris Matthews, who supports abortion rights. "I cannot let my presence imply support for anything less than the protection of all life at all its stages," said Bishop Daniel P. Reilly.

... which would be encouraging, were it not for this paragraph in the same story:

> Reilly said he is not questioning Holy Cross's commitment to Catholicism. He called the university "a great asset to the Diocese of Worcester and to the wider church," and said, "I am not questioning the fidelity of the College of the Holy Cross to its mission as a Catholic college or its dedication to the mission of the Catholic Church."

Clear, I hope? It should be, because it would be hard to find a more instructive specimen of U.S. episcopal leadership.

But Why Doesn't the Vatican Do Something?

June 6, 2003

Two imaginary dialogues:

PAPAL NUNCIO: Look here, Bishop, the papers say you've grossly mismanaged your diocese. Now what about it?

BISHOP (Response 1): All true, I'm afraid. The fact is that the only reason I became a priest is that I couldn't tell Mom I was queer. I've never had any particular interest in religion. The reason I was made bishop is that I was Cardinal X's golf partner. Probably it didn't hurt either that Cardinal Y was indiscreet with his housekeeper and found out later that she was my cousin. Of course I knew all about my diocese's underage abusers for the most part. But to tell the truth, I haven't always behaved perfectly myself, and there's a waiter in Provincetown named Fabio who could make life miserable for me if he ratted me out; in fact he threatened to go on *Good Morning America* if I didn't reinstate Father A—who helped him finance his condo among other things—after A got in trouble in his third consecutive parish. And once you start this game it's hard to back out: you have to tell more and more elaborate lies to cover the first ones, and you have to come down faster and harder on the victims. So right now the press and the DA suspect the truth, and I can't move in any direction without bringing the whole mess down on my head. There you have it, short and squalid.

BISHOP (Response 2): Lies, all lies! Your Excellency, I want you to tell the Holy Father that I am the victim of an anti-Catholic smear campaign. The liberal media are out to get me because of my spirited defense of the Church's teaching on the right to unionize.

Now ask yourself: Which response is easier to speak? Which response is easier to hear?

Is Off the Record Too Hard on the Bishops?

June 16, 2003

In the England of Henry VIII, every Catholic bishop except one abandoned the Faith and became Protestant. Would Catholics who accused these bishops of sloth, cowardice, and heterodoxy—in the months preceding the apostasy that proved them right—be guilty of scandalmongering? If it is always wrong to raise one's hand against the Lord's anointed, is it always wrong also to raise one's voice against him? Let's do a little stocktaking.

- A U.S. bishop pulls rank to bypass protocol and ordain his Costa Rican catamite to the priesthood, and fits him out with a beeper in order to summon him at all hours for sexual services.
- A U.S. bishop pays $450,000 of diocesan funds as hush money to a gay lover.
- A U.S. bishop throttles a male prostitute while the man is in the act of performing fellatio on him in his hotel room, this during a Knights of Columbus convention.

Note: The above incidents are not mere allegations but facts, admitted in each case by the bishop involved. There is no reason—absolutely zero evidence—to suggest that their brother bishops would have moved to depose them had not the scandals become glaringly public (in the last case, the bishop died before the story broke). In spite of this, some will console themselves by pretending that (a) steps are being taken "behind the scenes" to clean the stables; (b) the above-mentioned cases are flukes, and by a happy coincidence, all the rogues and heretics have been eliminated; or (c) public agitation against the bad guys was malicious and unnecessary because the normal oversight and discipline would have bagged them anyway.

As Christ's spotless bride, the Church is holy. She was holy in 1535, in spite of her rotten episcopacy. She is holy today, in spite of some of her ministers' lies, depravity, cover-ups, gutlessness. It would be great, of course, if the bishops helped us see and love her holiness by moving to rid themselves of villains in their midst before the first whisper of scandal reached the ears of the faithful. Either they can't or they won't. So how do the rest of us respond?

Many half-Catholics gloat over the Church's humiliation because they reject her teachings and hate the notion of ecclesial authority full stop. But many real Catholics—and this is true frequently in the Church's history—value the meaning of the bishop's office more than do the bishops who hold it; in remonstrating with episcopal frauds and timeservers they are defending the nobility of the calling of bishop, not spitting on it.

Here's Richness!

June 22, 2003

When the Stalin-era agrarian economy was at its nadir the economic propaganda of the Soviet regime, not coincidentally, was its most extravagant in celebrating prosperity. A sardonic proverb ran: If you want milk, fill your pail from the radio.

Last week's meeting of bishops ended as it began with prolix self-congratulation (for public consumption, at any rate) on the advances made in dealing with the child-abuse crisis. There was even an undertone of impatience at the less effusive enthusiasm voiced in other quarters.

The problem is not idleness or inattention—at least not of the bureaucratic variety. The bishops can point to an abundance of new policies enacted. What bothers the skeptics is the bishops' continued inability to demand a reckoning of their brother bishops. A few heads have been bared of their miters in the past two years, but always because the media or the law enforcement heavies did the bishops' work for them.

Or look at it another way. As a consequence of their criminal negligence, Bishops McCormack of Manchester and O'Brien of Phoenix were forced by the DA's office to relinquish some of their ecclesial authority. If this is a bad thing, why did their brother bishops permit it? If it is a good thing, why didn't they do it themselves?

If we take our pails to the radio, we can quickly fill them with policies. Is it a reproach to us if we're hungry for something more?

The O'Brien Twins (and How They Grew)

October 21, 2003

Archbishop Keith Patrick O'Brien, who will be retitled Cardinal O'Brien about five hours from now, publicly denies his public denial of the immutability of doctrine.

> Scotland's Senior Roman Catholic tonight strongly denied reports that he had called for the church to debate its teachings on celibacy, contraception and homosexuality just days after being appointed a Cardinal. Speaking on the eve of his elevation to the College of Cardinals by Pope John Paul II, Archbishop Keith O'Brien said he had been hurt by the allegations.
>
> He told a press conference in central Rome: "I would strongly object to the wrong reports that have been circulated about me round the world. I did not say anything against the Church's teachings at that mass (at St Mary's Cathedral in Edinburgh three days after he was named a Cardinal)."

Of course O'Brien didn't say anything *against* Church teachings; he merely suggested they should be changed. It is in extremely poor taste to take seriously what a bishop happens to say in the course of a Mass, as if it expressed his true mind on the matter. One should ask the director of archdiocesan media relations.

But for the three years' difference in their ages, we might imagine Bishop Keith was separated at birth from Bishop Thomas, quondam lord spiritual of Phoenix, who earlier this summer sputtered in indignation against folks who assumed that what he'd said under oath was meant literally. Faced with the prospect of prison, Thomas O'Brien cut a deal with the DA that included an admission that he had covered up incidents of sexual abuse. When the agreement (and confession) was made public, O'Brien blew a gasket and flipped back into full denial mode. Rod Dreher nailed him in his tracks:

> Bishop O'Brien, having signed a pretty straightforward statement, is now saying that the statement doesn't say what it pretty clearly says. I don't see any true contrition here. I see a venal creature who put his name to a document to save himself from the possibility of going to jail, and who, now that the danger of jailtime seems to have passed, wishes to disavow any responsibility for having done that.

O'Brien of Phoenix is no longer in a position to harm or help the Church. O'Brien of Edinburgh has at least ten years ahead of him as cardinal archbishop. Is it ungenerous of us to fear that, once the red hat has been safely pushed down onto his scalp, he will revert to his old ways and deny the denial of his denial? "I am only too willing," he assured his audience Monday, "to discuss and share my views with my peers and Pope John Paul II." Decent of him, but not exactly a rousing affirmation of orthodoxy.

Equivocation, however, is a two-edged sword. When O'Brien says, "I would hope that Catholics everywhere will join with me in respecting the decisions of the Pope," he may be less than pleased by those who take him at his word—that is, who imitate his own "tactical deference" by making purely verbal concessions to superiors while working to nullify their efforts. Perhaps the infection is contagious. Asked to comment on the elevation of the cardinal-to-be, the lord provost of Edinburgh responded with a sublime example of Caledonian diplomacy: "I think he will bring to the office the qualities that he has already displayed as Archbishop."

All too likely, milord.

Career-Threatening Ailments

February 13, 2004

"The most Rev. Thomas L. Dupre ... abruptly resigned yesterday as bishop of the Springfield Roman Catholic Diocese, citing health reasons."

Outstanding. Bishop Dupre bails out of his bishopric five years ahead of the statutory retirement age of 75 under the rubric of canon 401, paragraph 2, "because of illness or some other grave reason." He thereby joins a distinguished group of other "dash-2" retirees: Bishop Keith Symons (presently 71 years old), Bishop Patrick Ziemann (62), Bishop Dan Ryan (73), Bishop Joseph Hart (72), and Bishop Anthony O'Connell (65). All of the above stood accused of illicit sexual relations, with males, at the time of their premature retirement.

What if, one wonders, a bishop *really* retired for reasons of ill health—how would he announce it? Would he allow himself to be lumped together with the other dash-2s? Wouldn't he instead show up at his press conference holding a large placard reading NOT BOYS under his chin while his physician, under oath, gave us the exact stats on his PSA [prostate-specific antigen] or blood sugar?

Back in, say, 1973, both charity and common sense would have prompted us to assume that a bishop who announced ill health as the reason for his retirement suffered, in actual fact, from ill health, and that his illness was the true cause of his stepping down.

Times have changed. How much, you ask? Look at it this way: If you were a bishop who'd lived an upright life but had to exit tomorrow because of a dicky heart, wouldn't you make sure fifty or sixty of your episcopal confreres publicly attested to your probity? And if you were a bishop-friend of the man making the early exit, wouldn't you be downright eager to comply?

Is it ungenerous of us, before a case has been proved against him in a court of law, to class Dupre with other unsavory members of the boys-boys-boys brigade? Yep. But what goes around comes around: bureaucratic equivocation works both ways. We didn't give Dupre the dash-2 tag; the Congregation for Bishops did. And if his brother bishops believe we'd do Dupre an injustice in giving his dash-2 a negative interpretation, then it's their duty to instruct us—in plain speech, not ecclesiastical code—how it happens that in *this* instance the "grave reason" is a morally respectable one.

P.S. According to the Springfield *Republican* story linked [quoted] above, "[Dupre's] ailments are not considered life threatening, according to diocesan officials."

We can all breathe easier.

Bishops and Us

February 16, 2004

It's always sad, in Barnes & Noble, to see a thirty-year-old propped against the stacks while leafing through a book on How to Make Friends. If you need to ask, as the saying goes, you won't understand the answer. C. S. Lewis wrote, "That is why those pathetic people who simply 'want friends' can never make any. The very condition of having Friends is that we should want something else besides Friends."

The U.S. bishops' programs for "restoring trust" strike me as pathetic, and futile, for precisely the same reason. To adapt Lewis' words: the very condition of trusting a man is his total indifference as to whether you trust him or not. That is to say, we trust those who we know will tell us the truth regardless of how we'll react and keep their promises regardless of how they appear in the eyes of others. Only a confidence man asks himself, "How can I get this guy to trust me?" as a distinct endeavor from "What is the right thing to do in this situation?"

When the pertinent body is a collectivity, like a professional group, we trust the outfit that is harder on its own members than we ourselves would incline to be. "They fired Dr. Smith just for *that*?" "Captain Jones lost his command just for *that*?" When we marvel that what appear trivial lapses to those of us outside the guild are deemed career-ending offenses to those within it, and when we see that the guild not infrequently pulls the trigger on its own members even at considerable cost to itself, then we tend to think, "These are serious folks who have a serious mission—a mission they see more clearly than we do." And note: If they surprise us often enough by a severity towards themselves we don't fully understand, we can accept it as a good-faith decision if, occasionally, they show a leniency we don't fully understand. By acting consistently in conformity to objective standards—without reference to the impression it makes on us— they've *earned* our trust.

It doesn't matter, then, how many covenants are nailed to cathedral doors: every attempt to cajole trust from us is a reason for us to withhold it. As Dallas journalist Wick Allison asked the bishops two years ago: How can we trust you if you don't trust yourselves? And how can you trust yourselves if you can't remove the villains from your ranks?

The Mote-Plank Factor

April 17, 2004

Having vainly urged Boston auxiliary bishop John McCormack, throughout the late 1980s and early 1990s, to notify parishes in which known abusers had worked, Sr. Catherine Mulkerrin ruefully conceded, "I know I sound like a broken record." It's a distasteful task to keep sounding the same unwelcome note and earn the reputation of a crank. Most Off the Record bloggers will sympathize with Sr. Mulkerrin on the hardship of admonishing an unreceptive bishop. For all that, it needs repeating: Until the episcopacy addresses the serious moral problems in its own ranks, it will continue to lose its moral authority, which is the only authority it has.

In a discussion at Amy Welborn's blog, Rod Dreher put the problem of the "team player" bishops in a nutshell: "For the rest of their careers they'll be dogged by the Mote-Plank Factor every time they open their mouths."

The reference, of course, is to Jesus' hard saying: "Thou hypocrite, first cast out the beam out of thine own eye, and then shalt thou see clearly to cast out the mote out of thy brother's eye." It doesn't matter what subject the bishops may choose to instruct us on—abortion or gay marriage or capital punishment or homelessness or even fidelity to liturgical norms—at the barest hint of a call to moral seriousness or self-discipline they will be laughed off the stage.

Picture a newly married couple, presented with the Church's teaching on contraception. "Bishop, you seem not to grasp the hardships involved in following this teaching, the expense of a large family and the emotional cost of sexual continence. Where is the hardship in your own life or the evidence that you have called your brothers to austerity?" The Mote-Plank Factor.

Picture policemen in a big city force, urged to break the code of *omertà* whereby they perjure themselves and cover for one another

in incidents of brutality or racism: "Hey, why should I risk *my* job
and *my* neck by ratting out a fellow cop? I don't get into the head-
cracking stuff myself. Look at you bishops: what's the worst thing
that could possibly happen to you by denouncing another bishop?
Nasty looks. And yet there's not one example of your getting rid of
your own felons, for God's sake." The Mote-Plank Factor.

Picture a CEO, asked to delay relocating a factory out of concern
for employees too old to find another job. "Look, Your Excellency,
labor and production costs are 36 percent higher here than they are
in Carolina, and there'll be no factory, no jobs, and no pensions at
all unless I keep my costs down near the level of my competitors.
And don't give me the song and dance about 'justice'. I pay my
bills. Your man Rembert Weakland nicked half a million dollars in
donated monies in order to keep his gay lover sweet. That cash could
have gone a long way toward relief of the unemployed you're so
concerned about. If I'd fiddled with our pension fund to that extent,
even to create new jobs with it, I'd be in prison now. But Weakland
retired with full honors. He hasn't paid the money back. And he's *still*
in good standing. Now, Your Excellency, explain to me again my
obligations in social justice." The Mote-Plank Factor.

Here's the rub: we're writing as Catholics who *want* strong bishops, who think that it's a good thing that a bishop, like Jesus, "speaks
with authority, not as the scribes." But lots of people don't. Most
half-Catholics and all anti-Catholics are gleeful at the "team player"
approach because it means the teaching episcopacy will keep melting
down before their eyes, like the Wicked Witch after she was doused
by Dorothy. For the Frances Kisslings and the Garry Willses it's a
win–win situation: if the bishops cave and go into "healing and reconciliation" mode, reduced to "suggesting" that the Church's law
be followed—great, they're harmless. If they try to bluff and pretend
a baritone and a wagging finger will work the old magic—great,
they're laughingstocks.

There's one way forward. Bishops have to cut the cancer out of
their own midst, without a formal mechanism for doing so. That
means that those who have moral authority have to prevail on those
who don't to give over their miters. I know I sound like a broken
record.

The Peasants of Autun

May 4, 2004

Priests, C. S. Lewis wrote somewhere, are those men whom we set apart to minister to us as people who will live forever—forever, that is, in heaven or in hell. The sole reason for the existence of the clergy is to aid us in avoiding damnation and in attaining heaven. Often priestly work will include temporal remedies—Jesus was surely acting as a priest in healing the blind and sick—but temporal hardships are of themselves not impediments to salvation, and authentic pastoral work begins where temporal remedies leave off.

In the past fifty years, the possibility of damnation has all but disappeared from the clerical vocabulary, leaving behind a vacuum in which few bishops can explain to themselves—much less to others—why the Faith is important. A gathering of bishops calls to mind (for most of us) the picture of fleshy men in a conference room at the Omni Shoreham, with plastic name tags pinned to their lapels, peering apprehensively over their half-glasses at their programs while Sr. Sharon Euart leads them in morning prayer. Managers by training, socialists by conviction, they are clearly ill at ease with the "spiritual side" of the job, and it was pathetically typical that Bishop Gregory, when obliged to defend the existence of the Church, could find nothing more persuasive than her role as a provider of social services and community-building initiatives.

In broad terms, at this moment in history, those of us who believe in hell are governed by bishops who don't. This is analogous to being treated by a doctor who thinks death is a fable and disease an illusion of the patient. If we pester him long enough for penicillin, he'll give it to us as a placebo, but his heart's not in it. By the same token, bishops can get quite animated about battered women or water quality or even Bolivian debt relief, but when the conversation turns to sanctifying grace their eyes glaze over, their lips part, and they start blowing bubbles with their spit. With very few exceptions, they're just not interested in religion.

Let's be fair. Why *should* a bishop—I mean a bishop who thinks there's no such thing as damnation—be interested in religion any more than an employee of Disney's Magic Kingdom is interested in magic? If heaven is assured for everyone, if all trains are ultimately headed to the same station, your aim is to make the journey as comfortable as possible, working to keep doctrines as fuzzy and as few as the passengers will let you get by with. And when bad things occur en route, such as ministers' misbehaving with children, you don't worry about souls being lost; the name of the game is reconciliation: "Now, now, my little man, let's see that smile again!"

The Church has passed this way before, many times, and unbelieving bishops wax and wane like locusts. We've had it worse. I comfort myself with thoughts of 18th-century France, when Talleyrand, the atheist Bishop of Autun, bothered to visit his diocese only once in his tenure, spending the rest of his time in Paris in a life of Clintonesque dissoluteness. Today, as then, faithful and devoted bishops are scarce but not lacking entirely, and our job is to make of the others the best use that we can, remembering that "the unworthiness of the minister hindereth not the effect of the sacrament."

Did God love the peasants of Autun less than other Catholics, such that He wanted to imperil their salvation? No—but upright, devout, truth-telling bishops were not a gift He chose to give them. This gift has been withheld from us also, and as a consequence we have a difficult path to walk, neither giving in to discouragement nor becoming party to the lie that the rot is less serious than it appears. We have the promise, not that we'll succeed, but that we won't walk alone.

A Wholly Imaginary Cell Phone Intercept

May 9, 2004

CLIENT: Hello. Hello? This is the archbishop. Hello? Who's speaking, please?

N/A: You wouldn't remember my name. We met back in '77. At Fire Island.

CLIENT: You're mistaken. I've never been to Fire Island.

N/A: Oh yes you have. Remember that tall Irish busboy at Entre Nous? You came back to my beach house with Donal and me and a bottle of Tanqueray. In fact I still have some Polaroids of the occasion—a little overexposed, but then so was Donal. Hello ... You haven't gone to sleep on me, have you?

CLIENT: What do you want from me?

N/A: Nothing whatever. I'm just aware that you'll be asked to make some statements in the next few weeks about who can and can't receive Communion, and I wanted you to know that I respect the statesmanlike way you've handled yourself in the past, and that I'm confident you'll continue to earn my respect. My confidence *is* well placed, isn't it?

CLIENT: I ... I'll do what I can.

N/A: We can't ask more than that, can we?

Taking the Fifth

August 3, 2004

> KIM LAWTON: Some groups fear the bishops' energy and commitment may fade.
>
> ARCHBISHOP TIMOTHY DOLAN: Can't happen. Can't happen. We never, never, Kim, want to go through what we've had to do. We just can't do it. We can't do it personally. I think we bishops will collapse if we ever have to go through this again. And we can't, we just can't, in justice, put our people through that again. So, I don't think there's danger of us forgetting. (PBS interview, November 2003)

Shaken by public contempt consequent on their mishandling of sex abusers, the bishops—while the cameras were rolling—have collectively and severally pledged to "restore trust". Yet two of their number, Anthony O'Connell and Thomas Dupre, are currently refusing to respond to questions about allegations of *their own* sexual abuse of minors, invoking their Fifth Amendment protections against self-incrimination.

No one faults the bishops' attorneys for advising their clients to make use of this entirely proper tactic; they're simply doing their job. But the good of the Church is larger than her legal standing, larger even than the solvency of her dioceses and the liberty of her bishops.

It seems clear that shielding bishops from punishment and restoring trust are mutually exclusive alternatives: *either* you try to convince people you're interested in the truth, *or* you allow your brethren to keep mum in order to beat the diddling rap. You can't do both.

Is there a canonical mechanism by which bishops can force an unwilling brother to act contrary to his lawyer's sound advice and his own clear interest? Nope. But if they were serious about justice they could do it anyway. You send five bishops to put the case to Dupre or O'Connell in a room with no back door. If five fail to convince him, send ten. If ten don't work, try twenty. If he won't listen to twenty, bring fifty. The concerted moral pressure of his peers can make an ordinary man do extraordinary things—such as remain at his post in battle when only flight could save his life. Were it impassioned and sincere, such moral force couldn't fail to make a bishop risk telling the truth about himself, even knowing that he would suffer as a consequence.

Help me out here. Bishops Dupre and O'Connell refuse to reply to questions whose true answers they can't help but know, indisputably eroding the stature of the episcopacy and conceivably prolonging an objective injustice. Their brother bishops respond by ... doing nothing. Whose good is served?

Whosoever Shall Cause These Little Ones to Sin ...

May 31, 2005

An old joke recounts a telephone conversation between a college football coach and a high school prospect:

> COACH: Height?
> JOCK: Six foot five.
> COACH: Weight?
> JOCK: Two-sixty.
> COACH: Best 100-yard?
> JOCK: Nine point seven.
> COACH: SAT score?
> JOCK: 1600.
> COACH: You're perfect!
> JOCK: I lie a little.

In judging a man's reliability of character, truthfulness is not simply one quality among others—it is the medium through which knowledge of his virtue is possible. Once a man has shown himself to be a lying witness, it's a waste of time to interrogate him further.

Because the Church locates the charism of truth in the episcopal Magisterium in a special way, violations of truthfulness by bishops are especially distressing to Catholics. Faced with a flagrantly self-serving falsehood—say, Thomas Daily's testimony (under oath) that he didn't realize priests were criminally liable for molesting children—the faithful are momentarily knocked off kilter. *This* is the man who is transmitting God's will for us? Faced with the ensuing silence on the part of Daily's brother bishops, their absence of criticism or correction, the faithful take a second hit, blindsided from the other direction. *These* are the men who are transmitting God's will for us? The Christian concerned to unite himself to a reliable conduit of divine instruction is almost inevitably stunned.

CHRISTIAN: Number?
CHURCH: One.
CHRISTIAN: Godliness?
CHURCH: Holy.
CHRISTIAN: Range?
CHURCH: Catholic.
CHRISTIAN: Basis of authority?
CHURCH: Apostolic.
CHRISTIAN: You're perfect!
CHURCH: I lie a little.

Thanks be to God, it doesn't work that way. The charism is vouchsafed not to the person of Bishop So-and-so but to the episcopal college assembled around the pope with the purpose of teaching:

> The infallibility promised to the Church is also present in the body of bishops when, together with Peter's successor, they exercise the supreme Magisterium, above all in an Ecumenical Council. When the Church through its supreme Magisterium proposes a doctrine for belief as being divinely revealed, and as the teaching of Christ, the definitions must be adhered to with the obedience of faith. (*Catechism*, no. 891)

The reliability of the teaching Church is not contaminated by the perjury of her individual ministers. That said, it puts a huge weight on the faithful to make the act of theological abstraction needed to see beyond the personal untruthfulness of their bishop to the divinely protected deposit of faith in his custody. In plain terms, it's hard for Uncle Louie to watch Bishop Pinocchio lie his way out of a jam and still believe God is speaking through the same bishop in forbidding him to contracept or remarry.

Unable to handle this paradox—which the New Testament calls *scandal*, a stumbling block—some Catholics lapse into cynicism. ("Nobody believes the doctrine. It's all a power game.") Others contend that the lies of ecclesiastics are not lies at all or, at least, not really as grave as they appear.

The former tend to flatter themselves on their realism; the latter console themselves with their piety. Both groups lack the strength of faith needed to believe that the divine governance of the Church can coexist with appalling human frailty in her ministers. But both deserve a certain sympathy. Standing up under the encumbrance of scandal is a tough task to perform, and Someone who knew whereof He spoke was fierce in condemnation of those indifferent to burdens they bound on the shoulders of others, and He assigned millstones to those who caused little ones to collapse under the weight of their superiors' evildoing.

It matters.

How Bishops Are Made

September 29, 2005

Kudos to Mark Mossa for noticing this gem in the Code of Canon Law (332 §1): "If he does not have the episcopal character, he is immediately to be ordained Bishop."

As Mossa explains, canon 332 treats of the election of a pope, and stipulates that, in the case where the man elected is not already in episcopal orders, he is thereupon to be consecrated bishop.

And you thought we were close to getting an explanation for The Crisis? Well, so did I.

If I Were a Bishop ...

October 28, 2005

If I were a bishop, I'd write the following letter to the Bishop of Spokane:

Dear Bishop Skylstad,

I confess I was dismayed to read the following words in your *Inland Register* column of October 20: "There are many wonderful and excellent priests in the Church who have a gay orientation, are chaste and celibate, and are very effective ministers of the Gospel. Witch hunts and gay bashing have no place in the Church."

First, by referring to priests with "a gay orientation" instead of "a same-sex attraction", you cross the line from the descriptive and morally neutral to the political and morally problematic. This implies, even if it does not state, acquiescence in the self-understanding of those homosexual persons who call themselves gay. This is a disservice to those persons with same-sex attraction—not only those in your own diocese—who are struggling against enormous odds to live according to Church teaching, and whose resolve is seriously weakened by bishops who suggest "Gay is OK."

Second, it is hardly a secret that your own diocese is bankrupt—and that is because of your and your predecessors' catastrophically bad decisions about keeping sexually disturbed priests in ministry. Yes, I know some victims were female. Yes, I know most homosexual priests don't molest minors. But the fact remains that Spokane was buggered into bankruptcy by priests known to be deviant, and the underlying causes could have been avoided by unexacting prudential decisions well within the moral compass of an ordinary parishioner. Staggering naiveté is the kindest way of accounting for your own baffling action and inaction, and I think it behooves you, as head of a diocese bankrupted by sexual anarchy, not to touch on the subject of gay clergy at all, for any reason. I say this with the good of the larger Church in mind.

Then too, Bishop Skylstad, the admonition against "witch hunts" comes ill from your mouth. Most Catholics who read that line will recall all too vividly your predecessor Lawrence Welsh of unhappy memory. They'll remember the police report concerning the male prostitute Welsh throttled during an act of fellatio in a Chicago hotel room back in 1986. They'll remember the fact that it was the terrified prostitute that went to the Chicago police, who in turn contacted Spokane law enforcement only because of a long-shot connection with the Green River serial killer. You were Bishop of Yakima at the time, of course, but your comments on Welsh's behavior three years ago—"Obviously, he had a very serious drinking problem. Certainly, it's very sad behavior associated with that drinking. That would be my observation"—render your recent "witch hunt" language farcical. If, confronted with a bishop's sodomy and attempted manslaughter, you can't do better than "drinking problem", would you be able to put the right name to a witch even after she'd turned you into a bat?

Let's face it: in the only relevant sense, there are altogether too many witches on the prowl, and indeed "the witches" are the reason Spokane is not a solvent diocese today. We have to bear in mind, moreover, that the faithful can't help but take to heart the news reports, inasmuch as they've gone unchallenged except on trivial points. They know that Archbishop Hunthausen promised the Spokane detectives to get Welsh into counseling, and they know that, in spite of Hunthausen's awareness of the Chicago episode, Welsh was back in the saddle for the next four years. They know Welsh's drinking caused him to be retired as Bishop of Spokane at age 55 in 1990. Worst of all, though, we have to deal with the fact that after Welsh was deposed from Spokane he was almost immediately made an auxiliary bishop of St. Paul–Minneapolis. So tell me: How do we explain to the laity why a bishop can pull that kind of squeeze play, drink himself out of the ordinary's job, and still end up ministering to God's people as an auxiliary?

When folks put the Welsh saga together with the reasons for the Spokane bankruptcy, they're going to think along these lines: "I can see a couple of bad priests as an honest mistake. I can see a bad bishop as an honest mistake. Really stretching it, I could even see bounce passing the bad bishop to another diocese as an honest mistake. But the mistakes all hinge on a particular misjudgment no normal person would make. It can't be a coincidence."

What answer can we make? Not only is such a suspicion wholly justified, but to suggest that there is an "innocent" explanation borders on perfidy. Don't you see that—against this background, and especially in view of the added embarrassment of your election to the USCCB presidency—your remarks condemning "witch hunts" could hardly have come at a worse time? No one is taking a tire iron to effeminate clergy; your "gay bashing" line is preposterous. Most of the faithful are looking not for vengeance but for candid explanations. Your saying, in effect, "There is nothing to find behind that door," inflames the very suspicions it was meant to allay.

Bishop Skylstad, I have my own diocese to run, my own faithful to tend to. Many are shocked and bewildered by the negligence of us bishops. My own moral authority, and hence my ability to guide my flock, has been weakened by our collective equivocation and especially by our inability to purge our own body of ineptitude, villainy, and sloth. How can we call others to make heroic personal sacrifices when we can't confront the unpleasantness that would attend telling the truth about ourselves? Ultimately I'm going to have to answer to a higher tribunal than CBS News, and when I do, I want to be able to say that I lost none of my flock through my own deliberate inaction. With that in mind, I plead with you: pay your bills, and keep your head down, and don't fret yourself about the witch busters. The job belongs to others.

Your apostolic brother,
+Di

Sufficiently Clear?

June 11, 2006

"So just explain," Wolf Blitzer pressed Cardinal McCarrick, giving Uncle Ted the chance to back out of his position, "you think that you could live with—you could support civil unions between gays and lesbians, but you wouldn't like them to get formally married, is that right?"

Yes, yes, yes, gurgled His Eminence, and the audience loved him for it. Now the faithful are calling foul, and he's trying to put the toothpaste back in the tube, claiming that folks who understood his remarks in the context he went out of his way to provide are taking those remarks out of context. A 450-word clarification on the archdiocesan website ends with this apology: "I regret any confusion my words may have caused because I did not make myself sufficiently clear."

On the contrary, good sir: it's the clarity, not the unclarity, that's the problem.

What we're watching in operation is a familiar episcopal gambit, yet one that McCarrick has made a personal speciality. The game is to win the favor of the liberal media by addressing the hot-button issues in a "balanced" manner: that is to say, signaling sympathy for the heterodox position while uttering a few inert bromides that make indirect reference to the orthodox one. The heterodox innovation gets the media attention, as it was meant to, while conservatives who complain can be palmed off after the fact by pointing to the crumbs of Rotarian bonhomie scattered here and there in the same discussion. It's their fault, of course, for not giving their anointed shepherds the benefit of the doubt.

We saw this stunt three years ago in one of John Allen's columns:

> McCarrick, who named a woman chancellor in Washington and has appointed women to significant positions of responsibility in every diocese he's led, said he wouldn't be surprised if John Paul II, in his heart, would like to have women priests. "He's never said, 'I don't want women priests,'" McCarrick said. "He's said, 'I can't do it.' He's prayed, studied, and concluded that he can't call women to the priesthood."

Recognize the move? The telegraphed sympathies are clear: JP2's not really a bad guy. Deep down, he wants women priests just as much as you and I and Katie Couric do. But you know, the good man has looked into the matter and he just can't see a way to go with his heart on this thing. But give it time.

If, on the other hand, one of us ill-conditioned short-rib scratchers should be so tactless as to infer from the good bishop's remarks that the Holy Spirit is either (1) wrong, or (2) opposed to the Church on this issue, he'll be assured that His Eminence regrets any confusion his words may have caused.

Lies, Damned Lies, and the Bishops

April 3, 2007

"Insulting to all Catholics," protests the Archdiocese of Los Angeles, in reference to a tendentious and theologically leaky article in the

L.A. Times. The story in question centered on a tort lawyer's claim that Catholics believe the notion of "mental reservation" permits them to lie under oath to protect the good of the Church:

> "You really don't know," [plaintiff attorney Irwin] Zalkin said. "You put somebody under oath; you assume they understand that under civil law they would be committing perjury to lie. It complicates that process when there is a doctrine that allows for a lie to avoid scandal to the church."

I'd have to agree with those making the counterclaim that raising the mental-reservation question in connection with the Church's witnesses isn't a serious argument, but rather a lawyerly way of rattling cages. For all that, the willingness of ecclesiastics—and cardinal archbishops in particular—to perjure themselves is genuinely shocking. And the shock is delivered to serious Catholics who see their bishops as pastors of souls, not to the tactically modulated feelings of attorneys who stand to carry home a third of the white meat off the Church's carcass if the cards fall right.

Zalkin's suggestion that ecclesiastics have lied "for the good of the Church" is stupid—or would be stupid, were it tendered in earnest. It's not the Church that has benefited from the perjury but the perjurers themselves, who have in fact grievously harmed the Church in order that they might stay out of jail.

No one not a thorough cynic who has read through the depositions of Cardinals Law and Mahony can fail to be stunned by their readiness to perjure themselves. You find yourself gasping two or three times per page. Their testimony (while under oath to tell "the truth, the whole truth, and nothing but the truth") simply does not permit belief. Think of Law's failure to remember a memo he sent to the Vatican Secretary of State asking for the laicization of a priest who'd molested six boys; think of Mahony's inability to remember the two abuser priests he'd advised to flee the country, or to recall the police reports he'd received about Oliver O'Grady. One might possibly accept the fluke that both men suffered from some organic brain injury that impaired their memory to such an extent, but both men had perfect powers of retrieval when a past incident served to exculpate them from some misdeed—or even from a personality flaw. Were a man both harmed and helped by consistently fuzzy memory, or both harmed and helped by consistently sharp recall, we could take him at his word. But we can go through hundreds of pages of testimony by Law and Mahony without coming on a single instance where either their memory or their forgetfulness works to their disadvantage: to their *personal* disadvantage.

Why is this perjury so harmful to the Catholic faithful? Because of what's at stake in the oath that it violates. An Australian moral theologian told me that aborigines used not to be permitted to testify in courts—not because of an idea that they were racially inferior, but because it was thought that aborigines had no belief in an afterlife in which there was punishment for evildoers, and consequently the oath required of witnesses was meaningless.

Here's how that oath works: I, the witness, call upon God to send me to hell, eternally, if I do not deliver on my present undertaking, namely, to tell the truth, the whole truth, and nothing but the truth in answering questions in court. I'm mortgaging my soul in order to buy the power to be believed, even when appearances are to the contrary (that's where the "credit" is extended to me, as a function of my "credibility"). To default is to be damned. Nor can I do a bounce pass so as to lie in the witness stand to my advantage today, and then clear myself at confession tomorrow. My confessor has no power to absolve me—I deprived him of that power in taking the oath—but can only urge me to amend my testimony. A perjurer can avoid hell only by undoing his perjury: an act which is as public as his oath taking.

The upshot is that almost no perjurer can have both a well-formed notion of hell and, at the same time, a genuine belief in it. For this reason the indignant objections by lying ecclesiastics and their flak compound the harm by rendering farcical what is at bottom a grave situation. The following is from the *L.A. Times* piece:

> "Cardinal Mahony has always insisted and will always insist that honesty always prevails in giving testimony under oath," his spokesman, Tod Tamberg, said Friday. Tamberg said asking the question was "insulting and unprofessional" because it suggested that Mahony wasn't being honest.

And unprofessional. Right.

It should be noted, and figured into the calculation here, that not a single bishop has made anything like a robust defense of Mahony or Law (or Grahmann, or Daily, or Imesch, or McCormack ...). Now this is a loud silence. No bishop who read their testimony could fail to see how grotesquely improbable it must seem to the faithful. That means, if a bishop were really convinced that his brother was truthful, but that exceptional circumstances made it appear to the contrary—to the scandal of the faithful and the detriment of the Church—he would do whatever possible to remedy the situation. He'd phone other bishops and say, "You read Law's testimony? We can't let him take a hammering like that without getting the real story out somehow." But the fact is that the bishops have left the perjurers to hang from their own depositions, twisting slowly in the breeze of their perjury. They simply couldn't let this happen unless they were as convinced as Uncle Di that there's no honesty to rescue, no honor to defend. All the statements of all the spokesmen of all the dioceses put together don't outweigh that passivity.

"Insulting to all Catholics ...," thunders *The Tidings*. Is it?

Zalkin and company find the perjury a nuisance. The *L.A. Times* finds it a curiosity and a juicy addition to the Church-as-hypocrite file. The perjurers themselves find it important to their self-respect and indispensable to the project of avoiding an early retirement with an orange jumpsuit and weed whip. Whom does it harm? Those Catholics who've never heard their bishops mention the possibility of damnation—for any soul, under any circumstances—and who now have excellent reason to conclude that their bishops couldn't care less.

Time for Personal Renewal

October 1, 2009

Back in 2004, you may remember, the Springfield (Massachusetts) Diocese announced that Bishop Thomas Dupre, "citing health reasons", was opting for early retirement under the provisions of canon 401-dash-2.

The word "health", it turned out, had a special ecclesiastical meaning. The reason Dupre resigned, local law enforcement agencies immediately made clear, was that he had sodomized two underage boys in past years and the DA finally caught up with him.

Diocesan officials hastened to reassure us that Dupre's ailments were "not considered life threatening". A beautiful example of the new transparency.

We return to the present. On September 27 Bishop Raymond Lahey of Antigonish (Nova Scotia) announced he too was taking a dash-2 retirement. "I have already left the Diocese," he said in a statement, "to take some much-needed time for personal renewal."

Ah yes. Personal renewal. It turns out that on September 15 Lahey had been found with kiddie porn on his laptop by border security agents. He has since been arrested. The "much-needed time" Lahey claimed to be seeking will mostly likely be spent under house arrest with a transponder around his ankle. If he believed in his own innocence, after all, he wouldn't have requested an early exit or tried to blow smoke to conceal the reasons for his departure.

Canon 401 §2, under the *Gaudium et Spes* dispensation, has become Joe Catholic's friendly emetic. Like a panful of tapeworms taken from a dog's stomach, the roster of dash-2 retirees provides a grim display of parasites that fed, too long, off the Church's bounty. As so often, it's a pity that secular law enforcement should be the agency that puts a stop to bad bishops. As so often, it's a pity that even after the remedy the bishops won't name the real disease for which it was applied.

Bishop Lahey's ailments, be it noted, are not considered life threatening.

Lahey the Indomitable

October 9, 2009

When Bishop Raymond Lahey was arrested for possession of kiddie porn after attracting the suspicion of Canadian border patrol agents, Terry Mattingly asked the apposite question: What was the trigger that led to the secondary search of the laptop hard drive of a Catholic bishop? Well, now we know:

> Bishop Raymond Lahey avoided eye contact, changed his vocal tone and gave evasive responses when a border agent at Ottawa International Airport questioned him last month about his electronic equipment....

The agent flagged Bishop Lahey for a secondary inspection because of his behaviour and the fact he was a man travelling alone who had visited countries known to be sources of child pornography, says an Ottawa police officer's application for the warrant on Sept. 23.

Dry the starting tear. It seems that the photos of ungarbed males the agents found on Lahey's laptop—in their preliminary inspection at the airport—were of ambiguous age. And here we see the bishop's mandatory Child Protection Training kick in. The same pastoral deftness that led Lahey to explain his sudden resignation as a quest for "much-needed time for personal renewal" prompted him to give the agents a reassuring explanation of his appetites: "'After being cautioned, Lahey admitted that the laptop belonged to him and that he was attracted to males aged 20 to 21,' the documents state." He likes 'em legal, see? We can all breathe easier. The news report goes on to say that law enforcement documents giving the contents of the hard drive "describe eight sexually explicit images involving boys who police believe could be as young as eight. One boy is described as eight to 10 years old with a dark complexion and another is a blond boy believed to be nine to 12, according to the warrant application. Two photos are said to depict oral sex and another two show sexual touching." Doubtless there are cynics out there who will dispute Lahey's sincerity in attesting the rather narrow range of his attractions, but your Uncle Di is persuaded that the defendant's deteriorating eyesight caused him to miscalculate the maturity of his ... love interests.

After all, if you can't take a bishop at his word, whom can you trust?

THE SEX-ABUSE SCANDAL

Here is Diogenes at his most acerbic. The abuse scandal—which might more accurately be seen as a scandal of episcopal negligence—outraged him, as it outraged every honest Catholic. Uncle Di recognized instinctively that the cover-up aggravates the crime, and the cover-up—self-serving statements from the hierarchy to the contrary notwithstanding—still continues.

Down with Memory Lane!

March 22, 2003

A puzzling sentence from an earlier story in the *Boston Herald*: "Bernard Cardinal Law's attorney moved yesterday to put off Law's testimony in a civil case until after the cardinal goes before a criminal grand jury next month, explaining after that he fears Law might 'inadvertently contradict' himself and open himself to a perjury charge."

Please, teacher, could you please explain why, if the cardinal's anticipated contradictions would be inadvertent, what purpose is served by *delaying* his testimony before the grand jury?

Honor

April 7, 2003

Today's Mass reading of the story of Susanna and the unjust judges prompted this thought experiment: imagine that you're a regimental officer in the British Army in India, say, in 1880, with civil jurisdiction over a certain area. A brother officer is accused of assaulting a native woman. An official inquiry produces no usable evidence, so it comes down to her accusation versus his denial. He offers you his word of honor as an officer that he is innocent. Staking your own honor on that of your fellow officer, you let him off. Later it transpires that he was guilty of the outrage, and that you, consequently, were complicit in the perversion of justice to the harm of an innocent victim. How could you *not* resign your commission? How could your brother officers let you keep it?

Scapegoating the Abusers

March 26, 2003

Heads have rolled as a consequence of the Air Force Academy sex scandal. Four new senior administrators have been appointed. So which member of the Senate Armed Services Committee declared, "It's not just a change in leadership. It has to be a change in values from top to bottom"? The junior senator from New York. Presumably the cadets will henceforth be instructed in that profound respect for women showcased in her own household. She insisted, "We don't send (cadets to the academy) to become part of a fraternity where they defend one another and protect one another against criminal activities that keep going on."

No one laughed.

In itself, the senator's Pat Schroederite opportunism is not surprising. Scandal entails payback, and few politicians grasp that fact better than she. That said, Juanita Broaddrick and Katherine Willey might object that few people are in a worse position than Mrs. Clinton to climb on a soapbox and rail against silent complicity in criminal activity. How does she get away with it? Because everyone recognizes that her purpose is not to help the academy accomplish its mission but rather to change that mission fundamentally. This is how the culture wars are fought: subversion masquerades as reform.

Last June, the U.S. bishops gathered in Dallas to deal with a sex scandal of their own. Here too, the culture wars were engaged. Here too, the experts brought in for the fix were known dissenters, intent not on reinvigorating but on redefining the mission of the Church. Here too, irony was piled on irony, as Fr. Canice Connors, former president of the St. Luke Institute and former executive director of Southdown, not only gained a sympathetic hearing but later deplored the bishops' zero-tolerance policy in these terms: "In paying this purchase price for their moral credibility, the bishops in effect could be perceived to have become one with the voices of the media, unreconciled victims and a partially informed Catholic public in scapegoating the abusers."

Scapegoating the *abusers*? Five minutes' reflection on this extraordinary phrase, and the assumptions about human sexuality and responsibility that underlie it, will do much to explain the terms of the abuse crisis and its relevance in the culture wars.

Details

April 1, 2003

The manager of a Catholic diocesan newspaper resigned recently when auditors discovered that the paper's bookkeeper had embezzled funds.

> The weekly newspaper's editor, Steve Paradis of Longwood, a 12-year employee, was not involved in any wrongdoing, said Carol Brinati, a spokeswoman for the Catholic Diocese of Orlando. "He resigned because it occurred on his watch," she said.

Mr. Paradis' decision to stand down because of problems that "occurred on his watch" provides an instructive contrast with the decision of New Hampshire bishop John McCormack to remain in his position. Of course the situation is not exactly parallel.

- Paradis resigned three days after the arrest of his bookkeeper. McCormack is still in place, though his disastrous decisions go back to 1987.
- Paradis had no knowledge of his bookkeeper's misdeeds. McCormack knew of multiple accusations against the priests he cleared for reassignment.
- Paradis said, "I just felt that the best way for the newspaper and myself to move forward was to resign." McCormack said, "I cannot heal victims myself, but I am confident that I can help them."
- Paradis had responsibility for a newspaper office. McCormack has responsibility for the destiny of immortal souls.

In addition, one minor detail could occur to readers of the U.S. bish-ops' pastoral letter *Economic Justice for All*. Paradis may have a family to support.

Postmodern Pedophilia

April 7, 2003

Have you ever stopped to think *why* you don't want a child molester working in your diocese as a priest? As usual, you're wrong! Let Fr. Rossetti explain it to you (from *America*, September 9, 1995):

> Just as the banishment of lepers was fueled by medieval myths, the hysteria surrounding child sexual abusers is exacerbated by myths about those who suffer from sexual deviancies. Child molesters incar-nate our deepest childhood fears: We imagine them to be old, evil and malicious men. In our mind's eye, we see them as powerful and dark figures that lurk in the shadows and prey on the unsuspecting.... Our myths about child molesters come more from the projections of what lies within our own inner psyches than from the truth about who these men are.

Got that? Your view that molesters are evil and malicious is a myth, and—pay close attention here—this myth is a "projection" of *your* unresolved sexual fears. And all along you thought you were concerned about justice and charity!

Quis custodit custodes?

April 7, 2003

"Researchers have identified a pattern in the molestation crisis afflict-ing the Roman Catholic Church: most of the victims are older boys."

So begins an article by Rachel Zoll from March of last year. Hardly a surprising finding, you might think, but that's because you're not in the sex-abuse industry. The Vatican's recent symposium on child abuse delivered the "state of the art information" that—wait for it— "the majority of cases in the American crisis involve adolescent males

victimized by adult gay priests." And the concern we should have as
a consequence of these discoveries is increased protection for vulnerable boys, right? Wrong again. " 'What I'm afraid of is we're going
into this witch hunt for gays,' said the Rev. Stephen Rossetti, psychologist and sex abuse consultant to the United States Conference
of Catholic Bishops."

Rossetti, the former CEO of the St. Luke Institute, is the author
of the article mentioned below in support of "reintegrating pedophiles".[1] He was invited to address the bishops in Dallas this year, and
had a ringside seat at the Vatican symposium in question. Surprised?
Neither am I.

The *Boston Globe*'s Pulitzer

April 8, 2003

By February of last year, close observers were confident that office
wall space was being cleared at the *Boston Globe* for the inevitable
Pulitzer. The only surprise in yesterday's announcement was that
Donna Morrissey did not pocket an award for best supporting actress.
Some personal reactions to the prize:

- No one doubts that the *Globe*'s editors are as gleeful at the (literal) mortification of the Catholic Church as they are delighted
  by their Pulitzer. That said, what they find repellent about the
  Church is her unchangeable teaching—especially her moral
  teaching, and her sexual moral teaching in particular. In this,
  does the *Globe* differ greatly from the USCCB's Office of Communications? From *Commonweal* and *America* magazines?
- A necessary, though not sufficient, cause of the Pulitzer was
  Judge Sweeney's decision that the Archdiocese of Boston make
  public its records. Had she decided otherwise there would be no
  story, no prize, and no apostolic administrator.
- One unsatisfactory aspect of the *Globe*'s Pulitzer is that it obscures
  excellent reporting on the crisis by the other Boston daily, the

[1] See "Not a Parody", p. 198.

Herald. Journalists Eric Convey, Tom Mashberg, Maggie Mul-
vihill, and Robin Washington stand out in particular. Very often
the same stories fuzzily written by the *Globe* were eminently
lucid and intelligible in the *Herald*'s telling. It should also be
remembered that Kristen Lombardi of the *Boston Phoenix* was
onto the Geoghan scandal a good ten months before the *Globe*'s
blitz in January 2002.

- The *Globe* should be faulted for kid-glove handling of dissenting Catholics who posed as advocates for victims but whose
  "crusade for reform" was politically motivated and aimed at
  weakening the teaching Church. Simple objectivity requires
  that equal skepticism and scrutiny be directed at the motives
  and maneuvers of all contending parties to the dispute. When
  the same priest that leads a campaign to sack his bishop goes
  public in support of gay marriage, one expects an intrepid,
  Pulitzer-laureate reporter to ask a couple of obvious follow-up
  questions. Nada.
- A cardinal's red hat hanging in its trophy room was an obvious
  (and admitted) prize for the *Globe*, yet they have been strangely
  incurious of less sensational but equally serious aspects of the
  crisis. In March 2002 they reported the Jesuits' contention that
  accused abuser Fr. James Talbot's transfer from a high school in
  Boston to one in Maine was "routine", despite plausible claims
  that Talbot's reputation was known to officials before his move.
  Where's the clear-eyed, dogged, intrepid, Pulitzer-quality investigation, etc.?
- The *Globe* is to be commended for posting extensive (though
  selective) documentation on its website.

It has been noticed that winning a Nobel Prize usually spells the
end of the winner's creativity. It will be instructive to see whether
the Pulitzer has the same effect on the *Globe*, such that it rests on
its reportorial laurels. More interesting yet will be the forthcoming
books that describe the investigation from the inside, that tell us
about the stories we never saw, who spiked them, and under what
pressures. The problem, of course, is that there's no Pulitzer at the
end of *that* road.

Not a Parody

April 11, 2003

Perhaps [child molesters'] presence in society can ultimately be healing for us. They challenge us to face an unconscious and primal darkness within humankind. Our inability to face this darkness causes us to stereotype and banish all who embody our estranged dis-passions. In the past, this process spawned Molokai and a host of other human prisons. Today, we are banishing the child molester.

From "The Mark of Cain: Reintegrating Pedophiles", *America*, September 9, 1995. The Rev. Stephen Rossetti of the St. Luke Institute is one of the three or four experts who have taught the U.S. bishops most about child abuse.

Trick Questions

May 14, 2003

Cardinal Mahony's former flatmate Fr. Carl Sutphin is accused of abusing six boys in the 1960s and 1970s, according to a recent article:

Attorneys for Sutphin argued that it is unfair and unconstitutional for the government to file sex abuse charges after so many years. "It is difficult for anyone to recall what they did at specific times on specific days so long ago," lawyer Kay Duffy said after the hearing in Ventura County Superior Court. "We have charges from 30 years ago. We have a very elderly defendant. It's difficult to prepare a defense."

Well, I can't honestly recall what I was doing this day 30 years ago. But I can be very, very sure there were certain things I *didn't* do. My favorite specimen of clerical indignation at the outrageous temerity of trick questions is that of Msgr. Frederick Ryan, who was alleged to have abused a 14-year-old boy in the chancery office (Ryan was at the time vice-chancellor of the Boston Archdiocese): "Asked if he had sexually abused Garland, Ryan replied: 'I don't think that's a fair question. Let me find out what this is about.'"

Good point, Fred. They should at least let you have a look at your desk calendar.

Half of the Lies They Tell about Me Aren't True ...

May 15, 2003

"You can trust Dallas bishop Charles V. Grahmann in at least one respect: the man is reliably untrustworthy."

So begins this morning's editorial in the *Dallas Morning News*. That's the good part. The editorial goes on—with painfully well-aimed documentation—to condemn the diocese's "lies and evasions" regarding the most recent in its long series of wayward priests.

Ten years ago it was said, with justice, that the media elites hated the Catholic Church not for her vices but for her virtues, and media criticism of the Church could be taken as an excellent sign that she was doing her job. Happy days.

The Church will prevail, of course. Reform is inevitable. Weak, vain, and deceitful clerics will be replaced by sturdier and more honest men. It isn't anti-Catholic, however, to hope that the reform happens sooner rather than later. It isn't disloyal to hope that the changes come about through decisive intervention rather than the operation of blind Darwinian forces of sterility and spiritual disease. It isn't captious to hope that, when the crisis bottoms out, the faithful remaining might be 90 percent, instead of 15 percent, of their present number.

Applets and Oranges

July 20, 2003

> An Orange County Roman Catholic priest has been accused of having child-pornographic images on his computer, yet the Diocese of Orange continues to let him serve as a priest, using legalistic excuses why child porn doesn't fall under the diocese's "zero tolerance" policy. The diocese doesn't want you to know who the priest is, where he is serving or whether he is anywhere near children.

So begins an editorial by Steven Greenhut in today's *Orange County Register*. According to Greenhut, one Fernando Guido found kiddie porn on a laptop previously owned by a priest of the Diocese of Orange. He notified the diocese, which did the right thing insofar as it referred the matter to the police. The police decided not to pursue the matter, according to Guido, because the porn images may have been only pop-up ads. The priest was permitted to resume ministry. But now it gets interesting.

> In his letter to the DA, Guido explains his frustration: "I am deeply disappointed at the diocese because they decided to only give him 'psychological help.' But if history can teach us anything about these types of cases, one can see that this does not help. Many of the priests who have been convicted of child molestation or rape were given psychological help at one time or another. I would have wanted to see him ... removed from any activity where he has contact with minors. I just see him as a walking time bomb." ... Guido said the diocese told him the accused priest admitted having "sexual immaturities."

There are lots of holes in the story as reported, and it isn't clear whether the "psychological help" in question was diagnostic or therapeutic in nature, or whether the diocese has taken disciplinary measures with respect to the priest in question that it hasn't made public. From the information given it's far from obvious—to me, at any rate—that the diocese violated its zero-tolerance policy.

And that's the point. No policy, however meticulously enforced, can exhaust the number of ways in which a priest may render himself unserviceable as a minister of the Gospel. The *Orange County Register* pushes the pedophilia button as hard as it can in the editorial, and frames the story as a children-at-risk shocker. But even if the man in question is not a sexual threat to children or to anyone else, his dalliance with porn means something is seriously wrong with his heart, with his priesthood. We don't expect the newspapers to bother about what makes a good priest, but we might well expect the diocese to care.

Writing about the laws of prosody to be followed in composing poetry, Dr. Johnson said, "Rules may obviate faults, but can never confer beauties"—i.e., a poet may dutifully avoid any blunders in meter and scansion, and still come up with a bad poem. Analogously, the policies which the bishops enact in response to The Crisis may eliminate clergy who commit sexual felonies. That does not mean that the priests will be holy men. That does not mean that the spiritual harms caused by priests will be diminished in any measure whatsoever. The culture of moral defeatism that penalizes crimes but tolerates objectively disordered sexuality has enfeebled the priesthood and the episcopacy as well.

Parturient montes, nascetur ridiculus mus

July 24, 2003

After months of fanfare, and a grotesquely elaborate windup, Massachusetts Attorney General Tom Reilly has revealed that—wait for it—his subordinates are capable of reading the Boston Globe. The AG deserves a C-minus on his deplorably lightweight Report on the Sexual Abuse of Children in the Archdiocese of Boston.

Not a single new name appears, and not a single new fact—indeed, there are very few facts at all, except for some fairly lame tabulations (789 purported victims, etc.). Contrast this with the report on the Diocese of Manchester by the New Hampshire Attorney General's Office, in which nearly every page has precise and well-documented evidence, with a minimum of heavy breathing for the benefit of the media.

Writing of the scandal sixteen months ago, columnist Ann Coulter said:

> It is a fact that the vast majority of the abuser priests—more than 90 percent—are accused of molesting teen-age boys. Indeed, the overwhelmingly homosexual nature of the abuse prompted the New York Times to engage in its classic "Where's Waldo" reporting style, in which the sex of the victims is studiedly hidden amid a torrent of genderless words, such as the "teen-ager," the "former student," the "victim" and the "accuser."

Coulter could have been speaking of the Reilly Report. While the gender of the victims is mentioned sparingly, the age of the victims seems to be eclipsed entirely. Nor do the words "gay" or "homosexual" appear in its 91 pages.

Perhaps we're close to the explanation for the report's curiously vague character. As Fr. Richard Neuhaus pointed out, the priest abuse scandal is an instance in which the media elites love the sin but hate the sinner. Given his political fealty to Massachusetts Democrats, and their significant others, Reilly is no position to connect the dots too clearly in this business.

Who gets a boot in the ribs from Reilly? Cardinal Law, obviously, plus Bishops Murphy, McCormack, Hughes, and Banks. What do they have in common? Coincidentally, they are all out of the picture, all out of range of his own responsibility. The signal is clear: the artillery discharge was for its fireworks effect. Nobody gets hurt. Nothing will change. The system takes care of its own.

Explication du texte

June 3, 2003

This clause from Bishop O'Brien's plea bargain merits reflection: "During the course of the grand jury's investigation, to this date, no credible evidence has been received that would establish that Thomas J. O'Brien personally engaged in criminal sexual misconduct." By this lawyerly phrasing we are free to infer that

1. evidence has been received that would establish that O'Brien personally engaged in criminal sexual misconduct, but the witnesses were not forensically credible; or
2. credible indications have been received that would establish that O'Brien personally engaged in criminal sexual misconduct, but it doesn't qualify as evidence; or
3. credible evidence has been received that would establish that O'Brien personally engaged in sexual misconduct, but such conduct was not criminal; or
4. credible evidence has been received suggesting that O'Brien personally engaged in criminal sexual misconduct, but it fails (note the qualification "to this date") to establish this as fact.

Is it possible that none of the above is true? If so, what conceivable purpose could there be for including such a sentence? This isn't the DA's press release, remember; this is wording agreed to by both parties, doubtless minutely studied by O'Brien's attorneys, and signed by O'Brien himself. It's unimaginable that O'Brien and his legal team would have consented to such a degrading formulation unless they were under compulsion—i.e., unless the alternatives were even worse.

So what do we do now? The Phoenix DA—and, with the DA's pistol to his head, the bishop himself—have written in six-foot letters for all to see that O'Brien was an active homosexual whose cover-ups were a consequence of sexual complicity or blackmail or both. We can (and most will) continue to pretend that there is a more innocent explanation. If so, we'll hand another tactical victory to the Ziemanns, Weaklands, Ryans, O'Connells, and other twisted bishops whose aggression and mendacity gave them decades of cost-free mischief at the Church's expense.

Privileged Communications

November 24, 2003

The Archdiocese of Los Angeles is fighting to keep personnel records from being turned over to a grand jury investigating sexual abuse.

> Lawyers for the archdiocese say their effort is not a cover-up, but rather a simple matter of law. They are asserting a First Amendment privilege of freedom of religion, an extension of priest-penitent confidentiality to cover communications between priests and their superiors, and adherence to the grand jury process that mandates secrecy. The archdiocese's attorneys characterize the legal battle over the church documents as "religious persecution."
>
> "The relationship between priest and church is a familial relationship, such as the husband-wife privilege. It goes to the heart of the ability to function as a church that has a celibate priesthood," archdiocese attorney J. Thomas Hennigan said. "These men, otherwise isolated from society, need a place to be able to discuss their innermost problems that is secure. It's not an effort to protect pedophiles."

In the many thousands of pages of documents that became public in the case of the Archdiocese of Boston, was there a single instance of a communication that approximates confessional secrecy—a letter, e.g., in which a priest writes, "Archbishop, I am asking that you find help for me in overcoming difficulties in the following area of personal weakness ..."? Apart from the archbishop's notoriously sympathetic valedictory letters to retired abusers, did the archived correspondence betray anything close to familial intimacy?

Perhaps it did, but if so the edifying documents were never scrutinized. The unmistakable impression left by the communications we have seen—including the e-mails between Cardinal Mahony and his associates that were hacked last year—is that of calculated managerial aloofness.

The problem is that confidential communications are often necessary—wholly apart from confessional matters. To give just one example, the U.S. bishops have consistently (and properly) defended the right to marry of persons canonically free to do so. In cases where one of the parties is an illegal alien, and application for a civil license would mean deportation, the sacramental marriage can be effected clandestinely—out of the view, that is, of civil authority. And of course the clandestine marriage must be recorded.

But if confidentiality is forfeited, such marriages are no longer clandestine. One would be proud to be a Catholic if a bishop were to say, "I prefer to go to jail for contempt of court rather than make our records public," and then the records revealed not priestly wrongdoing but priestly solicitude, e.g., for the marriage of illiterate farm laborers. But it would be an abomination if a bishop were to invoke clerical privilege *cynically and in bad faith* in order to protect active gays from public odium and himself from prosecution, and then—once the lies were exposed and the privileges lost—the Church were crippled in fulfilling her spiritual mission.

A Thought Experiment

February 21, 2004

Imagine a large suburban high school whose faculty and administration (considered a unity for present purposes) devises a series of programs to deal with the problem of student drug dealers. After some months of very mixed results it happens that a faculty member himself is arrested for selling drugs; then another; then two more in quick succession.

At a certain point the public will begin to feel, not only that the faculty is neglecting the students' interests, but that the core problem is within its own ranks. But at what point?

Suppose further certain complicating factors: that faculty members in almost every case are recruited and hired on the recommendation of two or three faculty acquaintances. That the faculty has for years been eerily ambivalent on the morality of recreational drug use. That students who complained that faculty had used or dealt drugs were often ignored, often reviled, and invariably saddled with such a high burden of proof that not a single student- or parent-initiated complaint resulted in disciplinary action against a faculty member. Ever.

Suppose that many of the student drug dealers were widely known to be teacher's pets. That many faculty members had been aware of student drug dealing but ignored it. That the pressure on the faculty to resolve the problem came entirely from outside its ranks, from clean students and parents themselves. That even this pressure was successfully resisted until law enforcement and media took notice of unconcealable crimes. That dealer students, when disciplined, were often given shockingly lenient punishments.

Suppose that it was wholly unknown for the faculty to identify and expel one of its own for drug use. That *in every single case* the faculty drug dealers were discharged only after an arrest by police or after overwhelmingly disgraceful media exposure.

Gives you a funny feeling inside, doesn't it?

Now imagine this. Not only does the faculty give absolutely zero indication that there is a problem that needs fixing in its own ranks, but it continues to speak exclusively—without exception—of a problem "out there", among the students, and continues to speak of itself as the perfectly obvious body to effect the cure.

Thankfully, no such school exists, or could exist. Education, after all, requires a measure of trust.

Healing and Forgiveness: A Primer

May 19, 2004

> A priest convicted of public indecency last year is returning to the ministry next week, the Archdiocese of Cincinnati announced today.... Archbishop Daniel E. Pilarczyk reaffirmed that the church demands and that he expects priests to live in celibate chastity. However, he noted, the Gospel also calls for healing and forgiveness.

Distinguo.

Case A. Say my neighbor's children, not liking the sound of my last name, pitch rocks through my living room window and yell insults. My sons grab baseball bats and start to head out the door to thrash the aggressors. I stop them and remind them that the Gospel calls for forgiveness, and as Christians we should not only forswear vengeance for wrongs suffered but accept injuries as a step toward reconciliation.

Case B. My children, not liking the sound of my neighbor's last name, pitch rocks through his living room window and yell insults at him. When my neighbor comes over to complain of my sons' mischief and asks that I punish them and pay for their damage, I tell him that the Gospel calls for healing and forgiveness, and insinuate that it is un-Christian of him to seek retribution.

Got the picture, Your Excellency? Now follow me closely here: Case A is GOOD. Case B is NOT GOOD. For a Christian, forgiveness is something the injured party freely offers the man who inflicts the injury, not an obligation the injurer exacts from the man he injured.

Now comes the tricky part, the conclusion few bishops seem able to grasp: if I use my Roman collar to gain your son's trust and then rape him, it's NOT GOOD for me to lecture you on your duty of forgiveness and reconciliation. And the same goes for priests who harm the faithful by gross displays of deviant sexuality.

Would a puppet show help make the point clear?

I'm Not as Think as You Drunk I Am

July 7, 2004

In the country of Freedonia, the Catholic Church is plagued by catastrophically harmful automobile accidents caused by her clergy. Every year dozens of innocent persons are killed by priests who run red lights or who cross the center line while driving, and hundreds more are left disfigured or crippled for life. The money paid in liability settlements is staggering—so much so that in certain places parishes and schools must be closed for lack of funds.

In 85 percent of the cases, the priest or bishop was drunk when he killed or injured someone with his car. However, despite the fact that Freedonian priests have a notoriously high level of alcoholism, and despite the fact that confirmed incidents of drunk driving by priests

are grossly disproportionate to the rest of the population, the Freedonian bishops loudly repeat the claims of therapists (in their hire)
who insist that, while alcoholism is a "risk factor" for drunk driving
accidents, it does not *cause* drunk driving accidents (which are attrib-
utable not to alcoholism but to poor judgment and impaired motor
skills). Alcoholics, it is chanted mantra style, are no more likely to
lose control of the Buick than anybody else who chugs two-thirds of
a bottle of Bushmills in five minutes.

Bishop Felix Sunshine, president of the Freedonian bishops' conference, has gained national prominence for his dramatic displays
of concern for victims of vehicular homicide, and has even invited
experts from Seagram's and Anheuser-Busch to lecture his colleagues
on motoring safety. Sunshine—who has trembling hands and a nose
like a red asteroid—truculently maintains that "those who want to
start a witch hunt for alcoholics" are motivated by ignorance and
malice and looking for a "scapegoat" on which to lay the blame for
the problem. The Seagram's and Anheuser-Busch people concur.

The crisis is given a special twist by the fact that the clergy involved
in negligent manslaughter are almost always repeat offenders whose
problems with alcohol and driving were known to their superiors—
although often, earlier mishaps involved only property damage or
injury to clergy-passengers, and so did not entail criminal prosecution. There is a poignancy in the scene of Freedonian Massgoers
slumped in wheelchairs and adjusting their braces and eye patches
while listening to a rancorous homily on their duty not to be judgmental: "As church, we are about giving chinners a shecond shance."

The Diocese of Askelon, after shelling out $53 million in per-
sonal injury settlements and faced with several dozen new claims,
declares itself bankrupt. Many laymen are distressed, despite Bishop
Sunshine's reassurance that no collection dollars were redirected and
that plaintiffs were paid out of a special toffee tin kept near the front
door and used for extraordinary expenses like Girl Scout cookies and
shoelaces. When, however, Sunshine nails a seven-point "Friends
Don't Let Friends Drive Drunk" covenant to the door of the Happy
Hour Lounge in Anglesea (requiring every priest to be driven by a
licensed private chauffeur at all times), the Freedonians put aside their
doubts, embrace the episcopacy in a new spirit of trust and openness,
and live happily ever after.

Bishops and Indifference to Suffering

May 22, 2005

Ancient Israel had no police force or DA's office. Thus, if you were the victim of an injustice, the only option open to you (apart from an ad hoc vendetta) was to try to get the attention of a judge. A person without wealth, family, or important allies found it all but impossible to bribe or intimidate a judge into looking into his case. For this reason the prophets insist that widows and orphans have their day in court, and denounce indifferent or corrupt judges who attend only to the mighty.

> Every one loves a bribe and runs after gifts.
> They do not hear the case of the orphan,
> and the widow's cause does not come to them.
> Therefore says the Lord, the Mighty One of Israel:
> I shall vent my wrath on my enemies, and avenge myself on
> my foes. [Is 1:23–24]

Most Catholic bishops—and what I say about bishops applies throughout to superiors of religious congregations—view themselves as champions of the downtrodden and take sincere satisfaction in their hospices, their charities, their work for senior-friendly legislation, etc. They would reject with indignation the accusation of indifference to human suffering—especially regarding widows and orphans—since a good portion of every working day is devoted to relieving such suffering.

Yet good intentions and altruistic energy can coexist with colossal moral blind spots. In fact, the higher one's moral self-image, the more difficult (it would seem) to come to terms with misdeeds that violate that image. We see painfully concrete examples of this in the bishops' handling of clerical sexual abuse, brought into focus yet again by last week's California revelations. How is it that the same person who spends hundreds of hours a year lobbying, say, for family health care, can receive a letter from a poor divorcée claiming that a priest is molesting her child, and then ignore the problem, or hand it off to a flunky, or send a growling letter demanding proof, or silently relocate the priest among other divorcées with other vulnerable children?

Fully conscious villainy accounts for some cases; blackmail or fear of blackmail for others. But I suspect that, in most instances, the reason for episcopal injustice was the dilemma of weak men faced with an overwhelming Inequality of Consequence.

Here's what I mean. At some level, every U.S. bishop has been aware of a huge problem with sexual irregularity among priests, of which child abuse was but one particularly sordid manifestation. But who wanted to be first to tackle the problem, to open an abyss of horror underneath his feet (and those of his brother bishops)? The negative consequences of facing the music were obvious and incalculably great. The negative consequences of the damage control approach, however, were largely invisible—because these negative consequences were largely in the spiritual order. It wasn't just a question of weighing the alternatives and following the line of least resistance. There was scarcely any comparison: on the one hand, a leap into a bottomless pit of woes; on the other, business as usual, a look the other way, a meaningful nod to a lackey, and tomorrow looks much like today. The only thing lost is souls.

Forced to account for their injustice against the weak, most bishops excuse themselves, saying, "If what is known now was known then, we would have acted differently." This is partly sincere and partly dishonest. What has changed is the level of public scrutiny—not the bishops' knowledge but ours. Yet it's true that it's hard to see as injustice what is common practice in one's profession, tacitly accepted by nearly all members. And again, most bishops have a congratulatory self-image as *vindicators* of the oppressed. In these circumstances, it's an all-but-impossible psychological feat to view oneself as one of the sneering, corrupt, bribe-taking judges of the Old Testament, contemptuous of the widow—even when you have her handwritten letter on your desk pleading for justice. Margaret Gallant's plea to Cardinal Medeiros about John Geoghan still hurts to read after 23 years:

> Our family is deeply rooted in the Catholic Church, our great-grandparents and parents suffered hardship and persecution for love of the Church. Our desire is to protect the dignity of the Holy Orders, even in the midst of our tears and agony over the seven boys in our family who have been violated. We cannot undo that, but we are obligated to protect others from this abuse to the Mystical Body of Jesus Christ....

[Geoghan's] actions are not only destructive to the emotional well-being of the children, but hits the very core of our being in our love for the church—he would not gain access to homes of fallen away Catholics.... Truly, my heart aches for him and I pray for him, because I know this must tear him apart too; but I cannot allow my compassion for him to cloud my judgment on acting for the people of God, and the children in the Church.

My heart is broken over this whole mess—and to address my Cardinal in this manner has taken its toll on me too.

The "cry of the poor" doesn't get any clearer than that. Yet the bribe that made Medeiros and his brothers avert their eyes was not financial but something closer to the bone. When an injustice is so blatant as to scream for remedy, and that remedy entails facing the music at the heart of one's own life, and that in turn means tearing up the fabric of a whole lifetime of moral compromises, the injustice never becomes "real"—it's just too easy to go on pretending. An aphorism of Nietzsche applies here: " 'I have done that,' says my memory. 'I cannot have done that,' says my pride, and remains adamant. At last—memory yields."

Almost all bishops can admit to mistakes; almost none to iniquity. After the recent release of diocesan files, abuse victim David Guerrero is quoted as saying, "I would say Bishop [Michael] Driscoll's a sick, immoral person to allow something like this to take place." On his diocesan website, the same Bishop Driscoll insists, "I am completely and wholeheartedly committed to the safety of children."

They're both right.

Healing What? Protecting Whom?

June 24, 2005

Remember when the apostles James and John, the sons of Zebedee, commissioned a post-Judas investigative report on the causes of treachery? Neither do I.

Bishops also agreed to spend up to $1.5 million from a $20 million endowment fund to partly fund a massive study on the causes of priestly sexual abuse. The USCCB hopes to raise the remainder of the cost of the study, slated to cost between $3 million and $5 million, from private foundations.

Is there a single Catholic on the planet—and I include the bishops' own mothers in the question—who really believes the purpose of this study is to discover—and not to camouflage—the causes of priestly sexual abuse? Bishop Howard Hubbard's private investigator charged him $2.4 million to come to the conclusion that allegations of sexual misconduct made against him had "no merit"—and nobody laughed. Here too we can be sublimely confident that the scholars whom the bishops commission will find the principal "cause" of sexual abuse to be insufficient attention to the notions of the scholars whom the bishops commission. Expect multiple appendices detailing improved reporting procedures, seminary screening for doctrinal rigidity, and recipes for Rice Krispies Marshmallow Treats. In the same spirit of confidence, let me foretell some conclusions the researchers *won't* draw:

- Apostolic Pro-Nuncio Jean Jadot (1973–1980) significantly damaged the U.S. episcopacy by the appointment of young, gay-friendly bishops who formed a self-defense network still in force.
- The institutional "occasion" of the crisis is not secrecy, but blackmail, in which secrecy is merely instrumental. A clergyman with dirt in his past—whether hetero- or homosexual in nature—is blackmailable and incapable of acting against the crimes of other clergy except under duress.
- Psychotherapists don't fix sins.
- Too many individuals employed in priestly formation were and are in the business because they like to be around young men. This is not unconnected with the grossly defective instruction common in post-WW2 seminaries.
- "Between men who want to have sex with adolescent boys and men who do not want to have sex with adolescent boys, the former are more likely to have sex with adolescent boys" (Richard Neuhaus).
- Blackmail is not eradicated by systemic change or bureaucratic adjustment: firings (or firing squads) are necessary.

While Bishops Dupre and O'Connell are still refusing to testify about their own sexual abuse—with their brethren at least tacitly consenting—$1.5 million–plus is going into the pockets of those who will almost certainly not tell us what Dupre and O'Connell can tell us about "the causes".

Trust restored yet?

Priestly Formation in L.A.

November 17, 2005

The *L.A. Times* has a bruising story on St. John's Camarillo, the seminary of the Archdiocese of Los Angeles. The grenade graf says, "About 10% of St. John's graduates reported to have been ordained in the Los Angeles Archdiocese since 1950—65 of roughly 625—have been accused of molesting minors," and the article goes on to paint a picture of sexual anarchy (largely, but not entirely, homosexual) on the seminary grounds. One former seminarian reports that he often could not use the dorm bathroom at night "because it was occupied by men having sex." Many L.A. priests interviewed claim to have been oblivious to the situation when they attended St. John's, and it must be conceded that the *Times* wants to foreground the most lurid allegations, but on the other hand the picture is different in no important respect from that given in Jason Berry's 1992 book on The Crisis.

Among several lines in the story worthy of comment, this one struck me:

> J. Michael Hennigan, a lawyer for the archdiocese, conceded that exaggerated claims alone cannot account for the large numbers of alleged abusers in some graduating classes.
>
> "There were a couple of years at that seminary where lightning struck," Hennigan said. "I doubt we'll ever figure out why."

"I doubt we'll ever figure out why." That sounds less like a man who has been flummoxed in his search for an elusive answer than one with zero appetite to find the answer in the first place. Is it really impossible to find out the causes?

When U.S. State Department official Alger Hiss was finally exposed as a Soviet agent in 1949, the government departments for which he worked did not simply give a "Who wudda thunk it?" shrug and move on to business as usual. Researchers made an extraordinarily detailed examination of Hiss' entire career, asking above all, "Whom did Hiss bring into government work? Whom did Hiss promote or recommend for sensitive tasks? Whom did Hiss try to torpedo? Who went out of his way to advance Hiss' career?" The premise, obviously, is that a security failure is rarely an isolated occurrence, that other miscreants will have escaped detection, and that by taking back-bearings one can discover some of the still-hidden villains among those whom the known subversive regarded as friendly. In the case of Hiss, both those he helped and those who helped him included men who turned out to be fellow Communists—in addition to many dupes, of course.

Granted, a diocese lacks trained investigators and subpoena powers to conduct a full-scale government-style investigation. But then, a full-scale investigation isn't called for: we're talking about 625 men. If they wanted to know the answer badly enough they could put the right questions to the right people and connect the dots that would explain how it came about that "lightning struck" when and where it did.

"I doubt we'll ever figure out why." I doubt you will either, Mike, especially if you know the answer already.

It Isn't as It Wasn't, or Was It?

May 16, 2006

An old blues number bore the elegantly pleonastic title "Do What You Did When You Did What You Done Last Night". Well, whatever Msgr. CB of the Vatican Secretariat of State did last night, he didn't do what he did when he done what attracted the attention of the Rome police, and then the Italian press, this past Thursday.

According to a story in *La Repubblica*, later amplified by the news service ANSA, an office functionary of the Secretariat of State was stopped by cops while cruising late at night in a park known to be frequented by obdurate Albigensians. He fled, denting three cars in the chase, then got into a fistfight with the cops. The story supplies the edifying detail that the cleric, identified only as "Msgr. CB", excused himself to the police on the grounds that he was scouting only for adult schismatics—not minors. We are an Easter People.

Yesterday the Holy See Press Office issued a statement so art-fully packed with escape hatches as to defy translation. A coarse approximation:

> Being in receipt of the necessary information from the Secretariat of State, this Press Office is in a position to [*in grado di*] make it clear that the information disseminated this morning by the newspapers concern-ing an ecclesiastic working at the Vatican is wholly without foundation.

If the first you'd heard of the incident came from this statement, you could be excused for feeling less than fully enlightened. The statement continued: "To be foreseen is recourse to legal measures against those who have contributed to defaming the good name of said official."

Well, at worst the man's good initials were defamed, since his actual name hasn't made it into the media reports yet. At any rate, the newspapers announced they're sticking by their story. Strangely—or perhaps not so strangely, given Cardinal Sodano's superintendency of the persons involved—the Press Office has taken down Monday's statement from its website, and the link is now broken.

If you're one of those many Catholics who've been puzzled at how often the Holy See's own diplomatic corps succeeds in torpedo-ing the initiatives of the papacy itself, you may find the episode eerily familiar. Arguments from silence are weak, but presumably we're now meant to be free to think that the foundationlessness of the disseminated information is not on the brink of being demonstrated as expeditiously as it was yesterday morning. Clear, I trust? Either Monsignor didn't not do what he was said to have not did when he done it—or he did.

Through the Looking-Glass: A New Fragment

March 25, 2006

From an early draft manuscript of Chapter IV, recently found among Dodgson's papers at Christ Church, Oxford. Readers are reminded that

*state-mandated Vulnerable Minor Protection Programs were in their infancy
in the 1870s. Tenniel's illustrations, of course, belong to the edition of 1872.*

"So *much* obliged!" added Diddletwee. "You like poetry?"

"Ye-es, pretty well—*some* poetry," Alice said doubtfully. "Is it
very long?"

"It's long," said the Diddletwum, "but it's very, very beautiful.
Everybody that hears me sing it—either it brings the *tears* into their
eyes, or else—"

"Or else what?" said Alice, as Diddletwum had made a sudden
pause.

"Or else it doesn't, you know. The name of the song is called
'Talking about Touching'."

"Oh, that's the name of the song, is it?" Alice said, trying to feel
interested.

"No, you don't understand," Diddletwee said, looking a little
vexed. "That's what the name is *called*. The name really is 'Boundaries Are Beautiful'."

"Then I ought to have said, 'That's what the *song* is called'?" Alice
corrected herself.

"No, you oughtn't: that's quite another thing! The *song* is called
'We Have All Been Enlightened': but that's only what it's *called*, you
know!"

"Well, what *is* the song, then?" said Alice, who was by this time
completely bewildered.

"I was coming to that," Diddletwum said. "The song really *is* 'The
Ballad of Petey the Parrot'," he continued, giving his brother a hug.
Diddletwee smiled gently, and began:

> "Petey the Parrot served twenty-one months
> Of a rap for indecent exposure.
> His bishop paroled him and gave him a perch
> On his pear-wood episcopal crosier.
>
> He scolded the skeptics who labeled the bird
> Unsuited for pastoral placement:
> 'I'm giving him charge of the CCD staff
> And a suite in the chancery basement.'

Hide the eggs, Gwendolyn; hide the eggs, Tom!
  Hide the eggs, Kate and Kareem!
Petey the sinister Young Adult Minister's
  back on the pastoral team!
With an aawk! and a squawwk! twenty months and you walk,
  back on the pastoral team!

Petey was therapized, pampered, prepared,
Pronounced cured by professional weasels
Who shortly thereafter were found to have died
From a sorrowful shortage of T-cells.

The cops nearly nabbed him at Cock-à-Two's Bar
But Petey was just enough quicker
To fly through the window, and home, where he found
He'd been named archdiocesan vicar.

Hide the eggs, Gwendolyn; hide the eggs, Tom!
  Hide the eggs, Kate and Kareem!
Petey the sinister Young Adult Minister's
  back on the pastoral team!
With an aawk! and a squawwk! twenty months and you walk,
  back on the pastoral team!

When the parents complained that his ministry style
Included nonstandard relations,
The kindly old bishop asked Petey to screen
First his phone calls, and then his vocations.

It didn't take long for the entering class
To grow from near thirty to—zero.
Now Petey's a bishop himself, don't you know,
And described as 'the NCR's hero'.

Hide the eggs, Gwendolyn; hide the eggs, Tom!
  Hide the eggs, Kate and Kareem!
Petey the sinister Young Adult Minister's
  back on the pastoral team!
With an aawk! and a squawwk! twenty months and you walk,
  back on the pastoral team!"

"I like the cops best," said Alice: "because they were a *little* sorry for the poor hatchlings."

"They asked the DA to take them off the case, though," said Diddletwee: "Contrariwise."

The Legion of Christ and Its Founder

February 17, 2009

What do we know about the misbehavior of Fr. Marcial Maciel Degollado, deceased founder of the Legion of Christ? In strict terms: nothing. In part this is the fault of the Holy See, whose 2006 communiqué did not specify the wrongs in response to which it "invited" Maciel to "a reserved life of prayer and penance." In part it is the fault of the Legion of Christ, which issues assertions about Maciel while withholding the evidence on which the assertions are grounded. In place of publicly verifiable data—such as checkable documents and signed testimony—we have coy and ambiguous declarations based on informal confidential investigations. This is not knowledge.

In early February the Legion's spokesman Fr. Paolo Scarafoni announced that Maciel had sired an illegitimate daughter, now in her twenties. The CNS story reports, "Asked how the Legionaries came to know about her, Father Scarafoni said, 'Frankly, I cannot say and it is not opportune to discuss this further, also because there are people involved' who deserve privacy." This is a transparent falsehood. Scarafoni was in reality communicating, "Frankly, I cannot be frank about this matter." Tactical mendacity of this kind is beloved of Roman churchmen (think of the Jesuit General's claim that there is no conflict between the Society and the Holy See); it is not intended to be credible, but it serves as a kind of No Trespassing sign, warning outsiders that further inquiry along a given line will not be tolerated. Granted, however, that we don't and can't know whether Maciel's paternity is better founded than any other claim the Legion has made about him, the remarks that follow will assume that this minimal admission is true.

Maciel deserves to be reviled by the Legionaries of Christ. By "deserves" I mean his revilement is a debt of justice owed all Catholics by the Legion. This is not on account of Maciel's sin of sexual weakness, nor even on account of the sin of denying his sexual weakness. The fact of the matter is that Maciel was publicly accused of specific sexual crimes, and that out of moral cowardice he enlisted honorable men and women to mortgage their own reputations in defense of his lie. The lie was the lie of Maciel's personal sanctity, which Maciel knew to be a myth, and which the fact of his paternity (putting aside the more squalid accusations) proves that he knew. To the villainy of sacrificing the reputations of others, Maciel added the grotesque and blasphemous claim that the Holy See's sanctions were *an answer to his own prayer* to share more deeply in the Passion of Christ, as an innocent victim made to bear the burden of false judgment in reparation for the sins of mankind. The Legion cannot share Catholic reverence for the Passion and fail to repudiate Maciel's cynicism in portraying himself as the Suffering Servant.

Yet the LC leadership persists in allotting Maciel a role of (somewhat tarnished) honor: praising with faint damns, and suggesting that his spiritual patrimony remains valuable in spite of his personal life. This won't work.

Many of the greatest saints were repentant sinners. Yet not only did Maciel (as far as is known) go to his death without repenting, but he used wholesome Christian spirituality *as a tool in the deception of others*. Think of the Soviet mole Kim Philby: while he worked in the U.K.'s SIS [Secret Intelligence Service] and Foreign Office, his articulate patriotism may have inspired those he duped to a deeper love of country. Yet once he was unmasked as a spy, and after his patriotism was revealed as a contrived distraction from his real treachery, even those who were moved to genuine loyalty by his speeches would not continue to feed on them. And note: Philby's patriotic words would provoke the most shame and disgust precisely in the persons who found those words truest.

Or consider a woman whose husband ingeniously hid his infidelities from her for many years. Once she realized she had been deceived, the gifts he brought back from his business trips would be understood to have been instruments in that deception. Far from cherishing the jewelry he gave her, she'd feel that the diamonds now mocked the affection and fidelity they symbolized. By the same token, Maciel's addresses will be spiritually kosher—he was after all a highly successful deceiver. But those addresses dishonor the very truths they expound, and it's impossible that they can cause anything but distress and confusion in those who attempt to nourish themselves on them.

To repeat: the fact that he was a flawed priest is not the reason for repudiating Maciel. The Mexican priest-protagonist of Graham Greene's novel *The Power and the Glory* was enfeebled by lust and alcoholism and despised by those he served; yet, because of his concern for souls, he kept himself in the arena of danger and died a martyr. Maciel presents Greene's image flipped on its head: he was a Mexican priest with an internationally cultivated reputation for sanctity. He lived surrounded and cosseted by admirers, and yet in reality he held divine retribution so lightly that he went to his deathbed without undeceiving those he'd taken in, leaving behind him shattered consciences and wobbly faith.

When I speak of the Legion's duty of revilement, I do not mean they should issue so many pages of rhetorical denunciation of Maciel's sexual iniquities. What is required is an unambiguous admission that Maciel deceitfully made use of holy things and holy words in order to dupe honest and pious persons into taking false positions—sometimes slandering others in the process—in order to reinforce the legend of his own sanctity. Since Maciel's treachery was sacrilegious in its means and in its effect, he should posthumously be repudiated as a model of priesthood and of Christian life.

What is said above is predicated on the minimalist assumption that Maciel's siring of a daughter is the only canonical lapse that can be held against him. Yet he stood accused of sins much more serious, including the sin of *absolutio complicis*—i.e., of sacramentally absolving one's own partner in sexual wrongdoing. The Legion's leadership professes improbably comprehensive ignorance of Maciel's misdeeds, but even if they are in fact in the dark about Maciel's guilt in this area, they surely must understand that abuse of the sacrament of confession moves the debate over Maciel's priesthood onto an entirely different level than a failure in sexual continence. True, we don't expect *Newsweek* or NPR to focus on the gravity of abusing a sacrament, because for them sacraments are simply ceremonies. But we would expect orthodox Catholic priests to grasp the importance of the charge. Knowing what they now claim to know about Maciel's sexual delinquency, can the Legion confidently dismiss the accusation of abuse of the confessional? And if they can't dismiss it out of hand, how can they fail to address it, even obliquely, in their statements? How can they keep up the public patter of his "flawed priesthood" without the certainty—the *certainty*—that there are not souls out there that need concrete sacramental help, souls whose access to the sacraments Maciel may have blocked by his villainy?

The Legion leadership's piecemeal public disclosure broadens rather than narrows the general speculation about the extent of Maciel's crimes. Today and for the foreseeable future they're in the "half of the lies they tell about me aren't true" position. They have only themselves to blame. Whereas St. Augustine said, "God does not need my lie," the Legion's officialdom appears to base its strategy of teaspoon-by-teaspoon revelations on the contrary conviction: "God needs our falsehood, and yours as well."

Yet what are we to make of the Legionaries who aren't superiors and who remain under a vow of obedience to those who are? Are they complicit in the actions of their superiors simply by remaining bound by their vows? If Maciel has real victims whose urgent spiritual needs are being ignored or dismissed by the leadership, can the Legionaries who would wish to address those needs act on their own to do so? If not, what is the course an honorable man would take, and how might the Holy See make it possible for him to act in conformity with a well-formed conscience while remaining a religious in good standing? Many persons of goodwill who are associated with the Legion and Regnum Christi have called for prayers for Maciel's victims. This is entirely proper. But if you were a victim of Maciel, and had been denounced as a slanderer for accusing him, and that denunciation had never been unsaid, would you feel spiritually buoyed by the promise of prayers offered on your behalf?

Right from the Beginning

March 31, 2009

The NCR makes available some correspondence of Fr. Gerald Fitzgerald, founder of the Servants of the Paraclete, who was able to call a spade a spade even without the benefit of postgraduate research in the human sciences.

As early as the mid-1950s, decades before the clergy sexual-abuse crisis broke publicly across the U.S. Catholic landscape, the founder of a religious order that dealt regularly with priest sex abusers was so convinced of their inability to change that he searched for an island to purchase with the intent of using it as a place to isolate such offenders, according to documents recently obtained by NCR.

Fr. Gerald Fitzgerald, founder of the Servants of the Paracletes [sic], an order established in 1947 to deal with problem priests, wrote regularly to bishops in the United States and to Vatican officials, including the pope, of his opinion that many sexual abusers in the priesthood should be laicized immediately.

[chop]

In a September 1952 letter to the then-bishop of Reno, Nev., Fitzgerald wrote: "I myself would be inclined to favor laicization for any priest, upon objective evidence, for tampering with the virtue of the young, my argument being, from this point onward the charity to the Mystical Body should take precedence over charity to the individual and when a man has so far fallen away from the purpose of the priesthood the very best that should be offered him is his Mass in the seclusion of a monastery. Moreover, in practice, real conversions will be found to be extremely rare.... Hence, leaving them on duty or wandering from diocese to diocese is contributing to scandal or at least to the approximate [i.e., proximate] danger of scandal."

The Fitzgerald correspondence has in fact been known for some time. The *Washington Post* surfaced it six years ago, and OTR posted reactions several times. What may appear as Fitzgerald's prescience most of us would call common sense. He differs from today's experts on pedophilia in that he brought a Christian perspective to his work, showing concern for the salvation of his own soul and those of the priests in his care. And he was right where the St. Luke's approach was wrong. Had bishops and superiors taken Fitzgerald's advice to heart, there would have been some weepy ex-priests to care for, but there would have been no sex-abuse crisis.

So what happened? The bishops were persuaded to abrogate their moral duty and hand over the problem to the fix-it folks.

Self-described experts—like Fr. Michael Peterson, before he died of AIDS—convinced the clergy that moral revulsion at child abuse was un-Christian vindictiveness and theirs was the truly caring approach. The results are obvious.

More recently a new set of self-appointed experts (who, coincidentally, have the same conflict of interest as Fr. Peterson) are urging senior churchmen to abandon Catholic teaching on sexual morality in favor of the "scientific" solution of coaching the faithful in condom use. Like the pedophilia pros, the condom promoters attempt to portray Christian doctrine as obsolete, punitive, and conducive to misery. Like the pedophilia pros, the condom promoters have been willing to cook the stats to make their programs appear more successful than they are in reality.

In the 1950s, the orthodox Catholics whom progressives stigmatized as moral meatballs were skeptical that twelve weeks of therapy could turn a pederast back into an effective minister. Those meatballs were right. Today the orthodox Catholics stigmatized as moral meatballs reject the "dogs in heat" model of the human being, in which condoms are viewed as a matter of elementary hygiene; they believe that monogamy and fidelity can be accomplished by almost every person, regardless of circumstance. Once again, some of the clergy are being persuaded by the force of fashion to cede their moral duty to the experts. Once again, it's the meatballs that have it right.

THE LAVENDER MAFIA

Inseparable from the sex-abuse scandal was the scandal of homosexual influence among the clergy. As usual Diogenes concentrated his satire on the dishonesty that was exhibited by prelates who, rather than address the problem, sought to deny it. Uncle Di was initially pessimistic about the prospects for reform arising from an apostolic visitation of the American seminarians. He drew some encouragement from the 2005 Vatican directive that homosexual men should not be admitted as candidates for the priesthood (which he dubbed the "Doomsday Document"). But with time, as it became clear that bishops and seminary rectors would sidestep that directive, he lapsed back into his habitual pessimism. Meanwhile, during the years when Diogenes was writing, society was rushing to embrace the legal acceptance of same-sex marriage, to the detriment of family life and of the fundamental honesty that Uncle Di demanded.

What Problem?

May 7, 2003

A six-month-old *Boston Globe* article surfaces points of current interest:

> As a student at Harvard and then Yale, where different lifestyles mix uneventfully, Gavan Meehan found it easy and comfortable to be publicly gay. But after an inner tug to the priesthood drew him last year to St. John's Seminary in Brighton, his upfront acknowledgement of his sexual orientation brought a far different response.

There's an important point here: it's absurd to pretend that gays can put the toothpaste back in the tube when they enter the seminary and just toddle through like anyone else. If a man was openly gay in Cambridge, does he magically switch to a "none-of-your-business" category by crossing the river to Brighton? Are fellow seminarians who know his past supposed to pretend he was born 15 minutes before he crossed the St. John's threshold?

By March, amid a cascade of revelations about priests molesting children, Meehan's openness had become a source of discomfort for his superiors. The rector at St. John's, Bishop Richard G. Lennon, told him that some students were concerned about his homosexuality, said Meehan, who took the remark as "a warning that I had to somehow change my behavior." Meehan wasn't about to do that. Instead, he remained outspoken, complaining at school forums about homophobia and criticizing the seminary for a climate that he said punished openly gay students and protected closeted ones.

Imagine what life is like for a straight, orthodox seminarian in this setting. You must pretend gay seminarians are as chaste as the heteros, or else you are judgmental and unsuited for ministry. You must pretend the gays support Church teaching, or else you are judgmental and unsuited for ministry. You must pretend the closeted gays are not gay, or else you are judgmental and unsuited for ministry. You must pretend the holes gay faculty pick in Church doctrine are matters of purely academic controversy and are unconnected with personal appetites, or else you are judgmental and unsuited for ministry. You must pretend that gay candidates are accepted and "rigid" candidates are rejected by the staff simply for the good of the Church, or else you are judgmental and unsuited for ministry.

Now suppose you survive the four years' scrutiny and are approved by the staff for ordination. How intrepid a priest are you likely to be?

Silence, Subversion, and Trust

June 30, 2003

In an intentionally provocative column for the *National Review* online, John Derbyshire wonders aloud whether the Church will finish her days as "a gay dating service": "Organized Christianity began as a religion for women and slaves. It looks set fair to end, at least in the Western world, as a religion for homosexuals."

Derbyshire's own analysis of the problem is disappointingly, well, Anglican. Though aware of the danger to Christian doctrine posed by ministers pathologically hostile to that doctrine, his chief misgivings center on the threat to "tradition" in the broader sense: proselytizing gays will put an end to the comfortable, decorous, family-friendly ambience of churchmanship. Yet he rightly calls attention to the human dynamics, noting the paradox that, as their proportion increases within an institution, homosexuals become not less but more obsessed with their homosexuality. He propounds a sociological law apropos:

> Any organization that admits frank and open homosexuals into its higher levels will sooner or later abandon its original purpose and give itself over to propagating and celebrating the homosexualist ethos, and to excluding heterosexuals and denigrating heterosexuality.

To what extent is this a problem within Roman Catholicism? Well, to date no sitting bishop is a "frank and open homosexual". Some will conclude from this that we have no Derbyshire Problem at all. On the other hand, recent years have seen seven U.S. bishops forced out because of homosexual activity, while an eighth has died of AIDS. How many U.S. bishops chastised these men prior to their exposure? Zero. How many U.S. bishops had earlier given voice to a general concern about homosexual activity on the part of their brethren? Zero. How many bishops *today* admit that some of their brethren engage in homosexual activity? Zero. The upshot is that the silence (or inattention) of the bishops is meaningless, and from this a man can draw any conclusion he likes.

One thing is radiantly clear: they're not going to level with us. We will never read an article or see a press conference in which a bishop says, "Look, we figure we've got between five and fifteen sexually active gays in our number and probably another fifty celibate but seriously neurotic homosexuals. We're trying among ourselves to come up with the best way to help these men serve the Church and save their souls and keep the system intact in the process. None or few of the problem bishops tell us the full truth about themselves. It's a difficult, often bitter, conversation. We need your prayers."

It's not going to happen. Fine. But that makes the goal of "restoring trust" all the more elusive. As laity and lower clergy, we don't need to know everything, perhaps, but we need to know something. Specifically, we need to know that what happens behind the wall of silence happens in the service of Christ. In default of a demonstrably concrete example the situation will continue to deteriorate.

Imagine that, next November, 270 mitered men enter the U.S. bishops' conference meeting and only 260 emerge. Would we get a full and candid explanation of what went on? Of course not. But if the bishops could show that *something* was more important than saving face, the faithful would have a reason to believe that that something was saving souls.

Leadership

February 20, 2004

When the Massachusetts Supreme Judicial Court gave the green light to gay marriage, everyone, pro and con, realized that the Catholic Church was the only institution in the Commonwealth with a chance of mobilizing sufficient opposition to force a parlay. Lay Catholics instantly threw themselves into combat, only to look over their shoulders to find their commanding officers

> in seclusion ...
> AWOL ...
> retired ...
> ... for illness or other grave reason.

Yes, yes, one of the bishops who'd been publicly making the case that gay marriage was bad turns out to have a sordid history of homosexual encounters himself—another stinging humiliation, visited upon orthodox Catholics by the men anointed to govern, instruct, and sanctify them, with a prospect of more and worse defeats in the future.

One of the unidentified accusers said he was going public because he was offended by [Bishop] Dupre's prominent advocacy against gay marriage in recent months. "The level of anger and feelings of hypocrisy" pushed the victim, who is gay, to speak out, said attorney Roderick MacLeish Jr.

So how do Catholics respond? It's eminently plausible that Dupre was the most important contributor to this man's sexual problems, and the charge of hypocrisy is unanswerable. At present, Dupre is said to be at the St. Luke Institute in Maryland. Doubtless he'll get the conventionally rigorous therapy—twelve weeks with a Tickle Me

Elmo doll and a bottle of Bushmills—and will be back on the South-west Confirmation circuit, tanned and fit, in three or four years. We're about healing and reconciliation, remember?

Back in September a group of prominent bishops wearily agreed to give a hearing to conservative Catholics as a sop for having rigged a closed-door listening session for fellow liberals. When good guys present mentioned that Jesuit James Keenan had testified at the Massachusetts State House in support of gay unions, the bishops feigned shock and horror. Off the Record found this act extremely unconvincing at the time, and laid down this challenge: if the USCCB president were truly surprised by *and out of sympathy with* Keenan's plea for gay marriage, he could pick up the phone and dial the nuncio, who could get a public retraction from Keenan (or his superiors) by the end of the week.

Five months have passed. Notice any changes for the better?

"But does it matter how I happen to be dressed ... ?"

May 26, 2004

Why should a priest refuse Communion to a congregant who approaches him wearing a rainbow sash?

Jewish men are required to cover their heads on entering a synagogue. Consider the case of a man who tries to enter a synagogue on the feast of Simhat Torah wearing a Nazi *Stahlhelm* [steel helmet]. Most of us would think the elders justified in refusing him entrance. Why? Because bending steel in a particular way impedes worship of God? No, because the elders understand the *Stahlhelm* precisely as it is meant to be understood by its wearer, as an expression of contempt for Jews and Judaism. The key point is the *mutually recognized intention* in the wearing of a Nazi icon.

Prof. Michael Levin writes: "Just as reference is secured by a mutually recognized intention to refer ... so an insult is a word or a gesture used with the *intention* of causing affront through the recognition of that intention."

Would the situation change if the person wearing the Nazi helmet were himself Jewish? Only to the extent that one would acknowledge more complex psychological motivations behind the intention to express contempt. We can imagine a 17-year-old Jewish boy who showed up on Simhat Torah in a Nazi helmet, and most of us would intuitively recognize that there must be some deep-seated anger (directed at a parent, perhaps) at the bottom of the desire to wound, and consequently we might interpret the action as the product of pain and confusion rather than of true hatred. But the desire to wound is there for all that, and must be recognized. To allow the boy to attend services wearing the helmet would be grotesquely irresponsible indulgence.

Wearing a rainbow sash at Mass likewise is an action with a mutually recognized intention, in this case, that of expressing defiance of the Catholic Church's teaching against homosexual acts. It is not, of course, the equivalent of a perfectly univocal statement, any more than wearing a Nazi helmet is a univocal statement, but the intended expression of defiance is not in doubt.

Therefore: I do *not* refuse this rainbow-sashed man Communion because the sash implies that he is an unshriven sodomite. I refuse him Communion because the sash unambiguously expresses his defiance and rejection of Church doctrine, and, by entailment, his rejection of the Church as a reliable teacher of God's law, and, by entailment, his apostasy—in the literal, not the formal canonical sense: the rainbow sash is a declaration by the wearer that he "stands apart" from the Church. It makes not the slightest difference, then, if it's a gay man's 74-year-old mother wearing the sash in solidarity with her son who presents herself for Communion. I refuse her the Eucharist not because she failed her blood test but because she herself has declared, "I am not in communion with the Church."

Eyes That See Not

May 1, 2005

USA Today has an article on the upcoming apostolic visitation of seminaries:

> A Vatican evaluation of American seminaries planned three years ago in response to the clergy sex abuse crisis is expected to move forward under new Pope Benedict XVI and will likely tackle the polarizing

issue of whether gays should become priests. The appraisal will focus on conditions in the seminaries, including how instructors present church teaching on sexuality and celibacy, to look for anything that contributed to the scandal.

... The Vatican agency overseeing the project—the Congregation for Catholic Education—has already been given a list of recommended bishops and priests to visit the seminaries. Archbishop Edwin O'Brien of the U.S. Military Archdiocese has been appointed to coordinate the review.

I wish I had more confidence that O'Brien's the man for the job. There's no doubt that he knows the seminary scene—he was rector of New York's Dunwoodie seminary in the years 1985–1989 and again in 1994–1997, and rector of Rome's North American College in the years 1990–1994—the question is whether this counts for or against his ability to confront unpalatable truths. Remember the following story from the *Kansas City Star*'s series on priests with AIDS?

[New Jersey psychiatrist Joseph] Barone directed an AIDS ministry from 1983 to 1993 for students at North American College in Rome. While there, he set up an underground AIDS testing program. Over seven years, he tested dozens of seminarians. Barone gave them false names, drove them to their tests in an unmarked car and paid for the tests himself.

"I didn't know who they were; they didn't know who I was," Barone said. Of those he worked with, he said, 1 in 12 tested HIV-positive. By the time Barone left Rome, he had treated about 80 priests with AIDS. Most of them were gay, he said, and contracted the disease through sexual activity.

I don't know whether Barone is on the level or not, but after a bombshell of this magnitude we'd expect some pretty decisive action one way or the other. If the claim was true, there should have been a rending of garments, followed by lots of heads rolling at the NAC. If false, there should have been a rending of garments, a loud cry of "Calumny!" and a prompt but thorough rebuttal. If the claim was of uncertain merit, there should have been a rending of garments, followed by a room-by-room, closet-by-closet, drawer-by-drawer, hard-disk-to-blood-test investigation—then a rebuttal or a firing squad, as appropriate. What did we get? Head-scratching instead of garment rending. Hence that eerie feeling that no allegation, no matter how scandalous, is capable of provoking proportionately serious *action*—whether vindicative, corrective, or investigative—in response.

No one wants to come across as Chicken Little, panicking at every shadow and crying that the skies are falling. But bad things do happen—in Russell Shaw's words, "prophets of doom are sometimes right"—and if the skies have yet to fall on the U.S. Church, nearly a billion dollars' worth of the ground has disappeared from beneath its feet as a consequence of insouciant inertness, not to speak of the damage to the moral authority of its ministers. Catastrophe doesn't come any clearer. So what do our bishops want the faithful to make of a claim like Barone's? That it's false, and no big deal? That it's true, and no big deal? Or that it's no big deal whether it's a big deal or not? Most bishops (not all), in most crisis situations (not all), have acted as if the last were the case.

Your Uncle Diogenes has already voiced his skepticism about the visitation. Doubtless it will be carried out with punctilious attention to form. The problem is that men can conduct a minute examination and still fail to find what they wish very much not to find. (One thinks of Admiral Nelson at the Battle of Copenhagen, deliberately putting his telescope to his blind eye and saying, "Signal? I see no signal.") If the visitation team did find and report corruption at Seminary X, that might well lead to an ugly conflict with the responsible bishop. And that in turn could result in sacking the bishop in question—together, perhaps, with some shonky members of the team as well. Folks, if the record of the past thirty years is any guide, it won't happen. They'll take the course that's easier (in the short run) for all concerned. "Blackmail? I see no blackmail."

I sincerely want to be wrong here. I hope the *coup de Krenn* was not a fluke.[1] I hope next year at this time I'll be posting a blog apologizing to the team and eating my words. If I am wrong, the proof will be unmistakable: miterless heads and headless miters. It won't take long to find out.

[1] See "Say It Ain't So", p. 62.

The Gay Priest Imposture

October 11, 2005

This week's NCR has an interview with—don't be shocked—an anonymous gay priest. The editorial aim is to demonstrate the irrationality of the Church's stance on homosexuality; in fact, the article does just the opposite. A few observations:

- The priest interviewed identifies himself not simply as homosexual but as gay. He's not pointing to a condition but to an elected identity. Affirming this identity entails a rejection of the Church's teaching that the homosexual inclination is intrinsically disordered. To call himself a gay priest is equivalent to calling himself a Calvinist priest or a monophysite priest, which amounts to saying, "I'm Catholic, except where the Church is wrong." Well, so is Louis Farrakhan.
- Asked the reaction of gay priests of his acquaintance to the Doomsday Doc and the seminary visitation, the interviewee says, "They're angry and they're hurt and they're scared. They're terrified." Why terrified? How many Catholic clergy can you name that publicly acknowledge themselves as gay? Even priests like Robert Nugent of New Ways Ministry and James Schexnayder of NACDLGM [National Association of Catholic Diocesan Lesbian and Gay Ministries] stay one micromillimeter inside the declarative closet, on the grounds that their personal orientation is irrelevant to their politics. So what do they have to fear from a new policy, even supposing it called for defrocking gays?
- Asked if and how he "comes out" to his parishioners, Fr. X says, "There will be times when someone will say something like, 'Don't you miss having a family?' and I don't think I should lie to people. It's almost sinful to conceal those kinds of things …" He makes it clear that such revelation is an exceptional circumstance, which means that he does lie to people—or at least allow a false understanding to go uncorrected—for the greater part of his ministry. One can see the obvious reasons for this, but it points to the basic problem at the heart of the issue: no matter how sharply we draw the contrast between the condition of same-sex attraction on the one hand and the gay

lifestyle on the other, the real-world demands of Catholic ministry make it impossible for the homosexual priest to play all
his cards faceup all the time. Sure, self-selected groups of professionals and academics are cool with "out" homosexuals, but
don't kid yourselves, sexual openness will never go down with
First Confession prep. And that means concealment and deceit
are bred in the bone from the seminary onwards.

- Remember that there's a colossal asymmetry between hetero-
and homosexual men regarding the struggle of vocational discernment. The Catholic straight guy finds the prospect of giving
up wife and family a daunting one, and usually goes through
a wrenching period of self-testing to see whether he has what
it takes inside to attempt lifelong chastity. The man for whom
marriage is a threat rather than an allure is in the opposite situation: for him, the priesthood *solves far too many problems*. It
explains his wifelessness; it makes his parents happy; it mitigates
the prospect of loneliness. The ample testimonies to the reality
of seminary life make it clear that gay seminarians typically go
squirrelly after a year or two because they can't keep up the pretense that the priesthood was ever anything more than a means
to a self-gratifying end; they haven't undergone the spiritual
process of severing oneself from the world. God knows hetero
clergy have shown themselves pretty miserable in regard to chastity, but anyone who believes there's parity here is delusional.

- In performative refutation of his claims to sound churchmanship, the NCR's priest illustrates that mind-warping that exceptionlessly attends the move from "same-sex attracted" to "gay".
As in a room of distorting mirrors, every human perception is
twisted out of recognition in service of an occult personal need:

> You know Paul's image of the body? We are basically going
> against Paul's image of the body—we are saying we have no
> need of the hand or we have no need of the eye....
>   It's as if Jesus came back to the disciples and said, "Oh, by the
> way, the truth *doesn't* set you free."

Deny it if you will, but this kind of language betrays its author as
unambiguously as stiletto heels and a feather boa. It's Father's faith-
warping, not his sexual recreation, that renders him unfit to serve and

that vindicates the rightness of the Church's teaching. We're talking about a sickness, a disorder. Those afflicted with the disorder are being lied to on a massive scale. Speaking the truth in this situation invariably brings a hostile reaction, and the moral cowardice that makes peace with the aggressors typically flatters itself with the name of charity.

It's a fraud, folks.

The Instruction Arrives!

November 23, 2005

Seldom have I been happier to be wrong.

The Doomsday Doc—in what appears to be its final form—has been leaked, and contrary to my own dire prognostications, the Holy See has given us a doc that can hunt.

- The Instruction bases itself on the priest's "configuration to Christ" and the "spiritual paternity" that it includes. Thus the Church speaks to us about those truths of which she is a teacher—in fact the preeminent teacher—as opposed to speaking in terms of clinical psychology, where she is a pupil. The good that she is guarding is a spiritual good, and she views homosexuality as contrary to the affective maturity that is a component of this good.
- The Instruction makes it clear that no one can carry homosexual baggage across the seminary threshold. If your homosexual propensities were transitory and you've put them behind you, you can be given the chance to proceed. If your homosexual propensities are deeply rooted, you should be treated gently and with respect (*con rispetto e delicatezza*), but you don't get in the door.
- The Instruction's footnote number 10, in reference to the point above, cites the May 16, 2002, CDW letter, which said, "A homosexual person, or one with a homosexual tendency is not fit to receive the sacrament of Holy Orders." Its citation here indicates plainly that the CDW letter still has directive force and the Church teaching on which it is grounded has not been changed or "surpassed" in any substantive way.

- The Instruction tacitly dismisses the tendentious claims that homosexuality is innate, or unchangeable, or changeable only in rare circumstances. While it acknowledges that the disorder can be deep-seated in some persons, it maintains that it may also be just an adolescent hang-up one can leave behind. Here the Church's moral wisdom rescues her from the errors of politicized academic fashion. To treat adult homosexuality (except in rare cases) as a self-indulgent prolongation of juvenile weakness and infatuation may rattle some gay ideologues, but it's more realistic and more charitable than the standard APA account. In summary form, the Church is saying, "For the love of Christ, knock off the act and grow up."

This is as it should be. As the self-designation "gay" indicates, adult homosexuality is essentially frivolous, and no one can really take it seriously. Or better, the only circumstance in which we can take it seriously is in the case of persons who are trying to rid themselves of it.

There's a close analogy here with certain strands of iconoclastic feminism. When nuns tell you that you should give up monotheism and start sacrificing marigolds to Ishtar, you recognize they've been damaged somehow and feel sorry for them, but you don't deal in earnest with their theology. It can't take the weight.

The underlying rage, however, is very real. This is as true in the case of gays as of feminists. And this brings me to the controversial part of the Instruction. It says that men with transitory homosexual tendencies may be admitted provided such tendencies are "overcome at least three years before ordination to the diaconate." Note that the three-year plan applies to tendencies, not "activity"—as earlier reports suggested and as some of today's headlines erroneously repeat. If the proviso is read (as it should be) so as to exclude those whose tendencies have been actualized in mortally sinful ways, there's no problem. Taken otherwise, it seriously underestimates the anger and anarchic destructiveness that attend the gay lifestyle. As Robert Gotcher of *HMS Blog* pointed out earlier, "If the requirement is three years of celibacy before diaconal ordination, that means practically speaking no more than six months before entering the seminary." Thankfully, the text asks for a lot more than celibacy.

Are we closer to solving the problem? Not in the foreseeable future. The men asked to use this Instruction to guide their seminary admissions are the men who find the *Vagina Monologues* in keeping with *Ex Corde Ecclesiae*. But the Instruction seems to recognize this, insisting that "the candidate himself is the man most responsible for his own formation." Sure, a crypto-gay can lie his way through to ordination if he's devious enough. But if so, his choice for duplicity— that is, for adolescent dishonesty—performatively concedes the truth of the teaching he's trying to circumvent. But the good news is that there are honest men out there with the guts to tell the truth about themselves and (in Cardinal George's words) to let the Church be the place where Christ changes them. They've got a document they can work with, and we've got a document we can defend.

Backing Water and Blowing Smoke

November 30, 2005

A lot of bishops are twisting uneasily on their episcopal thrones today. The newly released Vatican Instruction excludes from the priesthood men with deeply rooted homosexual tendencies, and while it does not call for expulsion of homosexuals already ordained, the reasoning on which the document is based makes it clear that such men lack the affective maturity necessary to the spiritual paternity in which the priesthood is authentically lived out.

This deficiency does not affect the validity of the sacrament of Orders—homosexual priests validly confect the Eucharist and so forth—but they're not grown up in the way the Church would have them be. More pointedly still, the Instruction issues a ringing condemnation of tactical subterfuge—i.e., lying about one's sexual disorder: "It would be gravely dishonest for a candidate to hide his homosexuality in order to proceed, despite everything, towards Ordination. Such a deceitful attitude does not correspond to the spirit of truth, loyalty, and openness that must characterize the man called to serve Christ and his Church as a priest." Granted, these words are formally directed at men who are only aspirants to the priesthood, but undeniably they cut much deeper. Those bishops who have "deeply rooted homosexual tendencies" are not few in number, and they must be rattled by the Church's judgment that their own priesthood—while canonically valid—is spiritually flawed.

Bishops who are not themselves homosexual but who have welcomed homosexual priests are likewise in a bind: if they've advised homosexual priests not to speak about their libido, they fall afoul of the demand for authenticity; if they've encouraged priests to acknowledge themselves as gay they must admit the Church regards the priest as unfit and the bishop as flat wrong. Both sets of bishops—those gay and those gay friendly—have been caught out by the Instruction and will be struggling frantically to put the toothpaste back in the tube.

Pay attention to their use of the phrase "affective maturity", because this is the key term in the Instruction, and the Holy See and gay-positive clergy employ the phrase with radically contrary meanings. By affective maturity, the Holy See means the kind of psychological integration and adult equanimity that *exclude* homosexual tendencies; such propensities may have existed in a man's adolescence, but if he attains emotional maturity he has, by definition, put them behind him. Gay and gay-friendly clergy, by contrast, insist that affective maturity entails acceptance of whatever one's sexual orientation happens to be. For them, the homosexual who sees his libido as disordered and wants to free himself of it is *less* mature than the homosexual who has made the decision to live as a gay man, i.e., who accepts and affirms his homosexual tendencies as a given, as part of his identity. A self-proclaimed gay like Fr. Leonard Walker would be regarded by gay-positive bishops as a paradigm specimen of affective maturity, by the Holy See as a lamentable example of the opposite.

But it doesn't end there. Gay-positives insist that an indispensable condition of affective maturity is "comfort" with one's own sexuality (mature men are comfortable being themselves), and this in turn excludes opprobrium or aversion directed at a "sexuality other than one's own." In this view, a heterosexual at peace with his sexual identity does not object to gays as brother priests, any more than a white man at peace with his racial identity would object to blacks. That's why men like Fr. Timothy Radcliffe are keen to assert that those who oppose gays in the priesthood are affectively immature, and it is *they* who shouldn't be admitted to Holy Orders. Many bishops (and their fellow travelers) have been operating for years in opposition to long-standing Church discipline, anticipating that the discipline would change. It hasn't—and what we see now is the flailing of these men as they try to salvage their authority while looking for room to maneuver (the parallel with clergy who anticipated approval of contraception prior to *Humanae Vitae* is obvious). The *Washington Post* reports that Bishops Skylstad, Clark, and McCarrick have (predictably) declared that the Instruction does not exclude homosexual priests, while Bishop D'Arcy has (predictably) affirmed the contrary. The situation in Canada is much the same:

> Archbishop Weisgerber said he was pleased that the Vatican makes clear that the church is not questioning the priesthood of homosexual men who already have been ordained. He said he hopes it is clear that "the church is not saying you should not have been ordained."
>
> "So many members of the clergy, like men in the culture at large, are struggling with this," he said.

This is disingenuous, as Weisgerber is trading on the ambiguity of the deliberately equivocal phrase "questioning the priesthood". Validity is not at issue, but the Instruction makes it clear that homosexual priests—and a fortiori gay priests—are deficient in what the Church means by spiritual paternity. The Church has blocked one of the commonest exits, the "don't ask don't tell" ploy, by her insistence on "truth, loyalty, and openness" in these matters. Bishops, rectors, and spiritual directors can no longer give the homosexual candidate a wink and say, "You can proceed, just be discreet"—or if they do, there's no doubt but that they're complicit in the attitude of deceit that the Church has specifically reprobated. As USCCB president and a gay-positive bishop, William Skylstad will serve as a bellwether on the Instruction's implementation. He has opined that the document is "timely", that it urges a "realism", and that it "expresses a valid concern"—all of which are positive, but all of which can be said of a document the speaker wholly rejects. When it comes to the question of the Instruction's truth, Skylstad punts: "Bishop Skylstad said that the discussion in the media about this document raised the question 'whether a homosexually-inclined man can be a good priest.'"

No, the media discussion didn't raise the question, the Instruction raised the question. And answered it. Does Skylstad find the answer in the Instruction? He does not. "Bishop Skylstad said that 'the answer lies in the lives of those men who, with God's grace, have truly been dedicated priests ... &c.'"

That, boys and girls, is called blowing smoke. Expect more of the same.

Condition Rose

December 11, 2005

It's Gaudete Sunday, and Robert McClory dons tinted specs to pitch a fit about the Doomsday Doc.

> The Vatican's recent instruction on barring gays from the seminary may be the worst document issued by the church since it declared in 1866 (three years after the Emancipation Proclamation) that "slavery itself ... is not at all contrary to the divine and natural law."
>
> For centuries, gay priests, bishops, even cardinals have served the church and all its people with dedication and dignity.

Easy now, Robert, my lad. Let's do a little stocktaking here.

It's unlikely that you have discovered secret diaries in which, "for centuries," priests, bishops, and cardinals have confided they were gay. By what means, then, do you arrive at your conclusion? We're talking about those who served the Church honorably, remember, so that puts them below the normal historical radar. It seems to me there are two ways of proceeding.

1. You could assert what you elsewhere deny and, by looking for evidence of twee-ness or effeminacy among upright clergymen of the past, deduce their homosexual libido from their abnormality, from minor defects that set them apart from their contemporaries. This is doable, but I doubt it's a path you'd be inclined to take.

2. Alternatively, you could claim that upright homosexual clergymen, viewed from outside, are entirely indistinguishable from their heterosexual colleagues. How then can you know they existed? You'd need to argue that, in any given population of men, a predictable distribution of proclivities will obtain, and therefore a certain percentage will be homosexual. The fact that these men are all bachelors lends a prima facie plausibility to the claim.

Fine, so we posit a number of "stealth" homosexuals—chaste, unflamboyant—who are unidentifiable by any historical means. It won't do to quote Lady Fotherington's letter expressing suspicions about Archbishop LaCasse because, if she's right, His Grace was guilty of a lapse of dedication or dignity or both. So what we're talking about, Mr. McClory, is the color of cats in a dark room. "There's an invisible tortoiseshell in the cellar!" How do you know? "Well, the cellar looks empty, doesn't it? QED."

Now here's the crunch. Once you remove the rose-colored specs, you realize that these invisible homosexuals "look" a lot like what the Doomsday Doc has in mind in speaking of men with *tendenze superate*, tendencies that have been fully overcome. You can put such a guy next to a normal hetero priest, and if both are committed and honorable, they can live out their entire priestly lives in spiritual tranquillity, such that those not privy to their adolescence can't see a difference. So meet me halfway. I'll concede an intuitively reasonable number of *unidentifiable* homosexuals in the Church's past, if you'll insist that those in her future remain *unidentifiable* as well—if you admit, that is, that the DDD is right. Deal?

Not Up to Commonwealth Standards

June 1, 2006

Know anyone with the Italian surname of Esposito or Innocenti? Most of them are descended from an orphan taken care of by the Catholic Church. For centuries, Italian cities had hospitals where abandoned babies (*espositi, innocenti*) were taken in and cared for, and a number of them married and passed on to their own children a family name reflecting the foundling hospital in which they grew up. Nor was it always a grim existence; a good part of Vivaldi's music was composed to be performed by girls at the Catholic orphanage in Venice where, in the early 1700s, he was a music teacher. The circumstances of orphans raised under the auspices of the Church's charity varied considerably, no doubt, but her impulse to care for parentless children was such an obvious good that her liberty to do so was taken for granted.

Until now.

Maggie Gallagher writes that Massachusetts' decision to impose anti-Christian ideological restrictions on adoption services represents a first step toward putting the Church out of the Corporal Works of Mercy business:

> The question in Boston is not whether gays are going to be allowed legally to adopt. It is whether religious people who morally object to gay adoption will be allowed to help children find homes. This is not about gay adoption—it is about our fundamental commitment to religious liberty in this country.
>
> It is a crime to run an adoption agency in Massachusetts without a license from the state. To get a license you have to agree to place children with same-sex couples. For the first time in America, Christians are being told by their government that they are not good citizens, not worthy enough to be permitted to help abandoned babies find good homes.

The Catholic Church was tending to orphans centuries before there was such a thing as a secular state. Yet now the secular state has determined, in its wisdom, that it is the Church that risks harming the orphan by refusing to submit to gay adoption. So when this latest social experiment crashes ten or twenty years from now, who's going to be there postdisaster to pick up the pieces—the *human beings* collaterally damaged in the cause of political gain? The Harvard Committee on Gender Studies? The Rainbow Sash Movement? The Lambda Legal Defense crowd?

Think again.

Twelve Months On

November 29, 2006

Well folks, it's a year today that the Doomsday Doc was officially released, instructing seminaries that candidates with deeply rooted homosexual tendencies are unsuitable for admission to Holy Orders. In the months prior to the issuance of the document, Off the Record was not optimistic about the bishops' alacrity in implementing it. Cardinal George stated that the U.S. bishops had pleaded with Rome to cancel, or at least delay, the promulgation of the Instruction, but were turned down. In September of 2005, OTR suggested the bishops would manage to spin defeat as a ho-hum victory: "For the USCCB, the easiest tack will be to welcome the document publicly, simultaneously declaring that it amounts to a Vatican confirmation of their own efforts, back when the U.S. bishops fixed the problem (*of course* you remember!) three, or five, or seven years ago."

Obligingly, Cardinal McCarrick responded exactly on cue (December 1, 2005): "The Archdiocese of Washington *welcomes* the new guidance from the Congregation for Catholic Education on admission to the seminary, *which affirms the long-held practices* of the Archdiocese of Washington." The emphasis, *monsignori*, is mine. And the presidential candygram was [USCCB president] Bishop Skylstad's.

Generally forgotten in the public discussion that ensued was the accompanying letter to the bishops issued along with the Instruction by the Congregation for Catholic Education, a letter which gave some specificity to the Doc by insisting that homosexual men "are not to be appointed as rectors or educators in seminaries." The will of the Holy See in the matter is pretty clear. Notice all those offices mysteriously vacated over the past twelve months? The emptied desks, the puzzled secretaries?

Of course not. Remember the motive behind the U.S. bishops' frantic embassy to Rome: all the problems the Instruction was designed to address had already been put right.

Right?

Thus Saith the Lord, for the Time Being

October 5, 2007

Writing in the *Tablet*, Timothy Lavin delivers the thoughts of the premier Mexican Anglican:

> Meanwhile, the Anglican Archbishop of Mexico, Carlos Touche-Porter, sought to promote a middle way that "celebrates diversity" for the Anglican Communion at a press conference in London this week, writes Victoria Combe. Archbishop Touche-Porter said that the Latin American Episcopalian bishops—who have formed an alliance called

the Global Centre—had managed to remain unified despite different views on human sexuality.

"The solution is not a compromise but for the Church to remember that its primary mission is to witness the Gospel rather than discuss sexual morals," he said at the conference hosted by the British-based network Inclusive Church in St Matthew's, Westminster. He said he remained hopeful that the Episcopal Church would remain part of the Anglican Communion because to lose it would be to lose a "prophetic voice" in the Church. "We do not need to agree on every issue," he said.

Sorry, Charlie, you've got *that* backwards too. You can't call your preaching Good News until you grasp the bad news you hope to be delivered from.

Notwithstanding their efforts to ignore it, Touche-Porter and his allies are tangled in a hopeless predicament. There is no neutral ground here. It makes no sense—it's logically self-destructive—for a church to teach that an act that damns you today may ennoble you tomorrow, subject to a majority vote of its bishops and to indefinitely frequent political revision. If sodomy was contrary to God's will in A.D. 1840, it will be contrary to God's will in A.D. 2840, and for a church to deny this is to deny it knows God's will, which is in effect to deny that it is a church.

Let's try to take Touche-Porter's notion seriously for a moment. Can it really be the case (to borrow Fr. Raymond de Souza's language) that a gay Anglican, on waking some morning in the near future, must wait for the *Daily Telegraph* to arrive in order to learn whether the act he performed with his partner the evening previous was a mortal sin or a sacrament? Could a man really suspend his judgment on such a fundamental question until the results of a vote were in from the House of Bishops? Could he then accept and spiritually reorient himself in conformity to the winning answer as to the mind of God on the matter, not knowing whether or when it might be reversed in some future meeting?

The scenario is theologically grotesque, yet this is the package Touche-Porter and chums are asking us to buy. And while the crisis hinging on this incoherence is especially acute in the Anglican Communion, and may prove fatal to it, provisional Catholics like Andrew Sullivan occupy the same plot of quicksand. Gays ask the Church to welcome sinners (which she delights to do) and also to welcome their sins (which she can't). By urging the Church to change her teaching they are ipso facto asking her to cease to be the Church. The bottom line is this: what's at stake in the gay rights campaign is not some church in which gays want to share, but the Church they want to deny to the rest of us.

Healing the Rift

April 7, 2008

At the Los Angeles Religious Education Congress in 2006, key-noter Timothy Radcliffe, O.P., urged us to "let our imaginations be stretched" by watching *Brokeback Mountain*, etc. Radcliffe, it appears, stretches easy. At this year's congress he spoke to the question "Is Dialogue Possible in the Church Today?" In an interview with Busted Halo, the former Master General of the Dominicans explained in more detail how we can get beyond our divisions.

> BUSTED HALO: You've been criticized by some—and praised by others—for comments you've made regarding homosexuality, specifically with regard to the priesthood. How do you think this divisive issue could be better approached?

> TIMOTHY RADCLIFFE: We have to see that behind much of the furor is fear and these fears are comprehensible. There is a fear among straight priests of becoming a member of a small minority in what is perceived as a 'gay' vocation. There is a fear among some homosexual priests of being found out, a feeling of guilt and so on. We have to reassure people so that the issue can be faced calmly. If there is a fevered anxiety about all this, then it does not help people mature and face their own complexity. It is not the case that there are just these two groups, homosexuals and heterosexuals. People are complex, and have contrary motions in their hearts. Straight people may be tempted to strangle the little bit of them that responds to people of the same sex and fear gay people. But that is a disguised form of fearing themselves. And gay seminarians may be tempted to deny who they are, adopt an anti-gay rhetoric, and all that is highly unhealthy and deforming.

Got it. Straights should put aside their reluctance to accept gay demands, and gays should put aside their reluctance in making them. An ingenious solution.

Ad dubium

May 22, 2008

The Vatican Secretary of State has issued a two-sentence statement concerning the interpretation of the 2005 Instruction on the non-admission of homosexual persons to Holy Orders. In response to "numerous requests for clarification", the Holy See made clear what was clear from the outset, that the force of the prohibitions extends to seminaries operated by religious orders, mission territories, and Eastern Rite Churches.

Two or three years from now, in all probability, the Vatican will issue a further clarification affirming that the Instruction remains valid for Capricorns, redheads, and Edmonton Oilers fans. No one is fooled here. These are not good-faith doubts sent Romewards by genuinely perplexed ecclesiastics. The game is to stall implementation of unwelcome directives by finding textual ambiguities and feigning bewilderment, in the hope that, by the time the Church's cumbersome machinery of response has produced its answer, Pope Benedict will be dead and replaced by a man with a more enlightened view of the issues.

It's no secret that the old-line religious orders are the most fervid dissenters from the ban on homosexuals, and their superiors comprise a kind of Shadow Cabinet within the Church: hostile to the policy of the Holy See but outwardly deferential to its authority—and, most importantly, incubating in their ranks a parallel government and parallel apparat through which the "alternative" policies are discreetly advanced. The Shadow Cabinet's own term for this genial subversion is Creative Fidelity, and any housewife whose husband protests he was "creatively faithful" to her during his Las Vegas business jaunt will be able to gauge the degree to which the Pope is reassured by the euphemism.

Nor is the Vatican faultless as to its own responsibilities in the matter. Remember the much-ballyhooed "new and serious" apostolic visitation of U.S. seminaries launched in response to the clergy abuse crisis? The results of the investigation seem to have vanished into the ether. Those in charge managed to steer it to its conclusion without risk to any sitting bishop, and lay interest in reform has waned to the point where the findings can be safely entombed in a file cabinet until a new generation of prelates replaces those who were implicated. To put it in the (curial favorite) future perfect tense: face will have been saved.

In sum, it looks as if we're still stuck with the post-Conciliar truce: the Holy See holds fast, at least on paper, to the *vera doctrina*, while the clergy follows its own inclinations, pausing, when thwarted, to ponder what the meaning of "is" is. The faithful—watching the gap widen between Roman teaching and the convictions of the men Rome provides as their ministers—are presented with a distasteful choice between docility and orthodoxy. Those who wish to be sure of a welcome will decide that neither matters very much.

Marriage for All

April 8, 2009

In every nation, in every epoch, homosexuals have been free to marry. In every nation, in every epoch, homosexuals have been free to marry other homosexuals. Homosexuals have been prohibited, exactly as heterosexuals have been prohibited, from marrying persons of the same sex. There was no question of discrimination on the basis of orientation because the appetites of the consenting parties (as is the case in every contractual obligation) were beside the point. Until now.

Partisans of same-sex marriage pretend that marriage is a good they wish to extend to those it has been arbitrarily denied: hence campaigns named "Marriage for All" or "Marriage Equality". But the publicly dispensable good (the kind a marriage license gives you) has always been available. What they resent is the moral value accorded marriage—an honor markedly weaker today than in the past, yet still potent enough to cause gnashing of teeth among the innovators. That honor is what they want to abolish.

Imagine that the attitudes of a century ago—when marriage was accorded the power to ennoble sexual relations—could be beamed forward into the present. And imagine today's parents of a young man betrothed to another young man, urging him to remain a virgin until his wedding so as to preserve intact his and his fiancé's purity. Or imagine a same-sex couple, piously abstaining from fellatio or rimming during the season of Lent, only to resume it with prayerful joy on Easter morning. Simply to raise these possibilities is to see how grotesque they are. The decision to countenance same-sex unions is not to shift sodomy in one's books from the "immoral" to the "moral" column; it is to dispense with the category of sexual morality full stop. It is to rip up one's passport and renounce one's citizenship in the commonwealth of sexual morality.

Gay activists taunt the rest of us that conventional man-woman marriage is in a shambles today, and they're right. But their proposed innovation, as they really understand and rarely admit, is a choice for moral anarchy. Within their world there is no question of calling one act pure and another act impure, because the notion of purity has to be put to death before their project is embarked on. Chastity cannot be ennobling because to embrace same-sex congress is to debunk nobility. Even the photos from the Pride parades display a kind of sack-dance gloating over the dethronement of the concepts of purity and sexual integrity; it's a burlesque of those values that marriage— real marriage—was ordained to uphold.

Same-sex marriage is a war on honor. And it appears to be winning.

WHY BE A PRIEST?

What is the proper role of a Catholic priest, and why should a young man pursue that vocation? In a time of enormous confusion (and worse) within the Church, there were many bad answers to those questions. Diogenes found more than a few of them.

Please Leave Suggestions for Dialogue on My Secretary's Voicemail

May 15, 2003

The *National Catholic Reporter*'s Tom Roberts reflects on the low morale of priests and solicits the advice of Fr. Robert J. Silva, president of the National Federation of Priests' Councils:

> How to get beyond this awful moment? In a conversation over breakfast, Silva said he believes that priests and bishops throughout the country really need to engage in a structured dialogue if trust and confidence is ever going to be restored....
>
> Finally, and perhaps the most daunting task, said Silva, is that the church has to find a way to balance its obligations to be pastoral with the demands civil law is now placing on it. "We are not and cannot experience ourselves as a corporation or business institution. We are church."

Two questions:

1. If you were a priest concerned to shift the focus of churchmen *away* from corporate models of management to a more ecclesial pursuit of prayer, devotion, and moral probity, would you turn to something called the National Federation of Priests' Councils?
2. Unless you were the one controlling the microphone switches, would you voluntarily submit to "structured dialogue"?

The Way Forward ... into the Abyss

July 10, 2003

Ex-priest William Cleary reviews Dean Hoge's *The First Five Years of the Priesthood*:

> Early in his first chapter, Hoge asks how many recently ordained priests are homosexual (perhaps up to 50 percent) or if gay priests persevere in greater numbers (yes).... The heart of Hoge's research discoveries was summarized in an article published in NCR some months ago: "Hoge found that between 20 percent and 30 percent of priests left because they fell in love with a woman. Another 20 percent to 30 percent left because they felt lonely and unappreciated and could not abide by mandatory celibacy. And between 6 and 15 percent left because they wanted an 'open, long-term relationship' with another man. Between 30 and 40 percent left because they were disillusioned with their fellow priests or the hierarchy."

Think about the implications of having 50 percent homosexual priests. A very high percentage of the newly ordained—hetero and homo—will have mortally sinful sexual experience in their past; this is 2003, remember, when men typically begin studying for the priesthood in their late 20s. Most men will have episodes in their past that they would like to put behind them: sacramentally, by means of penance, but also concretely, so that they are free to teach hard teachings and to call others to lives of sacrifice. Can anyone fail to see how much harder it is for once-active gays to get this freedom than once-active straights? Consider, at minimum, the difference in the effect on the parish caused by the young woman at a picnic or wedding reception who announces, "Fr. Ron and I dated for six years before he entered the seminary," and the young man who says the same thing. Cleary again:

> Everything in the book suggests celibacy is the issue. Of course. Never again should we make sex or sexuality the enemy: It is instead the path of knowledge and even of wisdom. Giving it all up leads nowhere, and may lead to illness, in fact, in my humble opinion. Reverencing the revelation in sexual experience takes us in the only direction we have left. As precarious as is that path, it is the only one forward. Celibacy is natural and valuable in many contexts, not in the religious one,

even less for economic purposes. Plant such genetically engineered seed and it will yield bitter fruit indeed.

I know several married people who are obliged to abstinence because of the serious illness of a spouse. I have to say (to use Cleary's cant) that I am more impressed by the wisdom they gain through continence than by "the revelation in sexual experience." It must be an extremely difficult path to walk, though most seem to walk it with integrity. Does sex necessarily become "the enemy" for them? Of course not. It's one more of life's unchosen hardships. For priests it is a chosen hardship. One could hardly devise a better method of compounding the hardship than by dangling in front of celibate priests the prospect of relaxed discipline: that's the surest way to a crop of embittered, conflicted, and pathologically hostile subversives.

Aging without Grace

September 14, 2003

The *Milwaukee Journal Sentinel* reports that Bishop Wilton Gregory was the recipient of a petition signed by 14 priests opposed to obligatory priestly celibacy: "The Southern Illinois Association of Priests ... mailed a letter to Gregory on Friday, urging him to 'do all in your power to make the charism of celibacy a grace and not a mandated law for diocesan priests of the Roman Catholic church in America.' "

Anybody else find a theological problem in the proposal of a man's *making* something into a grace? Putting aside the bizarre tautological notion of turning a charism into a charism, if celibacy isn't already a free gift of God, how can a merely human endeavor ("do all *in your power*") make it so? Further, doesn't the wording imply that the petitioners regard their own (putative) celibacy not as a grace, but rather as a burden, or an imposition, or (at best) a personal lifestyle option?

We all know the Marvel Comix explanation that priestly celibacy was an 11th-century novelty introduced as a parochial cost-saving measure, etc., etc., but the simple fact of the matter is that most priests forgo marriage because Jesus Himself did. Celibacy is a radical, literal, not-very-sophisticated form of the imitation of Christ.

Much (not all) of the respect traditionally accorded Catholic priests stems from an intuitive recognition that their celibacy reflects not simply conformity to institutional discipline but a sacrifice modeled, however imperfectly, on the sacrifice of Christ. Of course, this notion fell into disrepute in the theology departments and seminaries of the 1970s and 1980s, when "ministry" came to be viewed as execution of discrete tasks (preaching, counseling, dialogue enabling) exercised by acquired human skills (e.g., training in theology and public speaking). In this scheme, what matters is whether the minister is a competent counselor or expositor of the Letter to the Romans; whether he, or she, is married or unmarried is irrelevant. You don't care whether the person who sharpens your lawn mower blades is unmarried provided the blades come back sharp. Why should you care whether the guy who dresses in flowing polyester for you once a week to paraphrase the Jerome Biblical Commentary is celibate?

When priests organize themselves into a regional professional association (like teachers or librarians) and draft a resolution or petition to exempt themselves or their successors from a pro forma obligation, clearly they see their priesthood not as a covenant but as a contract for commodities and services delivered. Everything's negotiable, and renegotiable, because everything that's given or withheld is less than and distinct from the Self.

But notice how faith and fidelity evaporate. If a husband asked his wife to do "all in her power" to make monogamy into "a grace and not a mandated law for married men," we could be pretty sure that his feelings about his own commitment were ... ambiguous. Almost certainly his wife would not feel flattered. Almost certainly she'd wonder whether her husband's support for optional openness was empirical and not purely theoretical.

Can We Talk?

October 12, 2003

L.A. cardinal Roger Mahony wins praise for openness and vision.

Some Los Angeles-area Roman Catholic priests are urging an open discussion on whether to allow married clergy as one solution to the growing priest shortage, and say they hope Cardinal Roger Mahony will raise the issue to church authorities nationally and in Rome. Calls to discuss the option of a married clergy came earlier this week at an annual assembly which drew about half of the archdiocese's 1,200 priests. Many priests lauded Mahony for allowing the debate on a topic considered taboo a decade or two ago.... "We have made an extraordinary shift in the last 10 years," said Msgr. Clement J. Connolly of Holy Family Church in South Pasadena. "It's a new day when we can even talk about this now with respectability and a certain reverence and understanding."

Many single women lament what they perceive as a shortage of men willing to commit to marriage. Following the lead given above, why don't we talk about dropping the monogamy and fidelity requirement for husbands? That would make matrimony a more attractive option for contemporary young men, who feel hesitant about binding themselves to what many see as an outmoded, late-medieval legal requirement. The institution of marriage itself would benefit from the change: think of the gifted and generous men who are scratched off the list of potential husbands simply because they're already married or reject the proposal to remain faithful. As teenage children begin to think about the prospect of marriage themselves, wouldn't it be wonderful for them to hear their parents debate, with reverence and understanding, the constraint of obligatory monogamy?

Tears of Grief and Anger

October 19, 2003

Chesterton once wrote that, in the eyes of the world, a priest is reckoned a knave for breaking his vows and a fool for keeping them. In his op-ed in today's *New York Times* ("Losing a Church, Keeping the Faith"), Andrew Sullivan attributes both the knavery and the folly to the celibate. Like most of Sullivan's lamentations on the predicament of gays in the Church, it is very well written and deeply dishonest. He affects to believe that the Church condemns "infertile" intercourse (full stop) and "emotional" as well as sexual relationships between gays—without further qualification. As a specimen of polemic, very adroit; as personal testimony, wholly contemptible.

Gay men are being deterred from applying to seminaries and may soon be declared unfit for the priesthood, even though they commit to celibacy. The American Catholic church has endorsed a constitutional amendment that would strip gay couples of any civil benefits of any kind in the United States. For the first time in my own life, I find myself unable to go to Mass. During the most heated bouts of rhetoric coming from the Vatican this summer, I felt tears of grief and anger welling up where once I had been able to contain them. Faith beyond resentment began to seem unreachable.

Putting aside the fact that many people besides gays are required to make painful decisions in order to follow Christ—decisions with consequences more far-reaching than any he contemplates—Sullivan fails to acknowledge the honesty and guts of those homosexuals who struggle against the odds to remain chaste, precisely because they believe God speaks through His Church. Yet Sullivan saves his compassion, not for those who heroically resist temptation, but for those who succumb.

Granted also that Sullivan is right in claiming that there are many gay priests who live duplicitous lives, there are also priests who not only keep their vows but who work (quietly and without public congratulation) to help homosexual Catholics understand the Church's teaching and live it with integrity. Perhaps Sullivan can dismiss them as fools—admittedly it isn't a shrewd career move. But must they be accounted knaves as well?

Sporadically Authentic Priests

November 6, 2003

Q. How can you tell your pastor's an archconservative?
A. He wears a collar even when he's not on the way to his arraignment.

An article in the *St. Louis Post-Dispatch* discusses the controversy caused by priests who are alleged sex abusers turning up in court wearing clerical garb.

Richard Waites, a lawyer and psychologist who heads a nationwide jury consulting firm, said that more often than not he recommends that defendant priests wear their collars to court.

"In general, jurors are looking for any person to be as genuine as possible," Waites said in a telephone interview. "And since the defendant is under a great scrutiny, he needs or she needs to be as genuine as possible and as authentic as possible."

By "as genuine as possible", of course, Waites means the opposite. He knows perfectly well the odds that some jurors—enough to acquit, at any rate—may respond to the uniform covering the defendant *instead of* the genuine article inside. One of my favorite examples comes from the U.K. *Telegraph* (October 20, 2000), regarding a priest from Wales who confessed to six counts of molesting a 12-year-old before he became a priest, and to indecent assaults on two 9-year-olds after ordination. His game was to get little boys to join a soccer club he had started: "Fr Joseph Jordan was a modern priest, always dressed in baseball cap, tracksuit and trainers. One mother remarked that the only time she had seen him in clerical garb was in the dock at Cardiff Crown Court."

Love these guys. When it's a matter of barhopping, or going to restaurants, or taking in a movie, they're invariably in civvies ("I find the collar to be a vestige of an antiquated clerical caste system that puts a barrier between me and the people I serve"). When their recreations finally catch up with them and they end up facing a five-to-eight for conducting underage Listening Sessions, what emblem of 1950s piety and propriety do they hide behind?

Why, how did you guess?

Good MORN-ing, Everyone!

November 23, 2003

Not infrequently, when I catch sight of khakis and running shoes under a priest's Mass vestments, I wish I could call a time-out and ask him what he believes is taking place in the Eucharist and what role his priesthood serves therein. Some weeks ago I posted observations on the nature of ritual excerpted from C. S. Lewis' *A Preface to* Paradise Lost, including this remark: "The modern habit of doing ceremonial things unceremoniously is not proof of humility; rather it proves the offender's inability to forget himself in the rite, and his readiness to spoil for every one else the proper pleasure of ritual."

Most of us, alas, are acquainted with priests who feel it their duty (or grant themselves the liberty) to make the Eucharist chatty, informal, spontaneous, commonplace. Awe is the enemy. The altar and its ministers are to be approachable. The celebrant who cracks jokes into the microphone from the presider's chair sends the assembly the message that, whatever might take place in the sanctuary, it's No Big Deal.

Many Catholics feel uneasy with liturgical informality and, without being able to put a name to the problem, intuitively understand that something important is missing. Here too Lewis' insight into ritual is helpful:

> A man performing a rite is not trying to make you think that this is his natural way of walking, these the unpremeditated gestures of his own domestic life. If long usage has in fact made the ritual unconscious, he must labour to make it look deliberate, in order that we, the assistants, may feel the weight of the solemnity pressing on his shoulders as well as on our own. Anything casual or familiar in his manner is not 'sincerity' or 'spontaneity' but impertinence. Even if his robes were not heavy in fact, they ought to *look* heavy.

The New and Serious Apostolic Visitation

December 20, 2004

The working document for the upcoming visitation of the U.S. seminaries—known in Vatican slang as the Eternal Sunshine of the Spotless Mind—occasioned some grim prognostications on our part. Yet I passed over the single ray of hope given by Bishop Nienstedt: his assurance that "a key element of the visitation is that any faculty member or student will be allowed to speak with the visitation team about the condition of the seminary." Provided there isn't an antecedent desire to bury negative feedback, this is a great step forward.

We're told that, as in the 1980s Marshall Visitation, a questionnaire will be sent to each seminary in advance, and then a visitation team (VT) will meet with the seminary personnel to evaluate the responses.

Any worthwhile visitation must be predicated on a firm recognition of the clergyman's fondness for the expedient lie. The VT has to take it as understood that the seminary staff is not going to report facts that are damaging to itself, period. The VT can use the questionnaire for curricular data, but no rector will ever write, "Our NT prof is a heretical Bultmannian, and our dean is dating the bishop's MC." If the VT wants to know the real picture, it has to go behind the scenes to get it. With that in mind, I propose the following:

- Require that, in advance of the team's arrival, every seminarian be given a copy of the questionnaire replies that the staff submitted to the VT. Reason: The questionnaire will tell the VT, e.g., there were three Days of Recollection last year; it won't mention that all three were conducted by a Sister of Loreto who's a part-time druidess. Seminarians can and will.
- Require a list of names and contact info for *all* former seminarians of the past decade, and require that the list be posted so current seminarians can complete the gaps where possible. Reason: Not all seminarians will have left or been expelled for reasons the staff wants known. Random contacts of ex-candidates will reveal info not available by interviewing only those who (1) have been "filtered in" by the system, and (2) are still cowed by the risk of discovery and dismissal.
- Require a list of priests, ordained in the past five years, who have left the priesthood. Find out why they left and, if possible, interview a few. Reason: The resentments and satisfactions of these men will testify both to the aims of those who formed them and to methods of selection and promotion.
- Ask for a list of the most prominent lay supporters and lay critics of the seminary, from both right- and left-wing perspectives. Reason: The view of the seminary among interested extern parties will help separate fact from gossip. If the bishop tells Rome his faculty is known for its orthodoxy, is that what the heads of the local CUF [Catholics United for the Faith] chapter and VOTF [Voice of the Faithful] group think as well? Make some phone calls and do some cross-questioning. "So-and-so says too many seminarians are second-career travel agents—what's your take on the situation?" Moreover, a consideration of those names left *off* the list will tell the VT a lot about what the diocese does not want known.

- Talk to the local pro-lifers. Reason: In every diocese in the U.S., pro-lifers have a vivid interest in the next generation of priests and an especially acute awareness of the gap between diocesan rhetoric and reality.
- Call the cops and the DA's office, and ask about recent relations with the seminary staff and students. Reason: They see and hear things others don't, and even their reluctances to respond to certain questions can point to areas of profitable investigation.
- Stage random visits of both faculty living quarters and students' rooms. Look for indications of a godly, sober, reasonably simple manner of life. Reason: Canon 282 §1.
- Conduct an open faculty discussion of *Dominus Iesus*, with the seminarians in attendance. Ask follow-up questions of faculty who say nothing. Reason: *DI* is a flash-point document, excellent at bringing up ugly and long-hidden doctrinal mutants from the lake bottom. If the seminarians tell you, "What he said at the round table was the opposite of what he tells us in class"—well, then you have something to discuss, don't you?

Bishop Nienstedt says, "I believe the seminaries today are not the seminaries they were 30 years ago," and insists, "I think that we have advanced tremendously." But the fact is that most of the priests and all of the bishops on the visitation team *were formed by the seminaries of 30 years ago*, i.e., at their nadir. The success of the visitation depends entirely on the will to confront unpleasant truths, and it's not mere tendentiousness to view the advance happy talk as an announcement that such will is lacking.

Premeditation

July 6, 2005

Look at me. Look at what an easygoing, modest, lovable guy I am. I'm a cazh priest serving a cazh god—a no-big-deal god, an earth-colors and coffee table god, a "sit back and make yourself comfy" god. No point in putting on a chasuble. My god doesn't subscribe to the Gammarelli catalog [please chuckle in knowing sympathy with me here]. Besides, it's a better tease if I do my own thing with the rubrics, agreeing with some and ignoring others. It shows I'm my own person and throws the faithful *just a little* off balance, which makes them uncertain enough to have to attend to ME and pick up their every ritual clue from ME, who am the most important Being at this event.

The trick is not to overdo it. If you go overboard with the disrespect, people tune out. Better to play off their expectation of a Catholic Mass, leading them on with the familiar and then shocking them with something baffling, mixing piety and impiety. Am I an obedient priest or a disobedient priest? Both. Neither. Doesn't matter. What matters is that the thoughts of the assembly won't be going heavenwards—as tends to happen when they get spiritual freedom from the Roman Ritual; rather, their thoughts and feelings are trapped in the here and now, within the cage I have built for them.

Cute, isn't it, the way I have the kids elevating the hosts like concelebrants? It shows I'm unconscious of my priestly dignity. It foregrounds my humility, and that's good. It also trashes the priesthood of the baptized. What—you thought it *emphasized* it? On the contrary, the priesthood of the baptized is signaled in bringing forward bread and wine at the Offertory, in which our common humanity takes part. No, by giving the patens to the boys to lift I'm actually making the point that unless YOU have a special and personal role in the Sacerdotal Show, YOUR priesthood doesn't count. In fact, the kids get pretty excited the first couple of times they take over bits of my duty, and then they feel bored and resentful when they fall back into anonymity in their ordinary parish Mass. And that's what I like to see. I'm singing a new church into being.

The problem with saying Mass by the book is that it *edifies*. That's a word that means "builds up". When the members of the assembly are edified, they are built up into an edifice which is of no single member's making; they're made into the Church—and that in such a way that their differences, far from being a source of division, actually work in a complementary way to form an organic whole. But that organic whole poses a serious obstacle to my personal project, in ways I'd just as soon leave unspoken. Better to blur. Better to obfuscate. Better to use the inherited respect of the faithful for a priest to lead them to a liturgical fork in the road, where they have to choose between obeying ME and obeying the Church, between sharing in the rite *I* concocted and sharing a rite given to the universal body. In the best-case scenario, some will tap into the anger and take positive relish in defying the Church. In the second-best case, they'll feel soiled by their timid acquiescence and transform the discomfort of their guilt into resentment against the Church, against the Church that asks such simple and "doable" obedience from them.

Don't you see? Obedience is the key to the whole game. The words and rubrics are so simple and so clear that any priest who wants to do so can offer a perfect Mass every time, and the faithful can offer a perfect Mass along with him. That means every variation from the words or the rubrics takes place *for a reason*. A noble reason? You should be ashamed even to raise the question. As a priest in good standing, could I offer you anything else?

The Problem of the Rigid Seminarian

October 23, 2005

Over the past thirty years or so we've often heard concern expressed by bishops, theologians, seminary rectors, and vocation directors that many candidates for the priesthood are unsuitable on account of their "rigidity". In these circles it goes without saying that rigid is bad.

But suppose, in place of the word "rigidity", we substituted the word *tenacity*. Immediately we see that tenacity can be a positive quality, something martyrs and confessors had, something laudable in any believer and eminently desirable in a priest.

Whereas rigidity is kind of a directionless term, negatively descriptive of its subject, tenacity is incomplete until we ask, tenacious of what? In the context of discipleship, we mean tenacious of principles, values, standards: in short, the truths of the Faith. So how is it that a Catholic who would have been commended as tenacious before, say, 1945, has come to be disqualified as rigid?

The kind of officer who excels in wartime often founders in times of peace; finding himself at a desk, he lacks the suavity, affability, and fondness for compromise that mark the managerial bureaucrat as promotable. When the game is no longer victory on the field of battle but cutting deals with patrons and rivals, the combat-veteran-turned-office-hack appears uncouth, awkward, and sometimes counterproductive in the eyes of his smoother colleagues. Since the Council, the Catholic clergy in the prosperous West has effectively transformed itself into a peacetime army, concerned not with fighting threats to the Church but with making life comfortable and consolidating political gains. The term "rigidity" belongs to the negative vocabulary of a peacetime army, "tenacity" to the positive vocabulary of a wartime one. The qualities that made Edmund Campion a hero in anti-Catholic England would make him a pastoral liability in Malibu.

Or so it may have seemed. Psychoanalyst Karl Stern, a Jewish refugee from Nazi Germany who converted to Catholicism, remarked how the experience of the concentration camps falsified many assumptions of prewar psychology. Stern says it was the conservative Catholics, the Jehovah's Witnesses, and the ultra-Orthodox Jews who endured extremes of stress without selling out, going mad, or collapsing, whereas the enlightened bourgeois typically lost all sense of selfhood and integrity in the maelstrom. Stern's point was that his fellow psychiatrists didn't realize the extent to which their model of psychological health was conditioned by the context of peacetime upper-middle-class urban life, so that the types judged by agnostic academics "most likely to succeed" crumbled disastrously in the camps, while nonadaptive persons, well accustomed to marginalization through tenacious—did someone whisper "rigid"?—adherence to principle, maintained their equanimity and character.

The Church in the West has enjoyed a half century of comparative ease, in which the agenda has largely been set by professorial Catholic clergy—men who dress, dine, recreate, and vote in ways indistinguishable from their heathen faculty colleagues, men who have had almost no price to pay for their highly adaptive Catholicism. It's not surprising that they should be alarmed by "rigidity" in their juniors. It's not surprising to read Fr. Richard McBrien lamenting a survey of seminarians that finds "many students resist 'the learning enterprise' because it threatens their 'preconceived ideas about theology.'" Yet, with some few exceptions, it's the professoriate, not the students, that feel threatened, and the source of the threat is not the students' inflexible ideas about *theology* (indicating rigidity), but their stubborn adherence to Catholic *doctrine* (indicating tenacity). These aren't 18-year-olds arriving dewy-eyed from a 1950s high school sodality; they tend to be college grads, sometimes converts, with personal experience of the false promises of the secular world, who have made an existential alignment with Catholic teaching. Regardless of theological maturity or naiveté, they know what they're saying no to.

We have to admit that some seminarians, by temperament, are wrapped too tight and can't handle conflict. I would call them not rigid, but brittle. Many are conservatives, but many aren't: brittleness is a characteristic of one's psychological endowment rather than one's convictions. Few would argue with the contention that brittle candidates are unsuited for the priesthood. But most of the men disparaged as rigid earned the label because they refused to join their professors and superiors in the doctrinal compromises that have guaranteed them such a comfortable life—perhaps the most comfortable life any Catholic clergyman has ever enjoyed. Like the blunt language of the combat vet, the intractability of the doctrinally tenacious Catholic is both an embarrassment and a threat to the accommodationist. And just as academic psychiatrists gauged mental health by adaptivity to their own bourgeois environment, so the seminary gatekeepers have measured "fitness for ministry" by the standards of success current in the faculty lounge, the theater lobby, the embassy reception. Blessed Rupert Mayer held his own in KZ Sachsenhausen, but he wouldn't go down well at Georgetown Law.

But we're preparing contemporary American men for contemporary American ministry, someone might object, and Malibu isn't Dachau. True. But Dachau wasn't *Dachau* until 1933, just a drowsy Munich suburb. Times change. And times are changing. Has hatred of Christianity faded in the last twenty years, or increased? Has the secular world grown fonder of Catholic doctrine or less so? Are your grandchildren likely to find their faith easier to live, or more difficult? Having answered these questions, ask yourselves which quality is more necessary in the priests who will minister to your grandchildren—tolerance, or tenacity?

A Primer on Vows

December 1, 2005

Here's an address I've never heard a new priest give, but wish I had. With appropriate changes, it applies equally to marriage promises and military oaths of loyalty.

Thanks to you all for coming today as witnesses to my vows of priestly chastity. I'd like to take this opportunity to explain briefly what a vow means and why your witnessing this profession is essential.

First of all, as a free man with a free will, there is no act enjoined by the vow that I couldn't perform perfectly well without it, no act proscribed by the vow that I couldn't avoid perfectly well if I'd never professed it. So why take it at all?

No one takes a vow to eat when hungry or to drink when thirsty. All vows (oaths, promises) involve commitment to duties that, at least on some occasions, are difficult to fulfill. No one is obliged to assume such a commitment, and no blame attaches to the man who judges the prospective hardship too great for him and declines to embark on it. But I've noticed that a life free of commitment is also devoid of meaning, and conversely, those whose commitments entail the gravest hardships are precisely the persons whose lives really *matter*. It's a risk I'm free to decline, but a risk I'm willing to take.

Now pay attention: I'm staking my reputation on the undertaking that I'll keep my vow, even where it's difficult to do so. And that's where you come in.

Every person, the Church teaches, has a right to his good name. And I claim that right from you as fellow human beings. In concrete terms, I ask for the ordinary freedom from slander, detraction, and rash judgment that you should extend to any person. And since I'm embarking on a commitment that is potentially difficult to keep, I'm asking for your goodwill, and the benefit of the doubt, in situations where gossip or ambiguous circumstances link my name with infamy.

However, by my vow I am indemnifying you against the eventuality of your backing me when I've let you down. I am hereby forfeiting my right to a good name *if I break the commitment* to which you are witnesses today. Should I ever break this vow, *I give you my permission* to treat me with contempt, to hold me up for ridicule, to broadcast my iniquities on television, radio, or the Web. You may decide to forgo any or all of the above, but should you take them to the furthest extent, *you do me no injustice.*

I can't pretend that I'm not anxious at the prospect of becoming the object of scorn. But this very anxiety will help me keep my commitment—and that's part of the reason I'm not making this vow in secret but have invited you here of my own free will. Further, I promise to defend your prerogative to exercise your right of contumely, if—which God forfend—I default on the undertaking you're about to witness. If I let you down, and if you then take a can of spray paint and write FATHER X SOLICITS MOLDAVIAN STEAMFITTERS TO

ACTS OF UNNATURAL VICE in Day-Glo orange letters on the side of my
rectory, and if our bishop rebukes you—I promise to take *your* side
against the bishop's. You'd be acting within the entitlement I give
you today.

I ask for your prayers as I pronounce this vow, and continued
prayers as I struggle to keep it. Any doubts about what we're here for?
Then do your job.

Le trou de gloire est arrivé, eh?

February 28, 2006

They're faithful priests, except where they're not. A group of Canadian clergy with what are euphemistically called "ecclesiological
problems" has nailed the Jolly Roger to the mast: "In an unusual
public dissent with their leaders, 19 Quebec Roman Catholic priests
published yesterday an open letter taking issue with the church's
opposition to both same-sex marriage and the ordination of active
gays into the priesthood." It goes without saying that these men
decided to take this bold position only after countless hours of prayer,
months of fasting, and a profound study of the Church Fathers, right?

"The signatories include the maverick, outspoken Father Raymond
Gravel. Father Gravel—who had a rough-and-tumble youth as a prostitute and barman in a leather bar before he entered the priesthood—
has often criticized the church's views on gays in the past." Now
is that a great job of vocational discernment or what? Consider the
scores upon scores of men turned away from seminaries on account
of "rigidity". I think we can agree there's precious little to fear in the
way of rigidity from Father Gravel, and that his bishop and vocation
promoter got themselves a man with the flexibility they desired. In
fact, Ray-Ray caught our attention a couple of years ago for his public
letter detailing the edifying recreations of his chums and colleagues:

> Father Gravel said the Vatican is wrong to say that homosexuality is a
> deviance. "Everyone knows that sexual deviations are not exclusively
> related to gays, but to everyone who has to live his or her sexual-
> ity clandestinely. In this matter, the clergy has become masterful, as
> numerous priests frequent parks, saunas and public washrooms to let
> off steam," he said in his letter.

Pretty much the level of spiritual perspicacity we expect from a man with Gravel's "maverick" background. So why is he still in good standing, still in active ministry, still writing open letters signed "Father"? There are two obvious explanations:

1. Fr. Gravel is blackmailing his superiors, or their superiors, whom he as a layman knew in his professional capacity.
2. Fr. Gravel's superiors, or their superiors, really think he's a good priest.

Uncle Di would like to hear from the "better to light a candle" bunch here. Tell me, which of the two possibilities reflects a more positive view of the episcopacy? Which is the more charitable opinion? Which explanation should a dutiful Catholic try to convince himself is the true one?

Sense and Celibacy

January 8, 2007

Fr. Donald Cozzens puts me in mind of one of those divers who takes higher and higher bounces on the springboard until he has everybody's attention, but then kills his jump, walks back off the board and robes up, still dry. As an author, he's penned a series of Prolegomena to Daring Stances, in each of which we are threatened with imminent candor. And spared. Recently Cozzens allowed himself to be interviewed about his latest book, *Freeing Celibacy*. No, he isn't calling for an end to mandatory celibacy. He says it needs to be "reviewed":

> The Rev. Donald Cozzens says the requirement is hurting the church at a time of priest shortages. "Many, if not most, of the inactive priests would be serving in our parishes if it were not for the law of celibacy," Cozzens writes in *Freeing Celibacy*.
>
> "Celibacy used to go with priesthood as fish went with Fridays," Cozzens said in an interview. "Over the past 40 to 50 years, I would argue that more and more Catholics are questioning the need to link celibacy with priesthood."

The fish-on-Friday analogy says a lot about Cozzens and his generation. He's a man of his time, and views celibacy in functional terms:
formerly a sign of Catholic distinctiveness but currently obsolete and
an obstacle to recruitment.

We're all familiar with Cozzens' attitude, though perhaps most of us
meet it in the celebrant at Mass. It's not as if they're obviously bored
or perfunctory, but somehow they communicate the feeling that the
real business takes place somewhere else. They seem bewildered, not
by the meaning of Calvary exactly, but that the faithful would find it
important. They don't understand genuflections or silences or prayers
said kneeling. They're embarrassed by awe. Their breeziness at the
altar as well as the Velcro on their vestments shows that, for them, the
whole Golgotha/sacrifice/wine-into-blood thing is No Big Deal.

Their priesthood means something different to them than it does,
say, to the faithful that show up at Mass during the week, whose eyes
tend to focus on host and chalice. It's a priesthood in which the gift
shop and the altar are simply two ways of reaching out to spiritual
needs. It's a priesthood in which there's no damnation from which
souls need to be rescued, a priesthood in which acceptance of self is
more urgent than contrition. Small wonder if, for Cozzens' generation of priests, asceticism in general—and celibacy in particular—is
hard to make sense of.

"Celibacy used to go with priesthood as fish went with Fridays."
There's nothing heretical about the statement, but what human good
does it invite us to recognize? It speaks to me of a mildly condescend-
ing and good-natured worldliness, with a wry smile for an austerity it
views as antique. And, after all, Cozzens' observations are eminently
sensible—sensible, that is, in a scheme in which mortification is
pointless (do Kiwanis fast?) because there's nothing worth dying for.

For a radically contrary view, compare the following remark of
Cardinal Emmanuel Suhard (Archbishop of Paris, 1940–1949), from
a retreat he gave to his own clergy, published in a book called *Priests
among Men*: "To be a witness does not consist in engaging in propaganda, nor even in stirring people up, but in being a living mystery.
It means to live in such a way that one's life would not make sense if
God did not exist."

Suppose the Church took the advice of her Cozzenses and, having
"reviewed" the discipline in question, made the change to optional

priestly celibacy. To whom would the change appear as eminently sensible? What would the new witnesses be witnesses *to*?

Yes, Minister

March 4, 2007

> Maurice Child's application was refused on the grounds, it was said, that in his interview with the Chaplain-General he was asked what he would do for a dying man, and answered: "Hear his confession and give him absolution." The correct answer was: "Give him a cigarette and take any last message he may have for his family."
>
> —from Evelyn Waugh's biography of Ronald Knox, discussing a High Church Anglican priest's attempt to enlist as a military chaplain at the outbreak of World War I

The Equal Employment Opportunity Commission recently ruled that a Jesuit chaplain at an NIH clinic was wrongly suspended and fired, and ordered his reinstatement. The ground of the ruling appears to be anti-Catholic animus on the part of the chaplain's supervisor. The more interesting (and still unresolved) problem is the self-contradiction in the notion of "multifaith ministry". From the *Washington Post*:

> Since he came to the center in 1994, [Fr. Henry Heffernan, S.J.] had been fighting the clinic's desire to have him minister to non-Catholic (as well as Catholic) patients and to have Catholics seen by non-Catholic clergy, according to testimony before the EEOC. Heffernan had made that point to his boss, O. Ray Fitzgerald, who felt that the priest's attitude was old-fashioned, according to the EEOC decision.
>
> "It just doesn't work," Heffernan said yesterday of so-called "multi-faith" ministry. "Ministers of other religions are personable, but when they interact with a Catholic patient, as far as the Catholic patient is concerned, it's a social call, not any sort of religious activity."

Heffernan's point is beyond dispute. A non-Catholic visitor can heal, comfort, and encourage a Catholic patient, but he can't *minister* to him in the strict sense. Regrettably, however, many half Catholics, including some senior ecclesiastics, see no ultimately decisive difference between religious activity and what Heffernan terms a social call ("the sacraments are about accepting who we are"), and the chaplaincy industry has done its utmost to flatten out the notion of ministry such that religious commitment—the chaplain's as well as his "client's"—becomes largely irrelevant. And note that, in this mindset, aspects of specific ecclesial conviction that resist the interchangeability norm become a threat to the professional ministry business. Back to the article:

> Evidence that Heffernan was targeted, the federal rulings said, included the fact that he was ordered to take elementary courses in chaplaincy before any other chaplains, despite having been a priest and hospital chaplain for years. When he refused to take the basic courses, he was suspended. He was suspended another time for going to the clinic to administer Mass to patients on his days off, something he said he did because he was concerned that Catholic patients weren't getting sufficient spiritual service.

Suspended for offering Mass for his patients on his day off. That tells us quite a bit about the contemporary *professional* approach to *professional* chaplaincraft. And we're probably safe in surmising that the "elementary courses in chaplaincy" Heffernan refused to take were principally intended as a program of ideological indoctrination and assimilation into the etiquette of the guild: can't have wild men on the loose saying unscheduled Mass and asking embarrassing questions about the lethally flawed logic on which the entire industry is built. As we've seen elsewhere, this aggregation of religious activity into professional associations also serves as a useful tool for progressives wishing to pressure the Church into change. Such associations conventionally insist on nondiscrimination based on sex, marital status, libidinal proclivity, etc., whence the restrictions the Church places on her ministers makes her a violator of employment rights or professional standards or both.

Take a look at the penultimate paragraph:

> Thomas Landry, interim executive director of the National Association of Catholic Chaplains, said most institutions are moving in the direction of multifaith ministry because it gives them more flexibility.

However, it depends on resources and the skills of certain chaplains, he said. "There is no template that fits every institution."

As far as one can tell from its website, the NACC is perfectly true to type: no stray fleck of Catholic belief intrudes on its severe professional banality. And Fr. Landry seems unfazed by the prospect of institutions "moving in the direction of multifaith ministry." But the Jesuit Heffernan's challenge remains unanswered: How does one go about multi*faith* ministry without abusing the notion of faith or that of ministry? A plurality of faiths entails a plurality of systems of belief that express incompatible truth claims. Sure, a chaplain can move around among those whose faith is partially in conflict with his own, and—if he is deft and the patient receptive—he may counsel, edify, and instruct. But truly religious ministry is going to be *ex opere operato*—i.e., not dependent on the gifts of the minister or the disposition of the faithful, and this relationship can obtain only between coreligionists. Yet the jargon of professional chaplains suggests that they're united, not in their passion for faith, but in their vagueness about how religious doctrine is important at all. Ministry is a snap once you clear that awkward credal business out of the way. One wonders whether "multifaith" is better termed "uni-doubt".

Hypocrisy?

March 19, 2009

In the current NCR, two officials of the Women's Ordination Conference condemn Pope Benedict's recent remarks urging respect for the dignity of every woman as "egregious hypocrisy". Why hypocrisy? Because women are not ordained priests.

Conventional secular wisdom, today, calls for the equality (often interchangeability) of women and men. A century ago it didn't. Since the Church offends conventional secular wisdom in this respect, she is regarded by secularists as antiwoman.

Even prescinding from the unchangeability of doctrine, the situation isn't so simple.

Flash back a century, when conventional wisdom in Europe and America vaunted Edwardian male complacency, and ask yourselves which public edifices would have been named for women. You'd find the occasional building named after a monarch (e.g., Victoria Hall), but almost all the rest would be Catholic churches dedicated to her saints: St. Anne's, St. Brigid's, St. Cecilia's, St. Dymphna's, etc.

Their unfriendly neighbors, remember, would have accused St. Anne's parishioners of *excessive* devotion to her womanhood ("Catholics worship saints ..."). The Church didn't receive congratulation for her "inclusiveness".

Does this consideration absolve individual Catholics of bias? Of course not. But it refocuses the question of who genuinely values the dignity of women: those whose enthusiasms for equality reflect the sentiments of the hour, or those who manage to find a place for the exaltation of women even when the social and cultural surroundings are hostile.

Cognitive Dissonance

April 9, 2008

I don't get it. Father prances up the aisle surrounded by song, incense, and banners; spins, dips, counterspins, pirouettes into the sanctuary; holds the Book of the Gospels aloft in a rapture of exultation.

And then in his homily explains that the events recounted never really happened.

A BLISTERING SCHOLARLY CRITIQUE

Alone among the items in this book, the following short essay appeared under Father Mankowski's own name. It is noteworthy for three reasons: First, the subject matter, research in biblical texts, is squarely in the field of his academic expertise—and thus this essay was not subject to Jesuit censorship. Second, despite the authoritative nature of its content, this essay appeared on the Catholic Culture site rather than in a scholarly journal—thereby illustrating the undue and undeserved influence that Elaine Pagels and her supporters have over academic fashions. Third, to the best of my knowledge, this devastating critique has never been answered.

The Pagels Imposture

April 26, 2006

Two weeks ago, at the height of the Gospel of Judas mania, a Google News search of "Elaine Pagels" plus "expert" scored 157 hits; she was the media's prime go-to person for a scholarly read on the import of the Coptic manuscript. Pagels was most often cited in stories such as the following from the *New York Times*:

> Elaine Pagels, a professor of religion at Princeton who specializes in studies of the Gnostics, said in a statement, "These discoveries are exploding the myth of a monolithic religion, and demonstrating how diverse—and fascinating—the early Christian movement really was."

I am going to demonstrate that Professor Pagels' media reputation as a scholar is undeserved, her reputation as an expert in Gnosticism still less so. The case for the prosecution will require some careful reading. Those who want to follow along with the sources at their elbow should find a copy of Pagels' 1979 book *The Gnostic Gospels* (New York: Random House). Those who have some Latin and a library handy may want the Sources chrétiennes edition of Irenaeus' *Adversus haereses* (ed. Rousseau and Doutreleau; Paris: Cerf, 1974, 1982) and can bookmark page 278 of vol. 211 and page 154 of vol. 294.[1] Others can get most of the gist from the translation available in vol. 1 of *The Ante-Nicene Fathers* (Grand Rapids: Eerdmans, 1951), with a finger in pages 380 and 439. OK, to work.

Pagels' *The Gnostic Gospels* is in large measure a polemic against St. Irenaeus (approx. A.D. 130–202), Bishop of Lyons and a Father of the Church, and is aimed in particular against the defense of ecclesial orthodoxy offered by Irenaeus in his work *Against Heresies*—which was written in Greek but which survives, for the most part, in an ancient Latin translation.

In a chapter called "One God, One Bishop", Pagels is concerned to show that the doctrine of monotheism and the hierarchical structuring of the Church were mutually reinforcing ploys designed to consolidate ecclesiastical power and eliminate diversity—specifically, the diversity that Pagels finds in the Gnostics whom Irenaeus was at pains to refute. Pagels claims that Valentinian Christians (disciples of the Gnostic Valentinus) "followed a practice which insured the equality of all participants" and put the bishop Irenaeus in a double-bind situation by ignoring his orders. Says Pagels (page 43; brackets, ellipsis, and emphasis are Pagels'):

> What Irenaeus found most galling of all was that, instead of repenting or even openly defying the bishop, they responded to his protests with diabolically clever *theological* arguments:
> They call [us] "unspiritual," "common," and "ecclesiastic." ... Because we do not accept their monstrous allegations, they say that we go on living in the hebdomad [the lower regions], as if we could not lift our minds to the things on high, nor understand the things that are above.

[1] Also available with facing German translation in Fontes Christiani 8/2 (ed. Norbert Brox; Freiburg: Herder, 1997). The benchmark critical edition remains that of W. Wigan Harvey, *Sancti Irenaei Libri quinque Adversus haereses*, Cambridge, 1857. The pertinent passages may be found in vol. 1, page 306, and vol. 2, pages 79f.; they display no significant textual differences from the edition of Rousseau and Doutreleau, or indeed from Migne (PG 7, pp. 760, 918).

Pagels' quotation of Irenaeus is tagged by an endnote reference which, on page 162, reads, "*Ibid.* [Irenaeus AH], Quotation conflated from 3.15.2 and 2.16.4." To put it mildly, an interesting method of citation. Let's look at the sources.

The first part of Pagels' quote comes from book III, chapter 15, of *Against Heresies,* where Irenaeus is arguing for the genuineness of the whole of the New Testament, here against the Valentinians:

> *Hi enim ad multitudinem propter eos qui sunt ab Ecclesia, quos communes et ecclesiasticos ipsi dicunt, inferunt sermones, per quos capiunt simpliciores et illiciunt eos, simulantes nostrum tractatum, uti saepius audiant.* [They give speeches to the crowd about those from the Church, whom they call "common" and "ecclesiastic", through which they entrap the simple and entice them, counterfeiting our teaching, that they might listen to them more often.]

From this sentence Pagels takes only the words *communes et ecclesiasticos ipsi dicunt,* omitting the larger context. Note that the "[us]" which Pagels inserts in her quotation refers not, as her context requires, to bishops, but to all the Catholic faithful: those who belong to the Church. After the ellipsis, her quote resumes midway through a sentence found in book II, chapter 16. In this chapter, Irenaeus is primarily concerned neither with the authenticity of Scripture nor with the Valentinians, but with the doctrine of creation propounded by another Gnostic heresiarch named Basilides. Once more, let's examine the text:

> *Etenim hoc quod imputant nobis qui sunt a Valentino, in ea quae deorsum Ebdomade dicentes nos remanere, quasi non adtollentes in altum mentem neque quae sursum sunt sentientes, quoniam portentiloquium ipsorum non recipimus, hoc idem ipsum qui a Basilide sunt his imputant.* [For that which the followers of Valentinus impute to us—claiming that we remain in the lower hebdomad, as if we could not lift our minds on high or perceive the things that are above, since we reject their own extravagant discourses—this very thing the followers of Basilides impute to them.]

We note that the last phrase is omitted and the order of the preceding clauses reversed to disguise the non sequitur—and for a very good reason: Irenaeus actually says that the same allegations made against the orthodox by the Valentinians are made against the Valentinians by their fellow Gnostics, the disciples of Basilides, and that's an embarrassment to Pagels' notion of the Gnostic-Catholic divide. To recapitulate: Pagels has carpentered a nonexistent quotation, putatively from an ancient source, by silent suppression of relevant context, silent omission of troublesome words, and a midsentence shift of 34 chapters backwards through the cited text, so as deliberately to pervert the meaning of the original. While her endnote calls the quote "conflated", the word doesn't fit even as a euphemism: what we have is not conflation but creation.

Rereading Pagels' putative quotation, you may have noticed that the word "unspiritual" corresponds to nothing in the Latin. It too was supplied by Pagels' imagination. The reason for the interpolation will be plain from the comment that immediately follows (page 44 in *The Gnostic Gospels*). Remember that she wants to argue that Irenaeus was interested in authority, and the Valentinians in the life of the spirit:

> Irenaeus was outraged at their claim that they, being spiritual, were released from the ethical restraints that he, as a mere servant of the demiurge, ignorantly sought to foist upon them.

Put simply, Irenaeus did not write what Prof. Pagels wished he had written, so she made good the defect by silently changing the text. Creativity, when applied to one's sources, is not a compliment. She is a very naughty historian.

Or she would be, were she judged by the conventional canons of scholarship. At the postgraduate institute where I teach, and at any university with which I am familiar, for a professor or a grad student intentionally to falsify a source is a career-ending offense. Among professional scholars, witness tampering is no joke: once the charge is proved, the miscreant is dismissed from the guild and not readmitted.

The Gnostic Gospels, like those portions of Pagels' later work with which I am familiar, is chock-full of tendentious readings and instances where counterevidence is suppressed. The example of "creativity" here discussed may fairly be called a representative specimen of her methodology, and was singled out not because it's the worst example of its kind but because it's among the most unambiguous.

No one who consults the source texts could give Pagels a pass, and that means she forfeits the claim to reliability as a scholar. Attractive as her ideological sympathies may be to many persons—including many academics—she does not deserve to be ranked with serious textual scholars like Claremont's James Robinson, and her testimony on the accuracy of inventions such as Dan Brown's *The Da Vinci Code* cannot be solicited without irony.

I am not calling for academic sanctions but, more simply, for clarification. Pagels should be billed accurately—not as an expert on Gnosticism or Coptic Christianity but as what she is: a lady novelist. Her oeuvre is that of fiction—in fact, historical romance. Had *New York Times* reporters sought Barbara Cartland's views on discoveries in Merovingian religion or paleography, most of us would find it odd, but we'd expect them to make it plain that it was romance, not history, in which she had the right to an opinion.

THE TRAGEDY OF MACDETH

As a grand finale for this remarkable collection, I was eager to offer readers a spectacular example of Father Mankowski's literary prowess. To appreciate the following satire fully, one must have a working knowledge of the American political scene in the 1990s in general, and of the Clinton White House in particular. But any reader should be able to appreciate the language, the meter, and the wit of this piece. "The Tragedy of Macdeth" originally appeared in the American Spectator *in August 1994 under the byline of Francis X. Bacon, identified as "a writer living in Vatican City". I am grateful for the editors' permission to reproduce it here.*

ACT I

Scene I—*A heath in Arkansas.*

[*Enter* MACDETH *and* LYONS, jogging.]

MACDETH

How now, my gentle Lyons, what's o'clock?

LYONS

My liege, the moon our sister Artemis,
like a T-cell new ruptured
by plaguy ill-bred pathogen hath done
dismissed herself from the field of play. [*Pushes button on wristwatch.*]
   Six-thirty.

MACDETH

Then let us canny falconers uncage
our Reeboks to th'unruly winds and speed
on wings of Taiwan-sculpted rubber hence,
lest time should turn our stomachs cuckold
and torpor the McBreakfast Special cheat.

[*Enter three* WITCHES.]

Yet stand I traitor to mine eyes or they
to me, who credit not their troth?
For these appear not women, nay, nor men,
but antecedents of the pronoun s/he—
three Deans of Gender Studies, it would seem,
the very substance of delirium.

1ST WITCH

Hail, Macdeth, all hail to the chief!

2ND WITCH

Hail, good-lookin'! Ro-mance on your mind?

3RD WITCH

Hail, Macdeth, both witness and defendant!
Art happy to see me, or is that a Title IX
enforcement order in thy pocket?

MACDETH

Stay, weird sisters! Download this riddle
into the syntax of propinquity.
For even as the wench of Little Rock
doth hide her charms in cotton-poly blend,
then bends with the remover to remove,
so too methinks your feignèd modesty
encrypts itself the better to reveal.

1ST WITCH

Lesser than Robert Reich, and stouter!

2ND WITCH

Wetter than Maxine's waters, and whiter!

3RD WITCH

Like Teddy for a spouse, but better wive'd!

WITCHES

All hail! [*Exeunt.*]

MACDETH

Hie thee hence to Lady Hillary,
knock twice—lest haste a Foster husband find—
and quaint her of this morrow's tidings.

LYONS

Good my Lord. [*Exit.*]

MACDETH

What joy, what horror must this be, that makes
my very scalp unseat itself, as when
the tempest scatters sickle'd wheat afield
or Cristophe runs his fingers through my hair?
What FDA-untested potion sacks
my intellect, and exiles high-enthronèd
Consciousness of Lack of Consciousness
of Class? Ambition, like a draught
of cannabis long held (but not inhaled),
doth prick resentment to a fury, who
gallops onward riderless, and comes
uncaptained frothing to her post. But let
our morning's revels look to botany;
if she's at Rose, then I'll with Flowers be. [*Exit.*]

Scene II—*The Governor's Mansion.*

[*Enter Lady* HILLARY *with* MESSENGERS.]

HILLARY

To Salomon go, and short my 20-years,
but do thou fetch me Deutschmarks in their stead,
that I might 'scape inflation's bloody tooth,
and like an alchemist turn dross to joy.

IST MESS.

I hear, your ladyship, and fly. [*Exit.*]

HILLARY
And thou,
ill-gendered knave, get thee to Madison
and teach our gentle cousin we would have
his ear.

2ND MESS.
I go. [*Exit* MESS. *Enter* LYONS.]

LYONS
My lady, by your leave ...

HILLARY
Fair Lyons, I wonder at thy charge, and see
thy face doth fax a message bearing not
the subtext of serenity.

LYONS
So foul
and fair a ball I have not seen. 'Tis foul,
in curving wide of deep left field; 'tis fair,
but in its agents of accomplishment.
For whilst I and thy noble husband did
this morning mark our wonted course afoot,
three pollsteresses squat and whiskered stood
bestride the path and croaked, All hail! All hail,
Mister President! I deem they be
so lipped the flaccid tennis balls of fate
through triumph's garden hose to inspirate. [*Exit.*]

HILLARY
Mister President! First Lady, I?
Say rather Empress, partnered with a drone.
By what defect of wit, what folly, what
dire presentiment, did I then yoke me
unto obscurity and shame? O come,
ye Wellesley-spawned Eumenides of spite,
unsex me here! Replace my blood with quarts
of chilliest testosterone, and butch

my hair, that no suspicious visitings
of NOW—nor journalists—might weaken my
resolve, or set me gagging Socks-like on
compunction's hairball.

[*Enter* FOOL.]

Fool! Varlet!
cross-gartered, mincing, single-witted knave,
remove thee from mine eyes, for but to gaze
on thy ill-favored visage acheth sore.

FOOL
Madam, 'tis I.

HILLARY
Methought thou wast another,
nearer in bond canonical, though more
remote in kind.

FOOL
Nay, nay, your ladyship,
for ne'er was cuckold made but in his horns
discernible, that shame be published by
his brow, or on his saxophone.

HILLARY
Thou art
an arrant whelp! Take caution lest I pull
the stripes from thine Adidas—but to lay
them on thy back.

FOOL
'Twould make thee whinny.

HILLARY
How?

FOOL

Marry, not as mare but as Mandela,
whose Winnie spurneth not the lash, nor yet
was vexèd by a friend whom time did not
incinerate.

[Sings.] An ANC[1] leader I knew
Asked her pals to a strange barbecue
  And explaining with sighs,
  'Well, smoke gets in your eyes,'
Ignited a dozen or two.
But let me set a riddle, for my head:
How dost thou in thy managements compare
to auguries of Carthage or of Rome?

HILLARY

Thy wit defeats me, naughty Sphinx. Make plain
thy lesson.

FOOL

          'Struth, that riches haply came
thy way unearn'd, in chicken futures.

HILLARY
                    Fie!

FOOL

[Sings.] A damsel of Lernerite fashion
Insisted on social compassion:
  'The market's degrading.
  It's insider trading
That pulls the postmodernist cash in.'

HILLARY

You're fired.

---

[1] African National Congress.

[*Enter* MACDETH.]

MACDETH

How *'bout* them *Hawgs!*

HILLARY
                        You're hired again.
And what blind beggary of fortune leads
thee here? No lickerous enticement to
thy fancy struts within these walls. No drab
awaits, no bawd, no trollop, slattern, slut
or concubine, no bacon double-cheese
with extra fries. Or haply hast thou lost
thy MasterCard, and cruel need restored thee
to our halls?

FOOL

[*Sings.*] *When she finds on her bed an intruder*
Like to Mandy Rice-Davies, but nuder,
   Slick Willie explains
   And forthrightly maintains
First I gave her a job, then I
     hey nonny hey nonny
     hey nonny nonny
     hey now Elizabeth Tudor!

MACDETH

Nay, tire me not in the habiliments
of wrath, nor taunt me with remorse's sting.
For now is the winter of our discontent
made Acapulco through the *New York Times,*
and any misdemeanors of the past
full deeply in the Metro section buried.
Indeed this very day intelligence
is mine, if I can but New Hampshire or
Nebraska buy, that Little Rock shall lose
both pimp and pimpernel, and Washington
a fan of Fleetwood find.

HILLARY

Let no device
remain untried, no artifice untested,
that ruth should beggar opportunity,
or honor's scruples pauperize success.
The siding from thy mother's mobile home
I'll sell, her dentures pawn, her Elvis lamp,
her Betty Crocker coupons liquidate!
Come Phaedra, come mistress mine Medea,
teach your willing daughter true resolve!
My husband I'll dismember for his pelf,
nor e'en his long-retirèd Jockey shorts
can rest unmortgaged, but shall serve
our purposes: as britches of contract,
brief harbingers of longings sated.

FOOL

[*Aside.*] That creditor be credulous indeed
who takes in trust such fell collateral.

MACDETH

If we should fail?

HILLARY

You fail! But do thou act
upon thy courage as it is thy wont
to operate upon thy hostesses,
and thou'lt not fail. Did not the bearded crones
give certain prescience of triumph?
Then play the man—or better, play the field,
and I shall summon manliness for both. [*Exeunt.*]

FOOL

'Tis passing strange, that Caesar, in his home
should tempt the 'why' of fate,
and stint the Y of chromosome. [*Exit.*]

ACT II

Scene I—*A cavern. In the middle, a boiling cauldron.*

1ST WITCH
Where hast thou been, sister?

2ND WITCH
Killing swine.

3RD WITCH
Porkers, boars, or gender-chauvinists?

2ND WITCH
Marry, all three, and at a single stroke.

1ST WITCH
How now?

2ND WITCH
Vin Foster lieth silenced on the crimson'd turf,
and husband, lawyer, Razorback alike
are dumb, reposing in the selfsame corse.

1ST WITCH
'Tis well and bravely done!
Then turn we to our order's liturgy,
lest Dee Dee's woe be changed to Limbaugh's glee.

WITCHES
Double, treble toil and trouble,
fan the flamers, prick the bubble,
in the cauldron boil and bake
Packwood's acne, Bobbitt's ache.
Lorena's shiv and Tonya's shank,
constituents of Barney Frank,
eye of World Trade Center bomber,
midnight snack of Jeffrey Dahmer ...

[*Enter* AUDITOR.]

AUDITOR

Oyez! Oyez!
[*Reads.*] 'Here be it noted in conformity
with H.R. 741 6(e)3:
Provideth funding for this curse, in parts,
the National Endowment for the Arts.' [*Exit.*]

WITCHES

... distill our brew with earwig venom,
compound with Amy Fisher's denim,
Teddy's poppers, Willie's toke,
Jonestown punch, Anita's Coke,
Janet Reno's rescue tactics,
Magic Johnson's prophylactics,
G-man's sting and he-man's stench,
powder'd harlot, Liquid Wench,
jaws of Jersey City mobster,
claws of Chappaquiddick lobster
(clutching in its briny clickers
Mary Jo Kopechne's knickers),
possum's blister, maggot's wen,
Susan Estrich estrogen—
Macdeth shall thus the networks charm
to spin the news and spare him harm! [*Exeunt.*]

Scene II—*The White House.*

[*Enter* MACDETH, HILLARY, MESSENGERS, *and* FOOL.]

MACDETH

Ah! for those departed too-brief hours of peace,
unwoo'd, infugitive, when sorrows died
more swiftly than they rose, and cank'rous cares
of state were bounded by the couch. O Arkansas!
Thy very hookworms prick my memory
as messengers of fragile joy, and lisp

in words more bitter for their sweetness
of pleasures I shall never taste again.
My desk, my Georgetown tie, my chiefs of staff—
all the massy dignities of state,
would I the most precipitously trade,
to purchase but an acre of my own
demesne, that uninhabitable past!

                    HILLARY
Art mindful of the time? We part anon
for Michigan to press down Polack gorge
the schemes of our firstladydom, lest he
or she wed his or her disquietude
to wit, and vomit our pretended physick.

                    MACDETH
The clock's a slave severer than his lord
and whoreson miserly, that spareth not
an hour for dalliance. [*Aside.*] A slice of bread,
a six of Meister Bräu, and thou, my coy
Miss Little Rock, electioneering in
the back of my Chevelle—'twas paradise!

                    FOOL
And how. Lend me a Whopper, nuncle, and I'll teach thee why thy
    office girls are known as possums.

                    MACDETH
So let me learn.

                    FOOL
Primo, for their wit and provenance.
Secondo, for that they counterfeit the dead.
Terzo, because they hold on to their jobs with their tail.

[*Enter* MYERS.]

Yet trippeth nigh calamity, I'll warrant.

MYERS

Mistress, master! Sir Vincent Foster comes
no more at your behest.

MACDETH

Subpoena'd?

MYERS

Slain.
For jury, judge, and executioner
unto himself he played, and furthe—

MACDETH AND HILLARY

I guess
we'll never, never, never, never know
what happen'd ...

MACDETH

... nor what melancholick flux
or humor darkened his estate ...

HILLARY

... nor how
his private woes were hid from public gaze
or friendship's many-eyed solicitude.
Do thou apprise our constables and scribes
that silence be their most becoming dirge,
nor naughty Democrat did e'er Pulitzer breed.

[*Exit* MYERS.]

FOOL

[*Aside.*] Full eager sextonry that love enroll'd
which fills love's grave afore his corse be cold.

HILLARY

[*To* MESSENGERS.] Fly! Fly! To those new-orphaned chambers go,
and savage there the relics of his charge!
What cannot be dismembered, kindle; rip

what won't be fed into the flame!
Be no leaf left familiar to his brother,
no scribèd pair of words conjoin'd.
Spare not the infant children of his pen,
lest all too soon they learn the art of speech
and prattle mortal secrets to the world.
His hard disk trash, his floppies formattize:
cut out the tongue of memory, and thus
turn Testimony mute; for so methinks
shall Justice keep her dreadsome sword
well scabbarded, when to her sightless gaze
is deafness full compounded! [*Exeunt* MESSENGERS.]

                    FOOL
Lady, knowest wherefore eagle gaol'd the bush-hog for a clumsy spy?

                    HILLARY
Nay, fool. Do tell.

                    FOOL
That bush-hog torched his house in seeming secret, then chid him
    not to look upon the smoke.
[*Sings.*] *Was ever brain so weightless yet*
    Lead bullets made it lighter?
Was ever Whitewater so clean
    That whitewash turn'd it whiter?

                    MACDETH
This dicing with doom's hit man likes me not.

                    HILLARY
Wouldst rather he yet lived? Nay, starch thy spine,
nor license fear to sully thy repute,
thy manhood, or thy BVDs (which, bear
in mind, shall not be fully amortized
'til '96). Do chasten thy trepidity,
for sawdust doth a queasy press corps feed,
and those who yet will not be stonewalled we
shall Stephanopoulize. [*Exeunt.*]

ACT III

Scene I—*A hall in the White House. A banquet prepared.*

[*Enter* MACDETH, HILLARY, *and guests.*]

MACDETH
Welcome, all. The majesty of state
doth well to feast her aristocracy
as roundly as she famisheth all else;
and you, dear guests, in breeding eminent—
I speak of triumphs in *salons de goût,*
not of the nursery—rejoice yourselves
in such delected trophies of success
as interest and merit shall incline.
For all ...

[*Enter* GHOST *of* KOPECHNE, *garlanded with seaweed.*]

KOPECHNE
[*Sings.*] *Larded with sweet flowers*
  Which bewept to the grave did go
With true-love showers ...

[*Enter* GHOST *of* FOSTER.]

FOSTER
[*Sings.*] *Some enchanted evening*
You will meet a stranger ...

[*To* KOPECHNE.] Hang it all, sweetheart, this is a private banquet.

KOPECHNE
Come I this eve when fêted be the SJC,
my inquest to appeal, to wail mine injury.

FOSTER
Senate Judiciary Committee? Aye, *next* Friday. This here is the
  American Bar Association.

KOPECHNE

Ah! Your pardon, sir. I guess I'll be avaunting.
I pray you kindly disregard this haunting. [*Exit.*]

HILLARY

Come, come, thou starest as a maddened bull,
or saddened steer, belike—continue, worm!

MACDETH

Canst disregard that gore, that loathsome gaze?
Alack the day, the hour, that seeth slain
my tongue, my appetite!

HILLARY
           Right cheerfully
discount we thy vice president, what though
he aideth our digestion not. Go to.

MACDETH

Welcome, all. The majesty of state
doth well to feast her true nobility,
our nation's flower; thus it is we come together to felicitate with one
accord our

[GHOST *sits in* HILLARY's *lap.*]

        necrophiles ... and doughnuts.

HILLARY

Still dumb?

MACDETH

Welcome, all. Full many peetsers have I laded
upon this board, nor scanted onions, peppers,
exter sauce—

HILLARY
      We hear.

MACDETH

—termaters, cheese,
eye-talian sausages with them little seeds
inside 'em, weenies, olives (green and black),
pimentos, cheese again, zucchini, mushrooms,
Velveeta, Spam, salami . . .

HILLARY
Dearest sir,
remember where we are.

MACDETH
. . . yea, *dolphin-safe*
salami! Onions, eyes of newts and toes
of frogs and wools of bats and Fightin' Hawgs,
Dancer and Prancer and Donner and Blitzen,
half a league, half a league, octave of Whitsun,
into the Valley of Dolls they rode,
valiant six hundred!

HILLARY
Friends, we beg your gracious leave. Our lord craveth . . . Health
   Care. [*Exeunt.*]

FOSTER
If madam's will alone could purchase health,
we'd see Kevorkian augment his wealth. [*Exit.*]

Scene II—*The White House, outside Lady* HILLARY's *chamber.*

[*Enter* MYERS *and* ELDERS.]

MYERS
Twice seven nights have I kept vigil here,
to watch my Lady break her rest in twain,
and rise, tho' not awaked, and wander down
this very corridor, supplied with five

or six erasers, then commence to rub
upon the patterned paper of the walls
with grievous haste and industry—as though
to bleach the White House with her blanks away.
She'll gain her couch again within the hour,
withal by sense or memory unpiloted.

ELDERS
Soft now, she walks.

[*Enter* HILLARY, *nightgowned, with a handbag, looking about her and pointing.*]

HILLARY
But here's a decimal.

MYERS
And speaks.

HILLARY
Yet another. And again.

[*Takes a bottle of Wite-Out from the bag and begins to paint her nails.*]

More dots, more dots. We've lots and lots of dots.
Thank heaven for Ko-Rec-Type, for we'd else
be dotty. Downright potty. [*Opens window.*]
We see stars. Stars and Bars. Stars *through* bars,
but for our privilege. Or are they dots?
Or both? Star, dot, star. Delete: star-dot-star:
We would thou couldst! And by a finger's touch
wipe clean the cipher'd night-skies of our past.

[*Sings.*] *O does eat dots*
And mares eat dots
And microdots eat ivy
Acquittal HIV-2, wouldn't you?

ELDERS

Now dat is one messed–up

HILLARY

Ho! A light ...
Nay, 'tis but a dot. Out, damn'd dot! [*Exit.*]

MYERS

Canst thou with thy leech's art uproot
this fever'd fancy from her mind? Is there
no surgery, no knife, this ill to amputate?

ELDERS

She needs *Lloyd* Cutlery, not scalpels, child:
I diagnose a sore 1040, jointly filed.
And, honey, that be Joycelyn's *ipsa dixit*,
'Cause if it ain't broke latex, I don't fix it. [*Exeunt.*]

ACT IV

[*The exercise yard of Ft. Leavenworth Federal Penitentiary. Enter* MACDETH *and* LYONS, *jogging.*]

MACDETH

How now, my gentle Lyons, what's o'clock?

LYONS

My liege, bright Phoebus knocks on Aries' door,
and begs admittance, pleading but an hour's
tarry in his house. [*Looking at the wall-clock
by the gate.*] Quarter to two.

MACDETH

Wondrous slow be time's unforward tread,
and whoreson recusant himself,
who lags and limps behind anticipation,

and goads her on while tugging at the reins!
I wonder what's for supper. Wednesday night
perchance we've chili dogs; full gladly could
I half a score internalize, but for
that Fuzzy in the ketchup bowl doth oft
his cut-leaf plug expectorate.

[*Enter* WITCHES *garbed as wardens.*]

WITCHES

Parcel for 6327.

MACDETH

We thank you for your pains. Belike compassion's tardy token, a
    sop to injur'd honor, balm in Kansas' Gilead—or Tootsie Rolls.

WITCHES

A gauge of love these presents be,
from Mrs. Edward Kennedy,
who (being to thy needs alert)
conveys this gift for your dessert.

Curdle milk and choler quicken,
Cripple limbs and deafness thicken,
Darken sight and temper sicken! [*Exeunt* WITCHES.]

MACDETH

Then take we merit's pulse ... *McChicken!*

[*Reenter* WITCHES *leading prisoner* FOOL, *in the guise of Ronald*
McDonald.]
                                                    Lo!
Doth fancy bend our vision to its will?
or is this fortune's jack indeed?

FOOL
                        The same.
My duty done, and doing five to eight.

MACDETH

How now?

FOOL

My mistress turn'd State's Evidence
against thyself—a pardoner's tale!—and so
indulgence purchased with the coin of thy
confinement.

MACDETH

What, 'twas so?

FOOL

And thereupon
she lofted Teddy to her highest Court,
who scarce was robed and wigged but wed again,
that Little Rock ne'er lack attorney's fees,
nor scandal's harpies vex Hyannis Port;
for by his zipper is he often tripped,
whose waitresses are tumbled more than tipped!

[*Sings.*] *Lest he come under feminist fire*
For indulging seigneural desire
  Disarmed he all blame
  by changing his name
to Ted Kennedy-Rodham, Esq.

MACDETH

Down, down I come, unwiv'd, un-amnestied,
to pay Whitewater's interest, and its deed;
'tis nobler that I quit this life in season
than breathe the air befoulèd by such treason!
Depart I now for heaven's caring shores ...

[*Takes drumstick out of box.*]

Mmf ... those exter tater tots are yours.

[*Stabs drumstick down his throat.*]

FOOL

Now croaks a noble heart. Goodnight, sweet prince,
that uttered blessing with thy last McBreath;
McFlights of angels do thy tonsils rinse
with Diet Pepsi, as befits McDeath! [*Exeunt omnes.*]

Finis